The Cylinder

For Tim

let's do something together,

and Rules for coming to Boulder!

Helmut 03/14

FLASHPOINTS

The series solicits books that consider literature beyond strictly national and disciplinary frameworks, distinguished both by their historical grounding and their theoretical and conceptual strength. We seek studies that engage theory without losing touch with history and work historically without falling into uncritical positivism. FlashPoints aims for a broad audience within the humanities and the social sciences concerned with moments of cultural emergence and transformation. In a Benjaminian mode, Flash-Points is interested in how literature contributes to forming new constellations of culture and history and in how such formations function critically and politically in the present. Available online at http://repositories.cdlib.org/ucpress.

Series Editors
Ali Behdad (Comparative Literature and English, UCLA)
Judith Butler (Rhetoric and Comparative Literature, UC Berkeley), Founding Editor
Edward Dimendberg (Film & Media Studies, UC Irvine), Coordinator
Catherine Gallagher (English, UC Berkeley), Founding Editor
Jody Greene (Literature, UC Santa Cruz)
Susan Gillman (Literature, UC Santa Cruz)
Richard Terdiman (Literature, UC Santa Cruz)

The Cylinder

Kinematics of the Nineteenth Century

Helmut Müller-Sievers

UNIVERSITY OF CALIFORNIA PRESS

Berkeley · Los Angeles · London

University of California Press, one of the most
distinguished university presses in the United
States, enriches lives around the world by advancing
scholarship in the humanities, social sciences,
and natural sciences. Its activities are supported
by the UC Press Foundation and by philanthropic
contributions from individuals and institutions. For
more information, visit www.ucpress.edu.

University of California Press
Berkeley and Los Angeles, California

University of California Press, Ltd.
London, England

Library of Congress Cataloging-in-Publication Data

Müller-Sievers, Helmut.
   The cylinder : kinematics of the nineteenth
century / Helmut Müller-Sievers.
      p. cm.
   Includes bibliographical references and index.
   ISBN 978-0-520-27077-0 (pbk. : acid-free paper)
   1. Literature, Modern—19th century—Themes,
motives. 2. Machinery in literature. 3. Mechanics in
literature. 4. Science in popular culture.
5. Cylinders. I. Title.
   PN56.M2M85 2012
   809'.915 23
                                        2011033138
Manufactured in the United States of America

21 20 19 18 17 16 15 14 13 12
10 9 8 7 6 5 4 3 2 1

In keeping with a commitment to support
environmentally responsible and sustainable printing
practices, UC Press has printed this book on
50-pound Enterprise, a 30% post-consumer-waste,
recycled, deinked fiber that is processed chlorine-
free. It is acid-free and meets all ANSI/NISO (Z 39.48)
requirements.

For J and s,
. . . ardorem cupiens dissimulare meum.

Contents

Acknowledgments

This book originated as a presentation in the fabled colloquium of Hans-Joerg Rheinberger's Abteilung II at the Max Planck Institute for the History of Science in Berlin in 2003. It was revived for a fellowship at the Institut für Kulturforschung in Vienna in 2006, where the director, Hans Belting, was a champion of the project and Ed Dimendberg first proposed to include it in the FlashPoints series. Most of the research was completed during a fellowship at the Getty Research Center 2007–8 with the help of its magnificent library staff. Correspondence, and finally a meeting in March 2009, with Francis Moon, the *spiritus rector* of KMODDL, the kinematics research group at Cornell, and the best expert of Franz Reuleaux's work, pushed the project toward completion. A Kayden Grant from the University of Colorado at Boulder helped defray the cost of image rights.

For anyone searching for an infallible means of testing who your real friends are, I recommend subjecting them, with no end in sight, to incessant talk of cylinders, rotation, and kinematics. Those who years later will still speak to you either have great patience or great powers of feigning interest, both excellent character traits in one's friends.

Among those who survived the ordeal and who supported the project in its various stages I want to mention in particular Marshall Brown, Robert Buch, Ruediger Campe, Tom Cummins, Heinrich Detering, Eric Downing, Peter Galison, Michael Gamper, Peter Geimer, Eva Geulen, Anthony Grafton, Sepp Gumbrecht, Michael Hagner,

Deborah Hodges Maschietto, Michael Hutter, Albrecht Koschorke, Karen Lang, Elmer Lewis, David Maisel, Ethel Matala de Mazza, Charlotte Metcalf, Gloria Meynen, Bob Pippin, Lois Renner, Simon Schaffer, Henning Schmidgen, Anette Schwarz, Mark Seltzer, Bernhard Siegert, Davide Stimilli, Ralph Ubl, Joseph Vogl, David Wellbery, Christopher Wild, Carsten Zelle.

Moving to the University of Colorado at Boulder not only has placed me in a physical environment in which one of the key concepts of this book, torque, can be experienced on rides up Lefthand Canyon but also has given me new friends, colleagues, and interlocutors: Adam Bradley, Chris Braider, Jeff Cox, Jill Heydt-Stevenson, Anne Schmiesing, John Stevenson, Davide Stimilli, and Paul Youngquist. My assistant at the Center for Humanities and the Arts, Paula Anderson, has helped greatly with the last versions of the manuscript (and assorted emergencies). Ed Dimendberg has accompanied this project with unfailing kindness, professionalism, and intellectual guidance.

PART ONE

The Prehistory and Metaphysics of the Cylinder

CHAPTER I

Introduction

The nineteenth century abounds in cylinders. Locomotives and paper machines, gasholders and Yale locks, sanitation pipes and wires, rotary printing presses and steam rollers, silos and conveyor belts, kymographs and phonographs, panoramas and carousels, tin cans and top hats—each of these objects is based on the cylindrical form, and each could be—and some have been—the starting point for a comprehensive interpretation of the epoch's culture. To state it in the form of a necessary condition, without the cylinder the Industrial Revolution, and the culture it brought forth, would be unthinkable.

How can we account sufficiently for this proliferation of cylindrical objects and processes? The answers given in the following pages are at the same time obvious and recondite, factual and metaphysical, technical and historical. In their most basic form, they amount to the proposition that cylinders allow the isolation, transmission, conversion, and application of rotational and translational (straight-line) motion in machines. The displacement of translational motion is necessary to do work; but since machines and mechanisms are (like their makers) finite, this motion has to be "returned." Translational motion has to be forced into reciprocating and rotational motion, while rotational motion has to be forced and anchored by straight guides and frames. The cylinder embodies both translational motion along its axis and rotational motion around its wall. Because every point on the cylinder's wall is equidistant from its central axis, the wall's surface is intrinsically flat and thus can impart the all-important motion of rolling.

On these bare kinetic explanations rests a vast edifice of historical and metaphysical dimensions. Philosophical speculation in the West begins with the dispute about the reality of motion as the elemental distinction between being and nonbeing. The genealogy of the cylinder reveals the opposition of rotational and translational motion as one of the starkest conceptual oppositions in Western metaphysics, one that until the Scientific Revolution and beyond was tantamount to the distinction between divine and human, perfect and imperfect, rational and irrational qualities.

This opposition—and the fact of its forced reconciliation in the cylinder—arises from an absence that for all its simplicity still is stunning: nothing on earth rotates.[1] Nothing in our life-world turns continuously around its own axis, least of all parts of our own bodies. That is why rotational motion is always forced, technical motion, and that is why the question of technics on its most fundamental level equals the question of whether and how to force continuous rotation. It is the epochal achievement of nineteenth-century machines and their cylindrical components to have made rotation universally available, and at the same time to have brought to light the limits of technics: it begins where the body ends. The machines born in the nineteenth century are not sufficiently understood as tools, they are not monstrous "projections" of human organs into the world. Rather, they disrupt the imaginary continuity of nature and human being and introduce with their motions a literally "inhuman" element into the world. The negotiation of the limits between human and inhuman motion is going to be the subtext of most of the object descriptions that follow.

Before exemplifying these propositions and looking more closely at the various cylinders that populate the nineteenth century we may do well to probe into the relations between rotation and translation, freedom and force, inhumanity and technics at the outset of the age of machines, and to set them in a historical frame that encompasses their theological, philosophical, and aesthetic dimensions. A singular and visionary text written at the inception of the cylinder's epoch will be our guide.

. . .

In 1810, Heinrich von Kleist published an essay entitled "Über das Marionettentheater."[2] It recounts an accidental conversation between the narrator and the *primo ballerino* of the local opera house, Herr C. When the narrator finds him watching the performance of a puppet theater in the public gardens, C. professes to be fascinated by the puppets' movements, and in the course of the conversation he outlines his idea that only a fully mechanized, unconscious body could be truly graceful. Both interlocutors go on to relate examples of the interference of consciousness with the grace of human motion, but it is Herr C. who most passionately advocates the elimination of all subjectivity from dance, going so far as to liken the goal of full mechanization with the return to paradise.

The text appeared, in four installments, in Kleist's own *Berliner Abendblätter,* one of the early daily newspapers in Germany still printed on hand-operated presses that could perform only translational up-and-down movements and on paper produced sheet by rectangular sheet. While the slowness of this process was the reason for the slight volume of the paper—not more than six to eight pages per edition—the Prussian censors made sure that the content consisted mainly of trivial police reports, epigrams, and Kleist's seemingly innocuous anecdotes.[3] There was to be no news that could foster unrest among the citizens, no opinion piece that would directly address the oppressed state of city and country. After the collapse of the Holy Roman Empire in 1806 and the subsequent trauma of French occupation, the governor of Berlin had justified strict censorship of the press with perhaps the most famous order in the German language: "Ruhe ist die erste Bürgerpflicht" (Rest is every citizen's first duty).[4]

"Über das Marionettentheater" is uniquely concerned with the state of unrest. It seeks to articulate in deliberately provocative ways the relationship between motion, subjectivity, and redemption. To propose an exhaustive account of motion *without* any regard to subjectivity and theology had of course been the goal of Newton's science of rational mechanics since the late seventeenth century; and a century later, Pierre Simon Laplace (for a brief time Napoleon's minister of the interior) had succeeded in purging Newton's theory of its last metaphysical remainders, such as the apparent irregularities of planetary orbits that required God's redressing hand.[5] Newtonian mechanics described a world in which all causes of motion were external to bodies and in which every motion, every change in motion, could be expressed in mathematical equations. Translated back into the realm of human history and community, the key concepts of rational mechanics—inertia, resistance, mass, collision, equation, revolution—could take on disturbing political overtones. The cult of reason before and during the French Revolution had all but deified Newton and had made ample, cross-cultural references to his achievements. After all, the emblematic mechanism of the *terreur,* the guillotine, harnessed gravity to do rationally what had hitherto been reserved for the extravagant demonstration of a sovereign's wrath.[6]

It was not the least motivation of Friedrich Schiller's project of aesthetic education—conceived shortly after the guillotine's bloody reign—to exorcise the specter of such mechanical politics.[7] Societies are composed of human bodies, Schiller insisted, and like all animal bodies they contain the principle of motion within themselves. What is more, human motion expresses a moral sense—sympathy—that mediates between the constrained mechanics of skeletomuscular motion and the unbounded freedom of the mind; it escapes all mathematical notations.[8] The aesthetic effect of this moral mediation is gracefulness—the ineffable quality of human motion that represents in the world of moving bodies what beauty is for stationary objects.[9] To move gracefully means to be in harmony with oneself, which in the gendered terms of Weimar Classicism meant to be a woman, or a man educated and graced by a woman. The outward representation of such harmony is dance. For Schiller, the remedy for a fractured and revolutionary society of colliding straight-line forces is the invitation to a dance in which individual and collective motions revolve around one another in a harmonious whole.

The thrust of Kleist's text against this fusion of motion, subjectivity, and grace—against the core convictions of Weimar Classicism—must have been easily detectable for readers in 1810. Herr C.'s argument that inhuman marionettes exhibit more grace in their motions than human dancers, that, in fact, every instant of reflection prevents gracefulness, aims straight at the center of Schiller's (and Goethe's) attempt to bridge the chasm between body and mind, to install aesthetics above mechanics. At the same time, however, Herr C.'s quest for grace in motion reintroduces into natural philosophy the very theological parameters that Newton and the Newtonians had sought to eliminate. When the two interlocutors equate the loss of grace with the expulsion from paradise, they shift the attention from the moral to the anagogical sense of the concept. In its theological context, grace in motion—*Grazie* or *Anmut*—is the sign of paradisiacal wholeness, an embodied reminder of the innocence that was shattered irrevocably by the desire for knowledge. Weimar Classicism, cheerfully proclaiming its own paganism,

held that paradise was just a mythological name for a historical forma-
tion, namely ancient Greece, that its loss was the result not of sin but of
a history of decadence decisively shaped by the Christian Church, and
that regaining paradise was, at least in principle, possible through a
reawakening of the aesthetic sensibilities of antiquity, such as the moral
feeling expressed in graceful motion. The notion of *Bildung,* so often
evoked in the context of nineteenth-century German pedagogy, expressed this hope for an individual and secular recuperation of grace.[10]
Kleist's Herr C. explores a radically different avenue to the restitution
of grace: rather than promoting aesthetic education, he speculates that
the return to grace will come as the result of a complete dehumaniza-
tion and mechanization of motion.

This hope in the redemptive power of mechanical motion, then, was
a broadside against Weimar Classicism, which, championed by Wilhelm von Humboldt and his *Bildungs*-reforms, had arrived in the Prussian capital just when Kleist published his short text. But the essay does
more than polemicize, and what it does in addition is what makes it
so interesting for our understanding of the future of mechanisms and
their relations to culture and aesthetics in the nineteenth century—a
future that is embodied in the cylinder and its kinematic properties.
For unlike Romantic writers like E. T. A. Hoffmann or Mary Shelley,
Kleist does not focus on the origin of motion or life in the puppets,
nor does he marvel at their mimetic and illusory power. He does not
mention the automata that delighted the eighteenth century before they
began to haunt early nineteenth-century literature with their imitation
of human consciousness and affectivity: he is solely interested in the
spectacle of their motion.[11] In the terms of nineteenth-century engineering, he focuses on marionettes neither as motors nor as tools but as
transmissions. Discovering generalities in the transmission of motion
is the purpose of nineteenth-century kinematics, a discipline as obscured by the awe of motors and the anxiety over mechanized tools as
is the understanding of Kleist's text by the biography of its author and
the speculations about its programmatic aim.[12] The genealogy of kinematics as an independent discipline is the subject of the next chapter.

It is true that the focus on kinematics in Kleist's text is hidden behind
what seem to be traditional hermeneutic and moral concerns. When
asked whether making marionettes dance requires artistry on the part
of the puppeteer, Herr C. claims that there is a "center of gravity" in
every motion and that the line traced by this center is identical with
"the way of the soul of the dancer."[13] To perfect the dance, then, the

puppeteer—Kleist calls him "the machinist"—must place himself in the gravitational center of the marionette. This hermeneutic imperative of empathy is draped in mathematical language: the lines of motion, C. says, are either straight or of computable curvature, and the fingers of the puppeteer and the motion of the puppets are related "rather like numbers to their logarithms or the asymptote to the hyperbola."[14] But this second-order grace is achieved by a sleight of hand. As Kleist— who once divided people into those who understand metaphors and those who understand formulas—knew very well, mathematical metaphors, conjoining algebraic precision and the vagueness of the "rather like" *(etwa wie)*, are inherently contradictory. As failed metaphors— catachreses—such figures of speech at the same time open and attempt to cover over a conceptual gap.[15] In Herr C.'s case, this gap appears earlier in his statement that every motion has a gravitational center. Within the basic parameters of Newtonian physics, only individual bodies, not motions, have a center of gravity: it is the imaginary, non-extended point in which, for the purpose of calculation, all of a body's mass is concentrated.[16] The mathematization of motion in Newton's rational mechanics—and with it the possibility of attributing grace to unforced motion—is based on the assumption that bodies can at the same time be treated as nonextended points that trace out curves in the Cartesian coordinate system *and* as massive atoms that are subject to the law of inertia. This latter law—Newton's first law of motion— guarantees the continuity of motion; the geometrical inscription, on the other hand, allows for the calculation of its form. "Gravitational center of motion," then, is the catachresis that reopens what historians of science call Newton's great synthesis—his ability to treat discrete, massive bodies like continuous geometric shapes.[17] In its attempt to cover up, the phrase brings attention to the abyss underneath the signal achievement of rational mechanics, the law of universal gravitation, by means of which the motion of physical entities is inscribed into the reversible and predictable grid of geometry.

Any endeavor to attack Newton's mechanics frontally would be quixotic, given its explanatory success and its consolidation and empirical verification throughout the eighteenth and the early nineteenth centuries. But the bulk of that success—for example, the prediction of the return of Halley's comet in 1758—was based on the motion of bodies so distant in a space so vast that indeed they could be treated as imaginary point masses. But what explanatory and predictive power do the laws of motion have for bodies moving close at hand—for bodies that can exhibit grace to human eyes? There is, of course, the anecdote of the falling apple at Woolsthorpe that the Newtonians kept reciting to underscore the universality of gravitation; but aside from ballistics experts, who would routinely experience the free fall of objects, let only find their translational motion graceful? What can Newton's laws say about objects that do not simply fall but move nonetheless, such as wagon wheels, water pumps, pendulum clocks?[18]

This is the point of Herr C.'s fascination with, and critique of, marionettes. In a double sense he interprets them as pendulums: first, because the puppet follows the hand of the "machinist" with the lag of a string pendulum such that the straight-line motion of the hand is translated into the lagging curve of the logarithmic or hyperbolic function; second, because the limbs of each individual puppet, "which are only pendulums," are not tied to "myriads" of strings and therefore follow the "gravitational center of the motion" in the puppet with a hesitation that inevitably results in "curves." For marionettes as pendulums, the law of gravity is literally suspended—they are "antigrav," as Kleist says—but the law of inertial motion persists. That persistence, and the lag that results from it, is precisely the reason for the marionette's imperfection: it grants an abode for the "last fraction of human volition"—later in the essay it is called "affectation" *(Ziererei)*—that threatens to interrupt the grace of motion. The only way to overcome this danger is to eliminate the effects of inertia as well, and that is exactly what Herr C. hopes for: "Yet he did believe this last fraction of human volition could be removed from the marionettes and their dance transferred entirely to the realm of mechanical forces, even produced . . . by turning a crank." The instantaneous transmission of motion by a crank suspends the effects of gravitational *and* inertial forces; it is the—often overlooked—ideal in Kleist's anecdote. Herr C. believes that perfect grace can be embodied, not in marionettes, but in crank-driven mechanisms.[19]

From the pendulum to the crank: it is hard to exaggerate the significance of this transition. Both are material objects built for a specific use, but both are also, in Hans-Joerg Rheinberger's felicitous terminology, "epistemic things": they embody ways of knowing and doing that exceed their functionality and historical employment.[20] Residing below the threshold of fully articulated theories, they can serve—as Herr C. shows with the pendulous marionette—as their material critique and challenge. The pendulum, beginning at the latest with Galileo's (mistaken) assumption that its period is isochronous and can therefore be used to translate space into time, has both spurred and defied the development of modern physics and mechanics.[21] Cranks, from an epistemic point of view, are the answer to the weaknesses of the pendulum: they seek to overcome the inertial lag inherent in pendulums through direct, continuous contact.[22] This means that their motions are defined, no longer by the forces governing Newtonian mechanics, but by their own shape. In the following pages we will see that the rudimentary shape governing the construction of all motion transmission, including the crank, is the cylinder. The pendulum is a passive instrument, but the crank drives a transmission. Hoping for a transition from one to the other, as Herr C. does, and discovering grace in fully contiguous motion, signals the advent of a new understanding and appreciation of machines.

Yet it is not only from the theoretical heights of such concepts as "epistemic things" that the transition from pendulums to cranks gains relevance. To the contrary, at the time of Kleist's writing this transition had become the crucial factor in the very real process of industrialization that was beginning to take hold in England. As we will see in greater detail in the next chapter, James Watt's decisive innovation in the design of steam engines concerned the manner in which the steam cylinder was connected to the working beam. Before his patent for the ingenious "parallel-motion" transmission, this connection consisted of chains or ropes—steam engines were, in essence, gigantic pendulums and were therefore limited to do lifting and pumping work.[23] Watt's transmission, which used the connecting rod as a crank, freed steam engines from this limitation and thereby turned them into the universal engine of industrialization. These new mechanisms, and with them the new era of motion control, would have been all the more desirable for someone living in Berlin in 1810: with his imposition of the Continental System in 1806, Napoleon had cut off the Continent from British imports and technical knowledge. The expression of a desire for a crank-driven mechanism also carried a distinct—and in Kleist's case certainly not unwelcome—whiff of anti-Napoleonic polemics.

Another dimension to Kleist's anecdote further connects the motion of the marionettes to the motion of machines and to the massive metaphysical and cultural shift they will bring about. While Herr C. concentrates on the two dimensions in which the puppets transform the linear impulse of inertial motion into the pendular "curves" of the limbs, the narrator notes that part of the naturalness in the puppets' dance stems from the way they dance "a round dance" *(die Ronde)*. "A group of four peasants doing a round dance to a rapid beat could not have been more prettily painted by Teniers."[24] The *ronde*—the *Reigen,* whose motion Arthur Schnitzler would famously use as a narrative figure in his eponymous novella—is a dance that represents not so much curvilinear as rotational motion. Facing and holding each other's hands, the dancers rotate around a common center; they experience, and by the grip of their hands counter, the centrifugal forces that Newton identified as "real" indicators of the immutability and absoluteness of space.[25] The rich cultural significance of this type of dancing can be gleaned from the scene in Goethe's *Werther* where the protagonist falls in love with Lotte while waltzing with her—the waltz, like the *ronde,* consists in a rotational figure the axis of which intersects the gaze of the dancers while their bodies form a virtual cylindrical space around them. We will encounter multiple avatars of this motion in nineteenth-century artifacts; what is important at the moment is the difference between circular or curvilinear motion—which Newton's mathematical success in calculating the orbits of planets and comets had explained as the sum of two compounding translational motions—and rotation, which is a genuine motion without translational displacement. This difference, as chapter 3 will show, is at the heart of Western valuations of motion, in which rotation has traditionally been associated with transcendence and divinity. The difference between a pendulum arrangement—like Newton's bucket, like the marionette—and a rigid linkage like a crank to induce rotation will become crucially important in nineteenth-century machines (one of the favorite apparatuses of the time, the chairoplane, uses both).

It is not simply a deconstructive metaphor to claim that Kleist's text itself resembles a machine that provokes and produces its own interpretations. Its composition, its logical and performative contradictions, even its mode of publication generate so much friction that attentive readers, like attentive engineers, try to supply argumentative lubrication to make the text and its arguments run more smoothly. The present account of the techno-historical subtext of the dialogue by no means seeks to invalidate or replace other attempts, nor does it claim to cover all or even most of the text's many facets. There are other aspects, however, that attention to the history of kinematics can also elucidate. The first is the convincing reading of the essay's arguments as a long poetological metaphor, in which Herr C.'s mechanized dancers function as the vehicle for the idea that bare, linear language could be converted into "round," troped language and vice versa, and that this could be done without the imponderable intercession of an author's intention. In fact, Kleist's linguistic companion piece to the "Marionettentheater," the equally performative treatise "On the Gradual Production of Thoughts Whilst Speaking" (Über die allmähliche Verfertigung der Gedanken beim Reden), advocates the same transition from pendulum to rigid linkage for the basic relation between language and mind. "Language then is not a rope, a brake on the wheel of the mind, but rather a second wheel rotating along parallel on the same axis." (Die Sprache ist alsdann keine Fessel, etwa wie ein Hemmschuh an dem Rade des Geistes, sondern wie ein zweites, mit ihm parallel fortlaufendes, Rad an einer Achse.)[26] German literary aesthetics at the time was fascinated with the prospect of mechanical transmission between poetic registers or "tones"; the idea that the difference between the genres, or the laws of prosody, or the sequence of a plot could somehow be calculated and reproduced mechanically held wide currency at the end of the eighteenth and the beginning of the nineteenth century.[27] At the end of this book we will encounter a less metaphorical attempt by Kleist to explain his vision of tragedy by means of a primitive machine; suffice it at the moment to underscore that the analogy between the movement of machines and mechanisms and that of poetic language is itself a standard trope of literary practice and criticism of Kleist's time.

The reason why this analogy could grip the thought of such a diverse group of writers and philosophers—this is the second aspect brought into relief through the history of kinematics—is its importance for theology, or rather for the philosophy of history that emerged as its secularized translation at the beginning of the nineteenth century. Common to both religious and secular thinkers was the idea that the language of paradise—or that of ancient Greece, for the "pagans"—had no need for the distinction between prose and poetry, between the linear language of propositions and the metaphor that always contains a moment of self-reflection, of turning round on itself in the act of establishing a relation. Edenic language in its undisturbed form was a language not of communication, where the intention of the author is always under the threat of dissipation and misunderstanding, but of simple naming: word and referent were indissolubly merged in one unit. This unity was torn asunder by the desire for propositional knowledge, theologically known as original sin. Poetic language, then, is both a mournful sign of lost unity and an expression of the desire to regain it. If a way could be found to heal the rift between prose and poetry, and if that process could be advanced and perfected by mechanical, that is, faultless, rather than inspirational means, humankind could indeed, as Herr C. and his interlocutor speculate, return to paradise through the backdoor.

This anagogical tendency of Kleist's text, well within the boundaries of idealist philosophies of art at the time, has a mechanical corollary that is important for any understanding of the age of machines. For the other consequence of the expulsion from paradise was the condemnation of the offended God: "Cursed is the ground because of you, in toil you shall eat of it all the days of your life" (Gen. 3:17). Work thus became the indelible sign of God's curse, a curse that—according to Christian theologians—could be lifted once and for all only by the apocalyptic destruction of the world. In the meantime, however, anything that helped to alleviate the weight of toil played a role in the drama of salvation. Therein lay the eschatological potential of machines that provided the background for even the most technical discussion of linkages and transmissions.[28] This potential was radically ambivalent, as were the debates it would provoke: either machines were seen as the means of breaking the sanctions of work and mortality that characterized all human life after the Fall, or they were hailed as the tools of emancipation with which human ingenuity managed to mitigate, and perhaps overcome, the curse of work. These positions were not necessarily articulated in theological terms—the ecological criticism of machines that started early in the nineteenth century substituted the integrity of nature (and later that of Being) for the will of God, and the awe of machines and engineering was certainly not anti-Christian—but they were part of a deeper reflection that accompanied the rise of machines. The provocative point Herr C. makes—that we will have regained grace, and with it admission to the Garden of Eden, to the fullness of life and language once we have installed machines that counter the trajectory of falling things—stands at the beginning of this history of interpretation.

Kleist's text, then, links the most mundane questions of motion transmission to the last questions of biblical hermeneutics. In the scenes between Herr C. and the narrator, it enacts a dialogue about the meaning of mechanisms, specifically about the relation between the induction of motion and salvation. In hermeneutic terms, this is the relation between the literal and the anagogical meaning of a term. Medieval interpreters of the Bible had simplified the multiple senses of the Scripture—they, too, were a result of the fall from grace—into four categories: literal, allegorical, moral, and anagogical. The classical example is Jerusalem. On the literal level, it is the historical city, on an allegorical level the church, on a moral level the soul of the believer, and on an anagogical level the heavenly city of salvation.[29] Kleist directly conjoins the literal and the anagogical sense of the marionette while disregarding its allegorical value—the puppet does not signify anything else than itself, whereas in Schiller's and Kant's aesthetics it signifies heteronomy and absence of feeling—and disdaining the moral dimension, which he belittles as "affectation." For the formulation of the literal sense, Kleist invokes, as we have seen, the mathematical language Newton had proposed to purge science from the three spiritual senses; in his anagogical questioning he envisions a reopening of the gates of paradise through the elimination of the literal, physical fall, the effects of gravity and inertia. In the hermeneutic tradition, anagogy wants to know how and when the injustices of the world will be righted, and what clues Scripture, or the book of nature, furnishes us to understand where we are in the history of salvation. Traditional anagogical interpretation, then, has as its vanishing point the apocalypse. Kleist's anagogy imagines a return to paradise without prior judgment and without prior destruction of the world.[30]

This vision of the anagogical role of machines motivated, as mentioned, a great deal of advocacy for and activism against machines in the nineteenth century, whether explicitly or not. It was accentuated by the new physics of thermodynamics, and in particular by the law of entropy: rather than a day of wrath visited on the world from the outside, apocalypse in the nineteenth century became a predictable, inevitable feature of the world conceived as a finite configuration of energy. Machines could either be seen as accelerating this end—if the focus was on the consumption and pollution of their motor—or as slowing it—if the focus was on the optimization of energy/motion transmission. The latter was the position taken by kinematicists, as the next chapter will show, and was behind their secret conviction that kinematics and its associated practices (like the emergent science of lubrication) had a key role to play in nineteenth-century culture.

The anagogical horizon of thermodynamics, of course, was not yet circumscribed at the time of Kleist, but the differentiation of machines into multiple senses was well under way. Already at the end of the eighteenth century, when the success of the steam engine had prompted further reflections on the nature and history of machines, French scientists had begun to discuss and institutionalize the analysis of machines in terms of their motor, transmission, and tool functions.[31] It was in this division that kinematics as the science of transmissions was first named and defined. While there are problems with this view—Where, for example, is the tool of a locomotive?—it survived as a heuristic approach throughout the century. It is tempting to speculate whether it was consciously modeled after the hermeneutics of Scripture, with the motor representing the literal engagement of the machine with the world, the transmission the allegorical transport of motion, and the tool the moral interaction of machine and man. Much less speculative is the assumption that cultural, social, and literary criticism of machines has focused almost exclusively on the first and last of these "senses." Motor criticism, so to speak, is concerned with the unnaturalness and danger of thermally produced power, with its outsized dimensions, and with its ecological consequences. A great deal of late Romantic affect against machines and industry, in Wordsworth, Raabe, or Baudelaire, is fueled by this thought. Tool criticism, as it were, is mostly concerned with the degradation of work, with the displacement of the hand from direct contact with the object of work, and with the social deformations ensuing from the factory system. Disraeli's novel *Sybil* comes to mind, or William Morris and the Arts and Crafts movement, but mostly, of course, Karl Marx, to whom later chapters will return.

Within this horizon, the concentration in the following pages on transmissions and their discourse, kinematics, seeks to fill a gap. The intention is certainly not to disregard other discourses on machines but to insist that there is an irreducible "transmissive" sense of speaking about machines and that this sense has been obscured by the disproportionate attention paid to motors and tools. Since in transmissions motion is transferred by contiguous contact, kinematics focuses on the form of machine parts and on the motions they can absorb and produce. Given their mutual constraint, these machine parts are bound by a synchronous, "analog" logic that radiates out both to the motor and to the tool and limits their form; but there is also a history of these forms that has rarely been told and that leaves an imprint not only on the machines but also on the objects they produce and on the culture in which they move. The titular result of this history is the epochal importance of the cylindrical form for a full comprehension of the nineteenth century.

In keeping with the superimposition of the parts of the machines and the senses of interpretation, the attention to transmissions could be said to explicate the allegorical sense of machines. It is certainly true that in a "literal" sense the transmission is the allegorical part of the machine—it is nothing for itself, it is designed to make motion "other," it refers from one part (the motor) to another (the tool), and so forth. We will encounter this literalization of allegories and metaphors throughout the following pages; *revolution, translation, horizon, freedom* all have very literal, three-dimensional meanings in kinematics. Another egregious example is the notion of *Gestell*, which in Franz Reuleaux's kinematics denotes the one member in a linkage that is fixated so that the others can move. We now know that Martin Heidegger read Reuleaux in preparation for his essay "The Question of Technology," which launched *Gestell* into conceptual orbit.[32]

Allegories are, in the tradition of rhetoric, extended metaphors. The late German philosopher Hans Blumenberg—perhaps Heidegger's worthiest and most powerful opponent—published his *Paradigms for a Metaphorology* in 1960 partly as a counterproject to Heidegger's incessant reliance on etymologies and to the obscurity of his concepts. His principal claim is that some metaphors, rather than supplementing or adorning concepts, are originary (Blumenberg calls them "absolute") and only later become hardened into the currency of concepts. The use of such metaphors can only be exemplified but not theorized (hence the title *Paradigms*); it is born from the initial speechlessness with which human beings confront the world. For Blumenberg, the usage and conceptualization of metaphors is an instance of technologizing *(Technisierung)* that helps reduce the complexity of the world to manageable and predictable features and that is later forgotten as such. In this view, metaphors and their extensions, allegories, are linguistic machines that help negotiate the anthropological mismatch between world and words. Since Blumenberg conceived of his writings on metaphorology as a technological history of the mind, it is only fitting that from his papers the volume *Geistesgeschichte der Technik (Intellectual History of Technics),* which seeks to open an avenue complementary to the project of metaphorology, was just published.[33] In these brief and suggestive essays, Blumenberg sketches out a history that pairs notions and practices in technics with their philosophical and theological counterparts, thus bringing them into a new state of oscillation and radiance. In his short histories, notions such as "invention," "law," "fall," "acceleration," and "imitation" are charged with a semantic energy that exceeds their use in either metaphysics or technics. The following pages aim to expand on this project.

The dimensions of hermeneutics, rhetoric, and theology implied in Kleist's text also help to situate the present project vis-à-vis the dominant discourse on nineteenth-century culture, the writings of Walter Benjamin and his innumerable followers. In his *Arcades Project,* the culmination of a long effort to unsettle the conventions of literary and cultural criticism, Benjamin read texts, artifacts, and practices of the nineteenth century like allegories, like words that refer to other words while their reference to worldly phenomena is obscured by ideological and theological forgetfulness. The purpose of this reading was to escape the hermeneutic ideology of the symbol for which every artifact is an expression of an ineffable individual and, increasingly throughout the nineteenth and early twentieth centuries, of a national spirit. Like Kleist, Benjamin saw in Schiller's celebration of such imponderables as "grace" and *Bildung* a stifling and potentially dangerous tendency to disable critical analysis in favor of affirmation and sentimental identification. To give an obvious example, calling a monument like the Eiffel Tower an allegory of industrial production rather than an expression of French spirit was a means of maintaining a critical distance to a cultural object and connecting it to other objects and phenomena (bridges, clocks, lighthouses) that it could in turn illuminate. Modern, commodity-producing societies, according to Benjamin's underlying argument, forget and indeed repress the allegorical function of their products in favor of the fetish of their originality and independence. Benjamin brought this insight to bear on the mode of his writing: the *Arcades Projects,* as much as we can determine from the methodological reflections it contains, was an attempt to reconstruct a network of cross-references that would convince readers, by sheer force of evidence, of the repressed inner coherence of industrial, social, cultural, and political production. Like Aby Warburg's contemporary *Mnemosyne* project, *Das Passagen-Werk* was to be an atlas of quotations that would reveal the allegorical fabric of the epoch.[34]

But Benjamin was not content just to reconstruct the kinematics of signification in the archives of the nineteenth century in Paris and Berlin. As we know from the very same theoretical reflections, as well as from his later essayistic and biographical writings, he experienced incessant translation, where every word and every object means something else and obeys only the parameters of communicative or transmissive functionality, as a deficient, fallen mode of signification compared to an ideal, paradisiacal state where every thing was in its place and every word, like a name, meant just itself. While Kleist at the beginning of the epoch of kinematics hoped for a return to paradise through the total elimination of (kinematic) freedoms, Benjamin at its end hoped for the messianic interruption of incessant translation. Although in his personal recollections Benjamin often expressed delight in the transitoriness of nineteenth-century phenomena—for example, in his childhood reflections on the large cylinder of the *Kaiserpanorama*—his "doctrinal" writings vibrate with disdain for the obliviousness and profanity of the epoch, for its aversion to the possibility of any messianic arrest of history. Unlike Herr C., Benjamin did not see any grace or hope in the motion of machines, nor did he expect redemption from mechanisms that could convert the translational motion of falling and alienation into the rotational motion of reflection and self-containment. That is why all of his key methodological terms—*standstill, shock, rupture, epic theater, flash point*—are antikinematic; unlike the dancer's crank, they all aim at interrupting rather than translating motion.[35] Benjamin's anagogy, unlike Kleist's, requires the destruction of the world of machines.

If the following pages adopt the perspective of the eccentric dancer rather than of Benjamin's messianism, it is not because of principled objections to its impetus but because issues such as apokatastasis (the most comprehensive rotation possible), justice, and salvation are just too vast for a modest book on mechanics and literary history. The restricted focus, and the empathetic admission that there may be a potential for grace in the products of mechanical engineering, allows for greater attention to details and to immanent developments, and it affords, hopefully, a more comprehensive view on phenomena that otherwise have seemed unrelated. In the resulting reassembly and rearrangement of disparate phenomena—in particular the integration of nineteenth-century narratives into the discussion of kinematics—and the use of multiple vocabularies to describe them I hope to convince the reader that there is a level of description that the prevailing literal, moral, and allegorical readings of nineteenth-century culture have not reached. It goes without saying that many of the phenomena here discussed have other than kinematic and literary dimensions; but, as both Kleist and Benjamin knew, the sphere in which to address such dimensions is not academic scholarship but political debate and action.

. . .

The following chapters will unfold and demonstrate the centrality of the cylinder in subsequent steps. After a genealogy of kinematics, centered on the presentation of its greatest synthesizer, Franz Reuleaux, a brief overview of the metaphysics of motion that issues in the rise of the cylinder rounds out the first part. The second part is chiefly concerned with demonstrating and illustrating cylindrical devices, showing the cylinder in its role as motor, as tool, and as enclosure, and arguing for the importance of the screw as the machined conjunction of translational and rotational motion. Spliced into these technical descriptions are readings of the epoch's greatest literary innovation, the realist novel, with Charles Dickens, Honoré de Balzac, and Henry James as the focal points. An epilogue attempts to situate this intellectual history of technics in the terrain of current scholarship and provides an outlook on the destruction of the cylindrical paradigm in the twentieth century.

A note on the photographs: with "literal" illustrations of these devices readily available on the Internet, a good portion of the images were selected to highlight the formal intricacies and inner relationship of the objects. These aspects became visible—heroically or nostalgically—only after the age of the cylinder had gone into crisis. Albert Renger-Patzsch in Germany and Margaret Bourke-White in the United States both seem to have been fascinated by the opacity and finality of the cylinder and the motions it embodied. With more patience (and a larger budget), the visual grammar of the cylinder could be traced on both sides of the Atlantic, with additional input from Soviet photography.

CHAPTER 2

The Rise of Kinematics

Kinematics is the science of forced motion, of motion in mechanisms and machines. Interest in such motion emerged once the concern with the origin of motion and the nature of motive forces moved from the domain of metaphysics to the newly energized discipline of physics. The steam engine diminished the eighteenth century's fixation on origins—debated in the innumerable Academy prize questions about the origins of motion, of species, of language, of ideas, of property—because it normalized the generation and harnessing of motion and because it focused attention on the measurability of relations between previously unconnected phenomena. Heat ceased to be a separate substance with separate properties; it became an effect of motion, but it was this effect in such a way that nothing was lost or unaccounted for in the transition from one state to another. The old distinction between cause and effect whereby the former was inferred from the latter in a metaphysical leap—there must be forces because there is change in motion—was superseded by strict equivalencies between contiguous phenomena—there is heat whenever there is motion, and vice versa: *causa aequat effectum*.[1] The *actio in distans* that governed, and bedeviled, Newton's mechanics gave way to processes that were conceived as contiguous or, as historians later would call it, analog.[2] Insofar as it translated every physical change into a fully measurable effect, the steam engine was, on a very fundamental level, nothing but a mechanism to transmit the "motive power of heat" present in the universe. Kinematicists, who conceptualized and facilitated this transmission, could therefore claim to be concerned with the very essence of machines.

What engineers had tacitly presupposed since the middle of the eighteenth century found its basic expression in the first law of thermodynamics: not only are forces convertible into one another, but such conversions also happen without absolute loss. The accounts of all transactions in nature are always balanced, nothing is added to and nothing lost from the overall sum. The law of the conservation of force confirmed that machines were calculable and therefore scientific objects and that the input in energy equaled the output in work minus the inevitable price paid to the environment in terms of evaporation, cooling, friction, and so on.[3] Their calculability as material systems in interaction with their environment distinguished nineteenth-century machines from the automata of the eighteenth century, which needed to be insulated against their environment, had an input consisting in some form of kinetic energy, and had an output that was not measurable—or, in the case of pendulums, clocks, and other instruments, was measurement itself.[4]

The interconversion and the conservation of force—as well as the interconversion of the knowledge of engineers, physicists, and physiologists—provided a finite frame in which translatability was a much more concrete and immediate concern than originality.[5] Of course, the question of the origin of force was not "solved" by this approach, but, in a fashion not untypical of the epoch's concentration on practicability, it was pushed toward the margins of metaphysics and religion. Under the auspices of the laws of thermodynamics, the earth, fueled by the heat of the sun, became part of a vast cosmic heat engine; the individual machines built on earth did nothing but intercept and utilize the stream of energy flowing through them. Cosmic heat, stored in subterranean coalfields, needed only to be reignited to provide energy for untold machines independently of their location.

Unfortunately, physicists also discovered that while forces could be translated into one another, the overall flow of energy was unidirectional and irreversible, from hot to cold. This second law of thermodynamics marked the beginning of ecological thinking; remarkably early, physicists and philosophers realized that human beings were, in the words of a French observer, "nothing but concessionaires" of the earth's finite resources.[6] Physicists, many of them devout Christians, scrambled to reconcile this inglorious dissipation with the biblical apocalypse, but the fact remains that ecological thinking is characterized by a renunciation of transcendence and divine intervention: while in New-ton's universe God still had to intervene to correct potentially cata-strophic irregularities of planetary motion, the fully analog and slowly stalling universe of the nineteenth century no longer had an opening for such correction. Not the origin of forces but their end became a major preoccupation for the epoch; entropy, the inevitable descent of all organization into undifferentiated matter and meaningless noise, was the flipside of the fully calculable universe.[7]

In this situation, kinematics as the science of mechanical energy ex-change and transmission rose quietly to prominence, not only because under the first law of thermodynamics every machine is a transmission mechanism anyway, but because under the second law the transmission is that part of a machine that can minimize entropy—by finding the best paths, by reducing stress on materials, and by avoiding as much as possible leakage through friction.[8] This is not its stated goal, and the first great theorist of the field, the German Franz Reuleaux, explicitly excluded all material considerations; but in the end he too dreamt of a totally negentropic machine, one that would run in perfect silence with the least amount of energy loss.

Modern kinematics owes its theoretical formulation and its forma-tion as a discipline to the emergence of new schools and curricula, par-ticularly in Napoleonic and post-Napoleonic France.[9] While France—to say nothing of Germany—lagged behind in the development and indus-trial deployment of steam engines, the Grands Écoles, founded in the wake of the French Revolution, were among the first institutions to reward engineers with academic positions and to urge mathematicians to think about the practical implications of mechanisms. Already in 1794, Gaspard Monge proposed courses on the theory of machines that would focus on the elementary mechanisms of force transmission: "By these elements are to be understood the means by which the direc-tions of motion are changed; those by which progressive motion in a right line, rotative motion and reciprocating motion, are made each to reproduce the others. The most complicated machines being merely the result of a combination of some of these elements, it is necessary that a complete enumeration of them should be drawn up."[10] The mathemati-cian Monge here identifies machine transmissions as instantiations of Leonard Euler's earlier observation that the motion of all rigid bodies may be broken down into translation along a straight line and rotation around an axis.[11] To transfer motion to act at any point in space and to act as translational, reciprocal, or rotational motion, the machine designer has to devise a chain of joints and linkages that best embodies and combines motions. Franz Reuleaux will later summarily call these chains cylinder chains.

The recognition of rotation as an irreducible and entirely technical form of motion meant that the moving object under investigation and construction could no longer be conceived as a mathematical point; points, lacking extension, cannot rotate. As Kleist's choreographic criticism had implied, the coherence and predictive success of Newton's mass point mechanics were in large part predicated on the fact that celestial objects in motion could be reduced to geometrical points because they were so far away and their orbits were so large; at close range and in rapid repetition, however, otherwise negligible imperfections (in the axial symmetry of an object, for example) were magnified and could quickly lead to the breakdown of a system of linkages. This is why standardization and precision tool making would take the place of mathematical solutions in nineteenth-century engineering.

Newton's celestial objects were moving along straight-line paths, or on paths that could be analyzed as the result of forces jointly impacting an imaginary center where all mass was concentrated. Rotary motion, by contrast, had to be conceived as the impact of two forces at separate points of an extended body. To reiterate, it makes no sense to speak of the rotation of a point, but neither does it make sense to speak of a single rotating force.[12] Louis Poinsot, also a product of the new French education system, argued that rotation should be viewed as the result of a "couple" of forces, acting equally from opposite directions on a line drawn through the center of a rotating body. Thus rotation can be quantified as the product of the forces times the length of the line on which they act: this is the measure of torque—a quantity unknown to the eighteenth century—which even today is the true measure of the output of machines, most prominently the automobile engine.[13] (A good example is turning a car's steering wheel: one hand pulls downward, the other pushes upward, and both are at an equal distance from the center of the wheel. Before the introduction of power steering, the diameter of steering wheels in heavy trucks was particularly large to help the driver expend less force in turning the vehicle.)

Kinematics relies on a still more restricted description of motion than that outlined by Newton and amplified by Poinsot. It is defined as a view of motion independent from the forces causing it. Since machines are, from one point of view, manifest attempts to eliminate random, or, as Franz Reuleaux would say, "cosmic," forces, kinematics is always "kinematics of machinery."[14] The text that is most often mentioned as the declaration of independence of kinematics, André-Marie Ampère's *Essai sur la philosophie des sciences* (1834), clearly recognizes this interdependence of machinery and geometric description:

> It [i.e., the new science of kinematics] should treat in the first place of spaces passed over, and of times employed in different motions, and of the determination of velocities according to the different relations which may exist between those spaces and times. Furthermore it should study the various instruments by means of which one motion can be changed into another; so that if one conceives of these instruments as machines (as is usually the case) one must define a machine not, as one customarily does, as *an instrument by means of which one can change the direction and the intensity of a given force,* but as *an instrument by means of which one can change the direction and the speed of a given motion.*[15]

While French theorists put serious efforts into founding and institutionalizing kinematics as a deductive science, British engineers were attacking its practical problems. Kinematically speaking, the rise of the steam engine as the motor of the Industrial Revolution was the result of a specific mechanism to "change the direction and speed of a given motion," more precisely the (reciprocating) translational motion of the piston, into the rotational motion of the working beam. It was invented by James Watt in 1784 and was immediately patented so that it could reach the open market at the very beginning of the nineteenth century. Only then could the proliferation of cylindrical machines in the nineteenth century really begin.[16]

This mechanism, commonly called "Watt's parallel motion," changed the steam engine from a pendulum into a fully rigid mechanism. It connected the piston that rose from and was pushed into the cylinder with the beam that pivoted on a central column.

The pivoting beam was part of the early architecture of steam engines, which were primarily used to pump water. Before Watt, only the downward stroke of the engine was powered: either the rapid cooling of the steam under the piston created a vacuum that pulled the piston down, or steam was injected above the piston. In this configuration, where the piston pulled on the beam (and the beam pulled on the pumping vessel), it was enough to use chains or ropes as a connection; they were run across the ends of the beam, and the kinematic conflict between the semicircular motion of the beam and the straight motion of the piston was reconciled—just as it was in Kleist's marionettes—by the slackness in the connection (fig. 1).

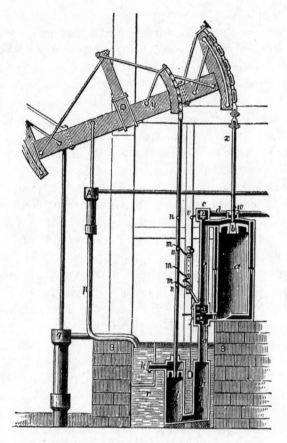

FIGURE 1. Watt's 1774 engine. The piston (and the valve gear) are connected to the beam by a chain; the power stroke can only be downward. Reprinted from Thurston (1902, 98).

This paradigm had to be changed when Watt began to power both the up- and the downstroke of the piston by using steam as a positive (expanding) rather than as a negative medium. Now the piston was pushing up on the beam as well as pulling it down; ropes and chains did no longer work, and a simple rigid rod without a mediating mechanism would have destroyed the machines in a very short time—if the piston were pushed along a line that deviated from the cylinder's axis, it would scrape against the inside walls, destroying its symmetry and losing the ability to seal and maintain pressure.[17] Even without these difficulties, the practical problems of boring or casting

accurate enough cylinders in sufficiently strong materials and of finding lubricants to minimize the inevitable friction proved very hard to
overcome for most machine builders in the late eighteenth and the very
early nineteenth centuries.[18] One of Watt's many advantages in the race
for efficient engines was that through his partner Matthew Boulton he
could intervene directly in the manufacturing of cylinders, asking for
more precision in boring and for stronger alloys.[19] To Boulton he first
announced his discovery that a rigid linkage configured the right way
could guide both the up- and the downstroke of a double-acting steam
engine without stressing the materials involved.

In a formulation at once revelatory of the truly empirical process of
engineering and of the stunning novelty of motion conversion, Watt
wrote of the contraption he called "parallel motion": "When I saw
it work for the first time, I felt truly all the pleasure of novelty, as if
I was examining the invention of another man."[20] Yet like so many
engineering advances in the nineteenth century, parallel motion was
an avoidance of conflict rather than an invention of something entirely
new. The mechanism simply caught two semicircular movements at the
point where they intersected along a seemingly straight path (fig. 2).
One was the movement of the beam O_A—A, which in kinematic nomenclature was called the crank (the *Kurbel,* of which Kleist's Herr C.
dreamed); the other was the link O_B—B affixed to an opposite wall,
called the follower. Both were connected by a third link A—B, the coupler. As the crank moved up and down, it led the follower into a mirror
image of its own motion whereby a point M on the coupler was forced
to trace out an elongated figure eight, the sign of infinity. If the proportions of the links were chosen appropriately and the movement of the
crank was restricted accordingly, M traced a line that was approxi-
mately parallel to the beam's support column. A piston rod, attached
to C, could push and pull in a line extending from the cylinder's axis.
Depending on the machine's architecture and size, Watt translated this
parallel motion horizontally by means of pantographs—linkages based
on the parallelograms that had long been used to translate writing and
drawing across a plane—which yielded other parallel points M′ able to
drive a valve train or an auxiliary pump (fig. 3).[21]

Watt's mechanism not only allowed for a potentially infinite increase
in power output but also universalized the use of steam engines just as
much as fossil fuel rendered them independent of natural location. The
four-bar linkage (the hatched line at O_B and O_A on the left of figure
2 indicates a fixed frame and counts as one bar, just like the "floor

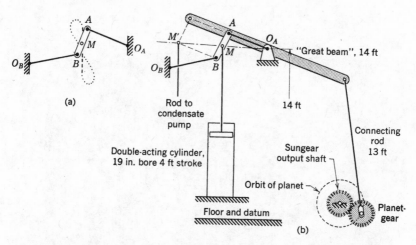

FIGURE 2. (a) Watt's "parallel-motion" linkage in schematic form: O_A—A is the beam's arm, acting as a crank; A—B is the coupler; O_B—B is the follower, anchored to a wall. The point M on the coupler will trace out a figure eight, part of which is "straight" and can be used to guide the piston rod. (b) The mechanism on Watt's engine. Point M is transposed to M' by means of a pantograph and there guides the rod of a pump. The sun-and-planet gear on the working side of the beam would be useless without the continuous motion provided by the parallel linkage. "Floor and datum" is what Reuleaux (and Heidegger) call *Gestell*. Reproduced with permission of The McGraw-Hill Companies from Richard Hartenberg, *Kinematic Synthesis of Linkages*, © 1964.

and datum" on the right) is the most economical way of mediating between translational and rotational motion. To repeat, such mediation is necessary because in a finite mechanism (unlike in the universe or in a gun) every translational motion needs to be "returned," every straight motion needs to be reciprocal or oscillating.[22] Using variants of the four-bar linkage, engineers could eliminate the working beam and configure machines for a hitherto unimagined variety of purposes—or else utilize the transmission as the machine's tool, as is the case in motorized vehicles. The slider-crank mechanism—an avatar of the four-bar linkage—became the most successful of these linkages: first in the locomotive, then in the internal combustion engine, it allowed the motor to produce nothing but rotation.

From a kinematic point of view, it is irrelevant where the motion of a mechanism originates and where it is utilized, as kinematics is not concerned with forces or with stresses on material that might result from the impact of forces.[23] Kinematic transmission functions without a fixed origin (such as straight-line motion) and without a determined

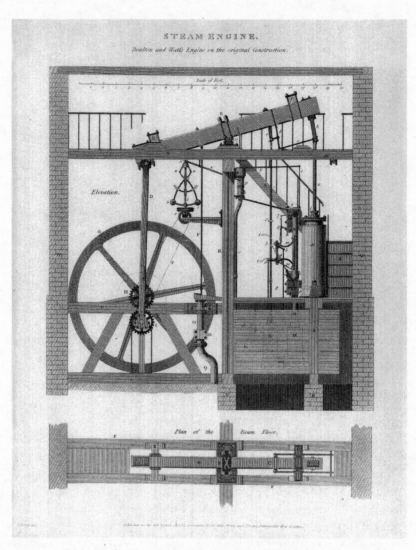

FIGURE 3. Drawing of a Watt and Boulton steam engine, after 1784. The parallel-motion linkage is on the right; on the left is the sun-and-planet gear driving a flywheel. Also visible on the left side is a governor, another of Watt's inventions. It rotates with the engine stroke and shuts down the steam supply if the machine runs too fast. © Science Museum / Science & Society Picture Library—All rights reserved.

FIGURE 4. Two of Reuleaux's teaching models. The curve traced by a point
on the coupler depends on the length of the links, and on which of them is
immobilized by the *Gestell*. Reprinted from Reuleaux (1876, 68, 71).

destination (such as pure rotation) but is concerned (to use Walter Benjamin's term) with translatability *(Übersetzbarkeit)* as such. All that linkages, and machines in general, need is a frame that determines the orientation of their movements; it generally consists in anchoring one link to an immobile part that in figure 2 is called the "floor and datum" but that in Reuleaux's seminal terminology becomes *Gestell*.[24]

The curves traced by a point on the coupler (the link d—e in the linkage on the left in fig. 4) are an instructive example of the irreducible empiricism and pragmatism in the construction of kinematic transmissions. They change in proportion to the length of the individual links and to the position of the *Gestell,* but the rate of this change and the bewildering variety of the resulting curves defeat attempts to describe them algebraically or in any other form of abstraction. This was true at least as long as the means of representing these curves were, like the mechanisms that produced them, analog; computer programs now can easily model coupler point curves, and the problem, like many others, has disappeared from the problem sets of kinematics students. Franz Reuleaux felt that the best way to teach the properties of four-bar (and other) linkages was to build (and license) an extensive collection of teaching models, which can still be admired, for example, in Cornell's Sibley School of Mechanical and Aerospace Engineering. Seeing these models in motion—or seeing Theo Jansen's fantastically inventive linkage "beasts" prowl the beaches in Holland—gives us a rare sight of kinematics liberated from the servitude to motor and tool.[25] They show that there is distinct grace and beauty in forced motion, as Kleist's Herr C. claimed with seeming contrariness. Uncovering the aesthetics of forced motion as an object of contemplation, as a driving force in mechanical engineering, and as an element in nineteenth-century literary culture is a goal of the following pages.

Such a goal was far from the mind of Franz Reuleaux, the great German synthesizer of machine design and kinematics; with his *Theoretische Kinematik* of 1875 he wanted to provide a space for kinematics on the curriculum of German research universities, which had been founded by men around Friedrich Schiller for whom all things mechanical were anathema. While experimental physiologists, despite operating with rather gruesome empirical remainders themselves, had managed to secure for themselves a prestigious place in the German research university, mechanical engineering was still relegated to professional schools and para-academic institutions. Reuleaux, who had traveled widely in Europe and in the United States, felt that German engineering products stood no chance in an increasingly globalized market and that it would behoove the Second Reich to centralize engineering training and raise it to a par with other academic disciplines.[26]

In the German context, any discipline wanting to graduate to a full-fledged science had to meet two fundamental requirements: it had to be in discursive control of its own principles and presuppositions, and it had to be able to give a coherent account of its own history. In the case of experimental physiology, for example, this meant that the dubious principle of *Lebenskraft* (vital force) had to be abandoned in favor of the first law of thermodynamics and that a careful rewriting of its history, especially with regard to Romantic visions of vitality (including Goethe's), would integrate physiology into the context of German intellectual history. Many of Herrmann von Helmholtz's popular lectures were devoted to this task.[27] In the case of mechanical engineering this meant that all contingent factors in machine design—such as the metallurgy of machine parts, the turbulences of power generation, the economic concerns of the manufacturing process, the social conditions of factory workers—would have to be bracketed, and the logic of machines developed deductively. Relying on the definitions by Ampère and other theorists, Reuleaux realized that an a priori deduction of the logic of machines could proceed only from the kinematics of machinery. The *Theoretische Kinematik* (translated into English in 1876 as *Kinematics of Machinery*) seeks to unfold this logic beginning with the most fundamental givens of material contact, and it invents a symbolic language in which machine elements can be classified and their combination be taught. At the same time—hidden in the vast body of his book—Reuleaux sketched a history of machines and mechanisms that emulated in scope the grand historico-philosophical designs of German historicism.[28]

With a good measure of irony, though not without systematic pride, Reuleaux reached back to the pre-Socratic sage Heraclitus for his most fundamental statement: "Everything rolls."[29] Everything in a machine is in contact with everything else in a motion that is at the same time rotational and translational. Motion in and of machines is always relative motion (anchored by the *Gestell* of its frame), and the successive positions of one extended body in relation to another can always be configured as one curve rolling off another. In the part entitled—with obvious reference to the opening chapter of Immanuel Kant's *Metaphysical Foundations of Natural Science*—"Phoronomic Propositions," Reuleaux demonstrates this relationship first as that between a moving and a fixed line. The successive positions of the moving line P—Q (or of any other figure through which a line can be drawn) with respect to the line A—B can be described by two separate lines: first, as the line between the successive points around which the line rotates (its poles) as it moves along the x axis in an imaginary Cartesian coordinate system (the line O_1, O_2, O_3 in the following illustration); and second, as the line between the successive points that indicate the rate of rotation along the y axis (the line M_1, M_2, M_3) (fig. 5).

Contracted from polygons into smooth curves, these curves fully describe the instantaneous position of the translating and rotating line P—Q in relation to the line A—B, which lies on the same plane (it is "con-plane"). Reuleaux calls these curves *Polbahnen;* his translator Kennedy calls them centroids (later changed to "centrodes").[30] The purpose of this abstraction is to show that the relative planar motion of any two bodies can be fully described once their centrodes are known, and that this relative motion can be described as a rolling.[31]

Machine parts, then, just make actual what is potential in any relative motion of two rigid bodies in a plane. Reuleaux operates with the abstraction of moving points and lines only because he strives for maximum generality—for the justification of his law that *everything* rolls. He is fully aware, of course, that the subject of kinematics is machinery: that is, an assembly of rigid bodies that have additional properties, even if one abstracts from material and from the forces to which they are subject.[32] The reciprocal rolling of the centrodes,

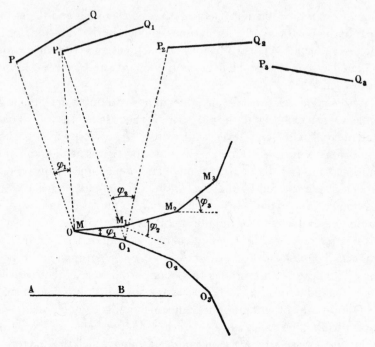

FIGURE 5. The relative translation and rotation of an extended body represented as the rolling of one body (P—Q) off another (A—B). Reprinted from Reuleaux (1876, 62).

as soon as it is conceived as being performed by two extended bodies moving in the same plane, must be understood as the rolling of one cylinder against another, for it is the cylinder alone that has an extended curved surface and a fixed axis of rotation.[33] Even if one of the bodies does not move, the other can roll on it, as a locomotive's wheel rolls on its rail (which is conceived as a cylinder with infinitely large diameter). The application of the Heraclitean law of rolling to the real world of extended machine parts therefore reads: "We may extend the law just enunciated for plane figures equally to the relative motion of solids . . . : Every relative motion of two con-plane bodies may be considered to be a cylindric [sic] rolling, and the motions of any points in them may be determined so soon as their cylinders of instantaneous axes are known."[34]

Even though the cylinder as an embodied motion is crucial for the understanding of the relative motion of extended bodies, Reuleaux introduces it in the first part of his theoretical kinematics without further comment or reflection. Far-reaching consequences of this conception could be explored: for example, the oscillation of *rolling* as an intransitive verb of motion and as a transitive verb denoting perhaps the most important industrial processes of the nineteenth century. Spheres, for example, can roll on one another (as they do in ball bearings), but only cylinders can roll something. Yet the cylinder, although everywhere present, is neither thematized nor generalized by Reuleaux.

It is worth reflecting for a moment on Reuleaux's "discovery" of centrodes, because it repeats on a higher level of generality the epochal shift from pendulum to crank that we have seen playfully discussed in Kleist's story about the marionette theater. Centrodes belong to a class of curves known as "cycloids," which are traced out by a point rolling on a circle, either on its periphery, or its interior, or outside its periphery as long as it is rigidly linked. The most prominent and universally visible example of such an (interior) curve in the nineteenth century was undoubtedly the motion of the crosshead on a locomotive wheel, which Heidegger rightly counted among the essentially technical motions.[35] But cycloids were of equally great importance for premodern astronomy, where the motion of the planets was conceived as their rolling on the surface of celestial spheres, and the apparent irregularities in their orbit were explained as epicycloids—as rotation upon a rotation that might look from the center of the system like a slowing down or an acceleration. Doing away with this extremely complex system and replacing it with the comparative simplicity of the earth's eccentric position and with gravitational forces acting instantaneously across the void had been Copernicus's and Newton's great innovation. The return of the cycloid in the nineteenth century, then, was a return of ancient celestial mechanics in the shape of machines and mechanisms—a return of a concept of cosmic grace and of cosmic coherence that characterized the newly closed system of thermodynamics.

The drama of this epochal difference was played out in the delicate frame of the pendulum clock. Galileo had initially thought that the period of the pendulum's swing was isochronous—that it would mark identical time intervals if all outside factors like friction were eliminated. Huygens famously proved this assumption wrong and showed instead that only if the pendulum was forced by an outside constraint (like a metal "cheek" on each side of the swing) to follow the line of a cycloid rather than that of a circle did it really count equal intervals. For Reuleaux, this episode strikingly exemplified the difference between theoretical geometry—descriptively accurate but practically worthless—and the theory of constrained motion *(Zwanglauftheorie)* that his *Kinematik* proposed to unfold.[36] This is the kinematic reason why Reuleaux, and many machine theorists with him, understood machines to be part of the cosmos, not artifacts alien to it.

Reuleaux also remarked explicitly that rolling always meant the rolling of one body on the surface of another.[37] That is, already on the most general level of his system, he conceived of kinematic phenomena as relations of pairs. This admission of an "original duplicity" differentiated the empirical approach of engineers from that of philosophers and theologians, who were committed to the search for first and singular causes. Reuleaux did not reflect on this stance; but he did carry it over into the second of his major contributions to the science of kinematics, the concept of kinematic pairs. If every motion in a machine was relative, Reuleaux argued, it could be conceived as the contact motion of one part against another. Therefore, the smallest element of a machine was a pair or couple (just as the smallest element in Poinsot's theory of rotation was a couple of forces). These couples, like the linkages on their plinths, had to fulfill certain conditions—one of their elements had to be the other's *Gestell,* the fixed element had to follow the form of the mobile element, and the joining had to exclude all other motions ("freedoms") except the one that was desired. The ideal couples to meet all of these conditions were the ones where one element fully enclosed the other—Reuleaux called them *Umschlusspaare* or enclosed pairs.[38]

The three elementary enclosed pairs Reuleaux deduced were by necessity all cylindrical. For when one body enclosed another and still needed to move, it could slide along the enclosed body's axis, rotate around it, or, ideally, do both. The three kinematic couples, then, were the revolute joint, the prism, and the screw-nut couple (fig. 6).

In a way that would become important when screw theory at the end of the nineteenth century generalized the motions of rigid bodies, these could be understood as versions of the screw: the revolute pair as a screw-nut pair with a thread tending toward zero, the prism as a screw-nut tending toward infinity. These three links exhausted the possibilities of enclosed pairs, since in planar motion—motion across a precise plane as is necessary in machines—no other motions than sliding, rotating, and their combination are possible. Indeed, "all three are well known in machine construction,—the screw pair both in fastenings and in moving pieces; the pair of revolutes in journals, bearings, &c. and the prism-pair in guides of all sorts."[39]

FIGURE 6. The three kinematic couples, from left to right: the revolute joint (which contains rotation, as in a wheel hub), the prism (which contains translation, as in a guide rail), and the screw and its nut. Reprinted from Reuleaux (1876, 43).

These couples by themselves did not yet have a determinate use; they were like the roots of words that were not yet inflected and connected to meaningful sentences. The next larger units therefore were kinematic chains—mechanisms in which cylindrical pairs served as joints. Watt's parallel linkage was such a *Zylinderkette*,[40] since it—like every four-bar linkage—consisted of four revolute pairs connected by rigid links; the slider-crank mechanism typically consisted of two revolute pairs and one prism pair. These cylinder chains transmitted and converted motion across the plane of the machine from the motor to the tool; they followed the same "phoronomic" laws as their elements and were fully determined (even though describing them mathematically remained difficult).

Mechanisms that employed the three cylindrical pairs were at once the basis and the ideal of Reuleaux's kinematics because they excluded all interference by outside (in Reuleaux's terms, "cosmic") forces and thus allowed for a coherent logic of machine elements. By calling his pairs *Umschlusspaare* and their combination "chains" *(Ketten),* Reuleaux invoked an embodied logic of material elements—*Kettenschluss* is, after all, the German word for syllogism.[41] The overall goal of *Theoretische Kinematik* was "kinematic synthesis"—which, in the wake of Kant's distinction between analysis and synthesis and with a view of making good on Monge's and Ampère's program, Reuleaux conceived as the science of deducing kinematic assemblages a priori, regardless of material or even of purpose.[42] Reuleaux coined a word to invoke both the exclusion of cosmic forces and the a priori necessity of kinematic design: *zwang(s)läufig.* It has since entered the German vernacular with the meaning "inevitable"; Kennedy translates it as "constrained," and Reuleaux in a note offers the Greek "desmodromic," which has caught on in certain engineering circles.[43]

Reuleaux was too much of a practitioner not to know that many mechanical linkages cannot be converted into cylinder chains with fully constrained pairs—ropes and belts and springs, for example, could not be enclosed, and the strain on the material in enclosed links often exceeded the metallurgical capacities of his time. Nonetheless, he understood the history of machine design to be a logical—a *zwangsläufig*—development from "force-closure" to "pair-closure." Force-closure, like the link between a cam lobe and a valve or between the wheel of a locomotive and the rail, is open to "cosmic" interference (valve float or wheel slip); pair-closure—its basic forms being embodied in the three cylindrical enclosed pairs—eliminates such interferences by systematically forcing motion in one direction to the exclusion of all others. The change from one to the other provides, according to Reuleaux, a parameter by which to measure progress in machine design: "The question now arises:—what is the special kinematic meaning or nature of the changes by which the machine has been advanced to its present degree of completeness? . . . I believe the answer to this question is:—the line of progress is indicated in the manner of using force-closure, or more particularly, in the substitution of pair-closure, and the closure of the kinematic chain obtained by it, for force-closure."[44] One way of describing this development in kinematic terms—and in terms provocatively contrary to liberal philosophies of history—is to chart it as the successive elimination of freedoms. For engineers, an object within three-dimensional Euclidean space has six degrees of freedom: it can move along the three axes of space and it can rotate around them. The motions of mechanisms (as opposed to those of a ship or a plane, from which many of the technical terms for the degrees of freedom are taken) are constrained to one plane, as in Watt's parallel mechanism, thus eliminating all freedoms except rotation around an axis and translation along it. These two freedoms, as well as their combination in the motion of a screw, are embodied, as Reuleaux had casually remarked, in the body of the cylinder.

Against this backdrop, the history of machine development, which Reuleaux inserted as a compact chapter into his *Theoretische Kinematik* and later dispersed over the second volume of the *Kinematik*, which appeared in 1900, amounts to a history of the progressive elimination of "cosmic" freedom.[45] "We have recognized and examined in certain pairs of kinematic elements the property of force-closure, by which a certain amount of kosmic freedom is left in the machinal system, and seen that it has been for thousands of years the aim of invention to limit or destroy this freedom."[46] Reuleaux's *Ur*-machine is a single cylinder: the fire drill, a pointed stick twirled by hands on a wooden cavity with the purpose of igniting the wood itself or fibers placed around it. So long as human hands twirl the stick, there is pair-closure only between the recess and the point of the stick. The next step consists in replacing the hands by a rope, which does not alter the nature of the closure but speeds up the rotation. Then a stone or a fitted piece of wood is placed on top of the rotating stick in such a way that all motion except rotation is eliminated. Now the twirling stick is part of a pair-closed chain that produces fire in a fully predictable manner.

A more contemporary but perhaps not equally felicitous example is the steam locomotive. It replaced the horse-carriage, which had been improved upon in various ways, for example in shock absorption and in the development of steering gear, but which was still beset by the potential disturbance of cosmic forces, such as uneven roads or drunken coachmen.

> Force-closure still remained, if nowhere else at least in the preservation of the direction of motion, which still demanded accustomed animals and an intelligent driver. Men naturally attempted to replace this force-closure by pair-closure. In the Railway the rails are paired with the wheels,—force-closure is used only to neutralize vertical disturbing forces. The step thus made in the direction of machinal completeness . . . was in reality no other than the uniting of the carriage and the road into a machine. The rail forms a part of this machine, it is the fixed element of the kinematic chain of which the mechanism really exists. . . . In opposition to this we have the problem of steam locomotion on common roads, which has been so feverishly taken up again within the last few years, but the solutions of which seem doomed to eternal incompleteness, for they are self-contradictory. It is desired to make something which shall be a machine, but in which at the same time the special characteristic of the machine—the pairing of elements—may be disregarded.[47]

To be sure, the pair-closure between the locomotive and the rail is only approximate: it is achieved by the weight of the engine (and in fact often breaks when the train has to climb a steep incline). What Reuleaux means by the inner contradictoriness of the automobile is that the wheels of the car cannot form a pair-closure with the road if the automobile is defined as a vehicle that can go anywhere by itself;

he mentions the recent discovery of wheels made of "India-rubber," which try to emulate rails insofar as "vulcanized India-rubber, externally flattened upon the road, serves as a smooth uniform surface for the rigid tread to run upon, thus corresponding generally to the rail of the railway";[48] kinematically speaking, however, the automobile is a failure because the pair-closure of its engine (the slider-crank-linkage) is stunted by the weak force-closure of its contact to the road. The further development of rubber wheels and the improvement of roads by means of another cylindrical machine, the steamroller, will alleviate this weakness, but every instance when a car spins its wheels or swerves off the road or just out of its lane is a testimony to the justness of Reuleaux's observation.

Although in the use of his terminology Reuleaux seemed to emulate Kant's critical philosophy, his view on the history of machines was Hegelian. Very much in the tradition of Hegel, Reuleaux tried to understand the history of machines and mechanisms as a slow but logically driven and often dialectical process toward maximum efficiency. His ideal was a machine, consisting of absolutely rigid elements connected by cylindrical pair-closures, that would capture and convert the energy flowing through the cosmos with as little noise and as little loss as possible. But this historical dialectic was the limit of his Hegelian leanings; in cosmological terms Reuleaux was thoroughly modern. Like Poinsot, like Auguste Comte, and like the foremost physicists of his time, he conceived of the cosmos, not as a living being (as Hegel still did), but as a vast machine driven by heat, in which the planets were the remnants of a linked planar mechanism. Perfecting transmissions, from this perspective, meant combating entropy in the only arena possible, namely by slowing down the dissipation of energy in fully linked, "pair-closed" machines.

Reuleaux also paid attention to the devaluation of human work. Like most engineers and scientists in the latter half of the nineteenth century, he was keenly aware of the destructive and dehumanizing potential of industrial modes of production and sought to confront the "burning question of our time, the question of the worker," with proposals of his own.[49] Characteristically, he saw the problem in the motor end of the machine: it is the logic of capital, he argued, that requires ever more powerful motors, which in turn lead to larger factories and more alienated labor. His own solution proposed smaller, yet kinematically efficient machines that would need fewer, perhaps even just one worker to attend them—automobiles, as it were, that did not move. We will see in chapter 5 how Karl Marx, unconcerned with the kinematic implications of factory work, shifted the discussion almost exclusively to the tool end of the machine.

Far more startling than the faith Reuleaux placed in the desmodromic progress of mechanization is the fact that he did not reflect on the shape that dominated every level of his investigation: the cylinder. We have seen that on the abstract level of phoronomy he conceived of relative motion as cylindrical rolling; on the elemental level of kinematic pairs he identified the cylindrical screw and its extremes as irreducible connectors; on the level of mechanical assemblies he developed a grammar of cylinder chains; and on the grand historical scale he began with an Ur-cylinder (the fire drill) and then described mechanical progress as the replacement of contiguous by cylindrical closures. Yet nowhere did Reuleaux look beyond the confines of kinematics and identify other cylindrical structures, such as rolling mills, the pneumatic tube delivery, or the tin can; nor did he ask why this shape, rather than any other, so dominated the machines and, as we will see, the culture of his epoch. This oversight is partly due to the natural myopia of the immersed witness and practitioner, but partly to the effort it takes to see that motions, and the shapes through which they are transmitted, are historically and culturally identifiable phenomena. Our view is traditionally trained on the motor or on the tool, not on shape-dependent transmission. The following chapter will begin to right this oversight by adding historical depth to shapes and motions.

The kinematic epoch that began so neatly in 1800 with the expiration of Watt's patent for parallel motion came to an end somewhere between the large-scale use of electrical motors, the discovery of radio transmission and X-rays toward the end of the nineteenth century, and the conflagrations of World War I. It was based on the visible, "analog" contact between moving parts and, more particularly, on the taming and conversion of rotation and translation. All of this was possible because with the emergence of the steam engine the kinematic problem of forcing and converting motion could be detached from concerns over the generation of power. The early French theorists of kinematics held out the possibility of devising a meaningful geometry of machine motion that would allow the construction of machines entirely on the drawing board. The experience of British machine builders showed that everywhere in the development of machines empirical factors would trump theoretical insight, in particular when the demands of the market and necessities of exploiting natural resources came into in play. Reuleaux, finally, sought to integrate practical and pedagogical concerns, but he also hoped that a grammar of forcing motion could be constructed that would allow the generation, the "synthesis," of transmissions, and with it the construction of machines for any purpose whatsoever. The unthought element in this entire development was the cylinder.

CHAPTER 3

The Valuation of Motions

The ubiquity of the cylinder in the machines and products of the nine-teenth century is due to its kinematic properties—its ability to force, transmit, and apply (to use a ethically paradoxical term) single-freedom motion. This insight translates the traditional triad of motor, transmis-sion, and tool into the kinematic triad of forcing, translating, and ap-plying motion. Kinematics, as Reuleaux's work shows, affords a view of machines from the inside out; much like the allegorical readings of old, which focus on intra- and intertextual relations, kinematics focus not only on the design and the necessities of individual devices but also on their interrelation, sometimes across several generations and avatars.[1] These relations are visible in the transmissions proper—for example, in Watt's parallel motion, in the driving gear of a locomo-tive, or in the mechanism of a front loader—while they also connect the kinematics of the motor (the cylinder of the steam engine), the new motions of the tools (the rolling of steel mills), and finally the objects these machines produce (the tin can, the pipe). Kinematics provides a standpoint from which to recognize in hitherto unrelated phenomena their underlying embodiment of motion. For example, it has often been argued that the nineteenth century, through its ability to machine and lubricate journal bearings, reinvented the wheel; but half-journal bear-ings were also used to allow the Galerie des Machines, an iconic iron and glass structure that spanned the largest interior space in the world in 1889, to expand and contract.[2] Just as we can think kinematically of the Galerie as a minimally moving wheel, we can think of the film camera as a lathe that carves light onto film, or of the fountain pen and the gasholder as the scalar extremes of a cylinder-piston assembly. Even the bridges of the nineteenth century, subject to so much debate, experimentation, and failure, conserve in the curvature of their arches and straightness of their carriageways the motion with which their parts were produced and with which they were launched from bank to bank—they, too, are frozen transmissions.[3] The Jena Romantics had the idea of breaking up the reification of the world by romanticizing it; kinematicizing the world of the nineteenth century similarly dissolves its massive structures, but it does so without introducing alien interpretive categories. Rather, we learn to see what Walter Benjamin has called the disfigured similarities *(entstellte Ähnlichkeiten)* that make up the coherence of the epoch.[4]

Yet kinematics discloses not only synchronic similarities across the epoch but also the profound historical and metaphysical conflict leading up to the forcing of rotational and translational motion in nineteenth-century cylinders. This conflict, the barest outlines of which are the subject of the following pages, has commanded little attention because techno-historical scholarship of the epoch has concentrated on kinematics' invisible other, the discovery and implementation of induction electricity—produced, to be sure, by the rotation of a magnet around a cylindrical coil, and hailed as a prime instance of convertibility. Electricity led to technologies and media that are no longer analog but, like an electrical spark, jump a gap. Telegraphy was its first successful application, and it is not hard to understand why it garners such attention—the difference between positive and negative, long and short, on and off, 0 and 1, seems to indicate a minimum of meaning amid the randomness of thermodynamic processes and thus to furnish the kind of interface between physical and intellectual realms that has long been the goal of modern natural science.[5] Of course, such processes, and their implementation in various media, are critically important, in particular for the archaeology of our own digital present; but scholarship rarely treats them as what they literally are, *dei ex machina*. Telegraphy, for example, depends entirely on cylindrical objects and processes—on the rolling of wires and cables, on the railway lines along which wires were strung, on the steamships from which they were laid across the ocean, and finally on the rotating drums in telegraphic transmitters and receivers. Similar kinematics underlie the development of the film camera.

The tactile and epistemological difference between analog kinematics and digital electricity is nicely captured in the reaction to the transition from gas to electrical lighting in private households around 1880. Early users of electricity remarked how uncanny it was to *switch* on the light, thus turning darkness to light (almost) instantaneously, rather than to open the tap and light the gradually emerging gas.[6] Both the unfathomable speed and the invisibility of electrical transmission raised concerns about the very fabric of the world. The growing popularity of all sorts of communications with invisible figures in séances is further testimony to the emergence of paradigms of invisible contact. Oswald Spengler, decrying the decline of the West at the beginning of the twentieth century, lamented that through electricity the bodies of machines "become ever more spiritual, ever more taciturn. The wheels, cylinders, and levers no longer talk. All that is important withdraws into the interior." Walter Benjamin, reading Charles Baudelaire's *Flowers of Evil* (1857), equated the disappearance of visible causation with the loss of meaningful experience, to be replaced by the (essentially meaningless) electrical sensation of repetitive shock.[7]

The disappearance of the machine from the visible, auditory, and tactile world imposes the question: If the electrical and digital age constitutes the far end of the epoch of the cylinder, and if that epoch began with Watt's invention of parallel motion, what came before its beginning? Looking backwards from the threshold of the epoch, we find that the distinction between translational and rotational motion, which is at the core of all kinematic endeavor in the nineteenth century, has a long and momentous history, a history that structures Western metaphysics and theology in significant, yet undisclosed ways. The threshold of kinematics was crossed at the moment when the double-acting steam engine required mechanisms that forced a compromise between rotation and translation. Of course, there were earlier attempts to tackle this problem, as all machines, regardless of their motor, are apparatuses for forcing motion, and water- and windmills in particular had long been outfitted with sophisticated transmissions that turned the motion of the wheels into all manner of reciprocal and intermittent motion. The steam engine, however, required the conversion of motions in both directions, from translation to rotation and vice versa, and it thereby raised the question of their relation to a general level. Theoretical kinematics attempted to deliver a priori rules of this forcing, but, despite Reuleaux's historical interest, it had no consciousness of its implications and antecedents. The following all too brief overview over the metaphysics of motions up to the nineteenth-century attempts to make up for this lack.[8]

The most influential early text in the valuation of motion, itself a *summa* of extended previous debates, is book 10 of Plato's *Laws*. Corporeal motion for Plato indicates a state of deficiency with respect to the immutable realm of ideas; it is a predicament of the world insofar as it is secondary, changeable, and imperfect. Nonetheless, not all motions are equal, and in the hierarchy of motions the best is that which reaches into immutability. This must be the motion of the soul, for the only relation that exists, in Plato's thought, between the world of ideas and the world of changeable and changing things is the soul. Its motion is the best; it is, like Newton's mass points, free in every direction, but it has the ability to originate motion. Only after this bridge to the ideas has been established—in a way that foreshadows Aristotle's concept of a pure origination of motion in the unmoved mover—does Plato rank motions in space. Rotation, combining rest (of the central axis) and motion (of the periphery) is an image of psychic motion and therefore the best possible corporeal motion. Below rotation Plato puts the continuous sliding or rolling motion of bodies in translation, followed by phenomena we would not recognize as essentially kinetic, like growth, division, and disintegration. A little further in the text (898a), he contrasts rotation and translation as motions appropriate and inappropriate to the soul, the motions of rationality and of irrationality respectively. In the cosmogony of Plato's *Timaios*—the most important of his dialogues for the Middle Ages—the demiurge endows the earth with rotation, "which, among the seven motions, is the motion most appropriate to reason and wisdom." The six other motions are the translational "freedoms" of a rigid body: back, forth, left, right, up, down. As translational motions they are nothing but "deviations."[9] The earth's rotation and the sphericity that results from it comprise the straight-line motions of the polygons of which the earth is made up—a contrast and tension that has found its most enduring image of the nested solids surrounded by spheres in Johannes Kepler's *Mysterium cosmographicum*.[10]

Aristotle accepts the hierarchy between rotation and translation but seeks to integrate it into a worldview that no longer posits a chasm between ideas and phenomena. The arguments in book 8 of his *Physics* for the eternity of motion, the primacy of locomotion over other forms of change, and the superiority of rotation over other forms of locomotion establish an uninterrupted chain of causes from the unmoved mover to cosmic and then to natural motions. Rotation is superior not only because it is the motion proper to the spheres of the cosmos but because rectilinear motion for Aristotle could never be continuous and infinite. In a spherical, finite cosmos it would at some point have to reverse itself, and this reversal—logically speaking, this self-contradiction—could be understood only as deficient. The linear rise of fire and the straight fall of a stone are motions that characterize the sublunar sphere, which is no longer in rotational motion.[11] Whatever their differences, for both Plato and Aristotle the hierarchies of motion are directly tied to the demands of onto-theology. The superiority and primacy of rotation derive from the fact that the coincidence of motion and stillness, of change and identity, of oneness and differentiation, is an indelible trace, or even a property, of divinity and reason in the cosmos.[12] The competing atomistic theory of particles falling in straight lines from which they are deflected by random inclinations was atheistic in precisely this onto-kinetic respect.

The disjunction between supralunar divine rotation and sublunar straight-line translation endures and is enriched in Christian kinematics by an anagogical dimension. Rotation is the motion of a redeemed world, of a world no longer disfigured by the gravitational pull of original sin. Nowhere is the divinity of rotation set against the drag of translation with more intensity than in Dante's *Divine Comedy*. After having endured the descent into the inferno, where the severity of punishment increases in proportion to the linear distance from the surface, and after having made the complementary ascent to the summit of purgatory, where the unburdening of sins follows the helical path of a screw, the voyager is finally led to the contemplation of ever more beautiful and intricate rotational formations, until he sees "quella circulazion" that is the godhead.[13] Dante's exaltation of rotation accords well with the doctrine of Thomas Aquinas, who adopted the hierarchies of motion from Aristotle and projected them onto the created world, as well as onto the history of salvation. Aquinas makes the additional point that rotation, unlike the translational motions of rising and falling, which are their own contraries, does not have a logical opposite. The circularity and infinity of rotation are visible signs of God's thought, manifest in the motion of the heavens and in the circle of incarnation, in which divine and human nature are indistinguishably joined.[14]

Taking into account these enormous ontological and theological investments in the opposition of rotation and translation, it is hard to see how the revaluation of motions initiated by early modern physics could have been more radical. Christian doctrine was appalled not so much by the statement that the earth moved as by how it was supposed to move. For with regard to both its cause and its form, motion in modern physics is godless: it is inertial, that is, uncaused, and it is, in its final formulation by Isaac Newton, purely translational.

Some transitional steps softened the radicalism of this new paradigm. One was the survival of Platonic theories of form. In a late dialogue, Nicholas of Cusa describes a bowling game in which the bowling ball is deliberately made imperfectly round so as to trace an unpredictable path. This leads the bishop to speculate on the implications of perfect rotundity, one of which is that a perfectly round body could not be seen. For since a perfect sphere would touch a plane only at one point, and points have no extension and hence cannot compose a surface, a perfectly spherical body would always remain invisible. Interestingly, Nicholas claims that this invisibility holds true not only for ideal forms but also for real bodies should they be turned perfectly round on a lathe. The dynamic equivalent to this thought is that a perfectly round body, once set into motion, whether rolling on a plane or rotating around its axis, would have no reason to stop moving. From the metaphysics of rotundity, then, the first ideas of "real" inertial motion arose.[15]

Another facilitating factor in the emergence of "natural" translations was that various discourses on natural motion tilted the angle of translational motion by ninety degrees: as the celestial spheres around the earth broke open, things moving in a straight line no longer had to drop into the pits of hell below man's feet but could also recede horizontally into an infinite distance. Striking images of this tilted and theologically neutral kinetics are the ever-shallower ramps onto which Galileo lets his bronze balls roll to demonstrate the laws of the free fall of bodies.[16] Earlier advances in horizontalizing man's worldview subtended Galileo's physical experiments. The most momentous of these surely is the "invention" of central perspective, based as it is on the horizontal coincidence between the observer's viewpoint and the image's vanishing point. This relationship, rather than imposing itself statically, is held together by the intromission (or extramission, as the case may be) of visual rays in the eye of the viewer. It is important to recognize that behind the static geometry of linear perspective is a kinetics of vision and of bodily motion, for in this manner the human body and its dimensions are connected to an increasingly linear universe.[17]

Leon Battista Alberti set this preference for horizontal lines in stone. In his foundational treatise *De re aedificatoria* he challenged the unfavorable etymology that derived the name of the builder's profession from the curve *(arcus)* of the roof *(tectum)*.[18] He asserted that rather than celebrating transcendence, as cathedrals do in their height and vertical intricacy, churches as well as representative *palazzi* and private homes should exhibit strong horizontal lines that converge on the altar, or on doors and windows.[19] These lines were understood as guidelines for visual rays on which the objects of vision traveled to and from the eyes. This inherent belief in the coincidence of geometric lines and natural motion found its most confident expression in Galileo's assertion that the book of nature and its motions was written in the language of geometry.[20] The relation of priority that Alberti established between the regularity of geometric proportions and lines and their embodiment in the motion of extended bodies would hold for many centuries, and in many fields. The house of memory, for example—the aid by means of which an orator would memorize the parts of his speech and their sequence—underwent an Albertian renovation: whereas ancient and medieval memory houses had regarded the difference between the rooms and the floors as an aid to memory, in early modern memory houses rooms were differentiated solely by their connection to other rooms.[21]

Also the active employment of the intellect was conceived as moving along straight lines with regular bifurcations and on a plane without curvatures. Early modern textbooks of logic often included bewildering diagrams showing the spatial array of logical relations as rectangles with any number of connective links.[22]

Ong insists that this linear charting of intellectual motion was deeply indebted to the invention of the printing press, and specifically to the rectangular uniformity of its page and its type. The rectangle of the printed page provided a coordinate system in which geometrical analysis and speculation on the extent of linearity and calculability could take place. The emerging systems of natural history sought to capture the variety of natural forms in catalogs that showed linear dependence of species very much like the diagrams of early modern logicians.[23] Works like Luca Pacioli's *De divina proportione* (1509) sought to arrive at a universal, geometrically modular typeface that in turn would be able to represent a universal language, actively sought by European learned societies at the time. Pacioli was equally convinced that the human face exhibited geometric proportions; neither type nor face was as yet subject to the kind of intuitive physiognomies that in the late eighteenth century would brush away all geometric and linear constructions.[24]

In the notion of proportion, however, the other, "Platonic" side of the new geometry came to the fore: proportion was "divine" insofar as it could not be assigned an exact number, yet it was an integral part of geometric patterns and, what is more, a sign of beauty. The circle and the sphere in particular embodied this rest of divinity in a world that was increasingly defined by numerical values. The relation between circle and square (and their relation to the human body, as in Leonardo's *Vitruvian Man*), the relation between the circumference and the diameter of the circle, and of course the golden ratio were favorite objects of speculation in the Renaissance, as were the Platonic regular solids and their relation to the sphere. Indeed, the ontological status of geometric relations and of the motions they embodied was discussed with renewed enthusiasm when new editions and commentaries on Plato's *Timaios* appeared in the fifteenth and sixteenth centuries. One of the key moments in this interpretation occurs in Marsilio Ficino's commentary on the *Timaios* from 1496. Commenting on the famous section on the origin of the world-soul (*Tim.* 36bc), Ficino claims that the natural motion of the soul is translational *(animae motum naturaliter esse rectum)* and that it is the task of intelligence (which itself is a gift of God) to bend it into rotational *(in gyrum)* motion.[25] The mysterious relation between the power of straight lines and angles and the nimbus of the sphere finds, as mentioned, a striking expression in Kepler's *Mysterium cosmographicum,* where the Platonic solids (composed of regular rectilinear modules) are encapsulated in ever-larger spheres to demonstrate the distance between and the orbital motion of the planets. Copernicus earlier had given a succinct summary of the metaphysics of rotation and sphericity when he stated that the sphere is the perfect form because it is without "joint" and that everything that limits itself—a drop of water, for example, but also the sun and the planets—does so in the form of a sphere The motion appropriate to this perfect form is, of course, rotation.[26]

All the trust put into the power and rationality of the straight line provided the ground for the assertion, first tentatively by Galileo and Descartes, then exhaustively by Newton, that motion along a straight line is the natural motion of any body in the universe. A corollary of this assertion is that space must be conceived as empty, homogenous, and infinite, since otherwise this motion would come to an inexplicable end. Alexandre Koyré has eloquently described the stages in this transition from the spherical cosmos to the infinite universe.[27] But the full acceptance of the translational motion paradigm came with some hesitations, and the objections all had to do with the nature of rotation. Although he established the idea of uncaused, inertial motion, Galileo for one could not convince himself that the orbits of the stars were just the product of two conflicting linear motions. His adherence to the Platonic idea of rotational and spherical perfection led him to reject the idea of a universe in which inertial motion could be conceived only as translational.[28] For Descartes, cosmic vortices carried planets around their axis, taking everything around with them into rotation.

Newton's "great synthesis," as we have seen in the discussion of Kleist's text, was based on a previous analysis, namely the drastic separation of kinetic phenomena from the aesthetic and theological considerations that had dominated scholastic science and theology and that still left traces on early modern physics. Some motions are not "better" or "more beautiful" than others, Newton declared; they are simply the result of the measurable impact of forces on mass.[29] With the concept of mass Newton could abstract from any shape or position and extend calculations beyond the reach of the observable. One might not know what distant stars look like, but one could be sure that they were composed of quantifiable mass because its effect—gravitational pull—was measurable in their orbits. This abstraction, together with the great distances involved in celestial mechanics, made it possible to treat any body as a nonextended point mass: for the purpose of calculation—say, to calculate the gravitational force of the moon—it sufficed to conceive of its mass as being compressed in a point at the center of the physical globe. Newton, an atomist, believed in the irreducible extension and indivisibility of physical bodies, but for the purpose of calculation this philosophical commitment could be disregarded.[30] He felt even more justified in reducing celestial bodies to points when he could show—as he did in the debate with the Cartesians over the shape of the earth—that a body of malleable matter rotating in empty space around its central axis would morph into a regular spheroid whose center of mass would coincide with its geometric center. Points, in turn, could become the stuff of geometry—their path could be described in geometric curves with perfect accuracy, and they could become subject to the predictive power of algebraic operations.

Newton was perfectly aware that there were limits to this mode of explanation; indeed, he was eager to point them out to counter the suspicion that he conceived of a fully mechanized, self-sufficient universe. One such limit was the implication of a void between bodies, and of forces acting across it. For rational mechanics to work, gravity had to act instantaneously and bodies had to be distinguishable from their surroundings; but how could such *actio in distans* be understood? How could motion change (as it did in Kepler's elliptical orbits) without any contact? Then there was the related question of whether the distances between the planets, placed as they were at the exact intervals that kept them from collapsing into the center *and* from flying off into space, could originate through mechanical forces. Newton enthusiastically embraced Bentley's suggestion that this might serve as a cosmological proof for the existence of God.[31]

As far as the motion of the planets was concerned, Newton admitted to Bentley that gravity would explain the centripetal factor of the planets' orbits, "yet the transverse motions by which they revolve in their several orbs required a divine Arm to impress them according to the tangents of their orbs." Since this did not necessarily include the rotational motion of the planets, Newton added "that the diurnal rotations of the Planets could not be derived from gravity but required a divine power to impress them."[32]

This cosmological argument had a mechanical counterpart in the fact that, according to Newton's second law of motion, any change of motion was proportional to the magnitude of a force impacting a body; both the impact and the resulting direction would be in a straight line. How could rotation originate from the impact of just one force?[33]

For reasons like these Immanuel Kant introduced a second "original" force besides gravitation into the fabric of the universe in his daring *Allgemeine Naturgeschichte und Theorie des Himmels* of 1755: the repulsive force. He blunted the audacity of this addition to Newton's mechanics by arguing that "these two forces are both equally certain, equally simple, and at the same time equally primal and universal. Both are taken from Newtonian philosophy. The first is now an incontestably established law of nature. The second, which Newtonian science perhaps cannot establish with as much clarity as the first, I here assume only in the sense which no one disputes, that is, in connection with the smallest distributed particles of matter, as, for example, in vapours."[34] To show the primordial interplay of these forces, Kant imagined the world "on the immediate edge of creation," when the universe was filled with matter at rest for a time "which lasts but an instant."[35] Since atoms were created with different specific weights, the heavier ones attracted the lighter ones and began to form "gobs" *(Klumpen.)*[36] All matter would collapse into one big gob were it not for the repulsive force that inflected the straight path of onrushing matter and sent it into an orbit around the central, that is, heaviest body. Applied to the formation of the solar system, the interaction of these two forces explained why all planets orbited around the sun in one plane—the central mystery for Newton in his exchange with Bentley. They were all remnants of the initial cloud of matter that had first collapsed on, and then been flung from, the heaviest gob in one part of the universe, the sun. The same had happened in countless other corners of the universe.

This "nebula hypothesis" was a theory with extraordinary explanatory power, justly famous for its range and daring: in one fell swoop it explained the origin of empty space (as the consequence of matter contracting), the spherical form of celestial bodies (as the consequence of the simultaneous rush of particles on a common center and the resulting rotation) and the common plane of all orbits in the solar system, resulting in a fully mechanical cosmogony.[37] But subtly it also reversed the question of the origin of rotation. In a later chapter, "Concerning the Origin of Moons and the Axial Rotation of the Planets," Kant makes the much-needed distinction between orbital motion ("Zirkelbewegung") and axial rotation ("Achsendrehung") and explains the origin of the latter as the result of particles impacting the already forming body, off-center and from opposite sides, and thereby keeping it spinning.[38] The diameter of the planet serves as a lever on which the particles exert opposite, yet equal translational force. Kant's hypothesis anticipates here the notion of torque as the product of the length of a lever arm and two opposite perpendicular forces: he argues, for example, that Jupiter rotates faster than smaller planets (like Mars), which can be explained only by the fact that it has a larger diameter: "If the axial rotation were an effect of an external cause [e.g., God's twisting motion], then Mars would have to have a more rapid axial rotation than Jupiter, for the very same power of movement affects a smaller body more than a larger one. We would quite correctly be surprised at this, since all the orbital movements diminish with distance from the mid-point, but the speeds of the rotations increase with the distance."[39] What needs to be explained, this theory implies, is not rotational motion (for it is a natural effect of the self-creation of the material universe) but its cessation. Why, then, do some planets rotate around their axes and others, like the moon, not? In the *Universal Natural History* Kant promises to solve this problem in his answer to one of the Academy prizes, and indeed he does so in a small essay of 1754 with a very long title.[40] There he shows that the orbit of the moon around the earth is the result of the earth's greater mass having dragged the satellite by its (now evaporated) aqueous surface and finally locked it into its present synchronous rotation. The same will happen, Kant knows, to the earth once the moon's drag on its oceans overcomes its rotational momentum.

The great conceptual problem of Kant's history of the heavens, immediately seized upon by the next generation of natural philosophers, lies in the assumption of two original forces.[41] A system based on two principles is unable to close itself off; it remains susceptible to the charge of contingency, to that which cannot be anticipated or grounded. This uncertainty is expressed in Kant's cosmogony by the curious temporal assignations of the "immediate edge of creation" and the "instant" of equilibrium—Kant cannot further account for their occurrence, nor can he explain why attractive forces operate first and repulsion follows later. According to the Romantic philosophers of nature, who succeeded Kant and who acknowledged their debt to his writings on natural science while eagerly moving away from his mechanistic thought, the principal motions cannot interact in such a desultory fashion, and, what is more, they must follow from principles that are valid for both natural and intellectual phenomena. Otherwise, the relation of nature to our understanding would remain inexplicable, and the system would again suffer from contingency. Rotation, this implies, cannot be the result of two supervening forces but has to originate together with the system itself, and it has to have a subjective manifestation.

This, at least, was the way the most scientifically inclined idealist philosopher, F. W. J. Schelling, argued. He neither accepted the contingent relation between attraction and repulsion at the origin of rotation nor countenanced the separation of mechanical causes from organic (and ultimately intellectual) ones. In his own rewriting of Plato's *Timaios*, *Von der Weltseele* (1798), he advanced the notion that the world was a "universal organism" and that its motions and interactions were governed by two forces that formed a polarity: one was the other of the other, neither existed by itself. Nature would not coalesce into solid phenomena if the tendency to expand were not checked by a "returning motion." These two polar forces—whose avatars, among others, were positive and negative magnetism and electricity, chemical affinity and repulsion, physiological irritability and sensibility—animated the universal organism and kept its soul in constant motion. Since Plato and Aristotle had already argued that motion originating from the soul was superior to all others, and above all that it could initiate rotation, Schelling could spend comparatively little energy on explaining the origin of rotation. If everything potentially rotated, it was rectilinear motion that required explanation.[42]

Schelling's *Naturphilosophie* underwent a few metamorphoses before he expanded his perspective even further and considered—in his *Philosophy of Revelation*—creation and the becoming of God as a process of rotational gestation. His followers and successors kept their focus on the primacy of rotation in the explanation of the natural world. Lorenz Oken, one of the most influential teachers of Romantic natural philosophy, declared confidently: "God is a rotating globe. The world is God rotating. All motion is rotational, and there is everywhere no straight motion any more than there is a single line of straight surface. Everything is comprehended in ceaseless rotation. . . . Straight motion is only the mechanical; such, however, exists not through itself. The more a body moves in a straight direction, the more mechanical and ignoble it is."[43] Hegel interpreted the solar system as a kind of cosmic mind, where the sun represented subjectivity in its most abstract form as self-relation (because rotation was motion that related only to itself); the moons, which circled their center of gravitation without rotating, were entirely other-related; and the planets, including the earth, combined both motions by rotating and orbiting at the same time. This figure of an initial rotation that exteriorizes itself in its component motions recurs at various junctures in Hegel, whose philosophical system in its totality has been described as depicting a multiplicity of spheres rotating around a common center.[44]

Similar thoughts animated Goethe, who, as we will see later, sought to identify spiral motion as the motion of organic growth: "The supreme thing we have received from God and from nature is life, the rotating movement of the monad about itself, knowing neither rest nor repose; the instinct to foster and nurture life is indestructibly innate in everyone; its idiosyncrasy, however, remains a mystery to ourselves and to others."[45] Goethe's metaphysical and poetic notion of free rotation already reached into the epoch in which rotation was broken down by the formula for torque. His contempt for rotating machines and for the pernicious acceleration brought about by them animated his last, resigned musings on historical progress in his novel *Wilhelm Meister's Travels*.[46]

The full intricacy of rotation's transition from divine attribute to mechanical necessity cannot be recounted here. All this fragmentary overview of theories of translation and rotation has attempted to show is that motions have their history. Properly speaking, of course, only their valuation undergoes historical change, but since these motions do not "exist" unless they are forced, their metaphysical value dominates their mechanical properties until the widespread use of engines reverses this situation.[47] The ubiquitous availability of convertible motion from the steam engine and the emergence of suitable transmission replace metaphysical speculation with the forced geometry of motion—with kinematics.

Still, looking back at the roles played by translation and rotation respectively, we can appreciate the irony that steam engines met a deep desire on the part of Romantic natural philosophers who had kept the cosmic dignity of rotation alive against what they perceived as the cold rationalism of straight-line mathematical physics. It is true that the intrusion of large machines into the life of the nineteenth century pushed most poets and thinkers to the side of the protesters and even Luddites, but this had to do with the steam engine as a motor—and hence as a thermodynamic polluter, in the widest sense—or with the machine as a tool that dispossessed human workers of meaningful and remunerative work. When the Romantics articulated their opposition to the motion of machines, it was to mechanisms as metaphors (or as translations, in the Latin and kinematic version): against the state as a machine, against mechanical thinking and art making, against automata insofar as they tried to imitate or supplant natural bodies and their motions and emotions.

As far as the purely kinematic impact of the new machines was concerned, there was agreement between engineers, philosophers, and artists that bringing rotation to earth and accomplishing its conversion into other forms of motion was in fact an epochal achievement. A continuous line of thinkers from Kant to Babbage to Reuleaux, and on to Lacan and Deleuze and Guattari, and an equally continuous line of poets from Kleist to Dickinson to Beckett and Wallace Stevens testify to this view. Baudelaire went so far as to see in the visualization of kinematic conversion an essential sign of modernity. His painter of modern life, like Kleist's Herr C., delights in depicting carriages in motion because "a carriage, like a ship, derives from its movement a mysterious and complex grace which is very difficult to note down in shorthand. The pleasure which it affords the artist's eye would seem to spring from the series of geometrical shapes which this object, already so intricate, whether it be ship or carriage, cuts swiftly and successively into space."[48]

Hopefully, this metaphysical background helps to mitigate the technicality of the following parade of cylindrical objects. For their early designers, these objects retained an aura in which the drama and the conflict between the motions—even when they were frozen in the architecture of early iron bridges and glass roofs—were still palpable. Kinematics seems an abstract science to us, but it fascinated the general public in the nineteenth century. One example is the kinematic quest for a mechanism that would produce straight-line motion. The inherent inaccuracy of Watt's four-bar linkage and the difficulties involved in predicting solutions mathematically had set off an eager quest for a linkage that would do for the straight line what the compass did for the circle. For while the drawing of a circle by means of a compass is a legitimate expansion upon the circle's definition, the drawing of a line by means of a straight-edge ruler is vitiated by circularity: how can the straightness of the Ur-ruler be guaranteed? In 1864, Charles-Nicolas Peaucellier solved the problem but was promptly ignored. Not ten years later, James Joseph Sylvester made the straight-line linkage the subject of his lectures at the Royal Institution, where "he spoke from the same rostrum that had been occupied by Davy, Faraday, Tyndall, Maxwell, and many other notable scientists. Professor Sylvester's subject was 'Recent Discoveries in Mechanical Conversion of Motion.'"[49] That this was by no means an obscure or unpopular topic can be seen from the account of a contemporary observer who described how on the occasion of the lecture he found "all the approaches to Albermarle Street [the seat of the Royal Institution] blocked by carriages."[50] In 1877, Alfred Kempe delivered his equally popular lecture on "How to Draw a Straight Line," in which he praised linkages in general for "their great beauty."[51] The conversion of motion through (often complex) linkages seemed finally to have attained the popular and aesthetic status for which Kleist had pleaded at the beginning of the century.

PART II

Cylinders of the Nineteenth Century

CHAPTER 4

The Cylinder as Motor

Cylinders appear in the **steam engine** in all three of its traditional parts: there is the cylinder in which the pressure of expanding steam lifts and pushes a second, inserted cylinder, the piston; there is the transmission, which is based on "cylinder chains"; and there is the cylinder as a tool in the all-important process of rolling. In addition, the boiler, one of the many cylindrical storage devices of the time, allows for the initial generation and compression of steam.

From a kinematic point of view, the cylinder-piston assembly in the motor achieves the isolation of translational motion along the central axis; since the cylinder wraps around the piston completely, it is an instance of "pair-closure," which Reuleaux heralded as the negentropic ideal that would overcome the "force-closure" of, say, a wheel on a straight rail. To minimize friction and wear, the piston rod must take the position of the central axis, and the piston itself must be fitted as tightly as possible into the cylinder.

In the cylinder-piston couple, as in many other mechanical devices, the cosmic—to use Reuleaux's term for interferences of unforced motions—coincides with the practical. Why cylinders as expansion or combustion chambers, and not another shape with a central axis, like a cube? The cosmic answer is that a shape without corners allows for a more complete utilization of energy, since steam or combustible fuel (the "flame front") expands in spherical fashion. (The same phenomenon, slowed down considerably, led the builders of silos to abandon rectangular shapes.) It is unlikely that this consideration was much on the minds of the early steam engineers, but a more practical one certainly was: cylinders can be bored by tools in continuous rotation, thereby achieving precision and uniformity and minimizing the loss of energy. One reason for the superiority of James Watt's early engines was the accuracy with which his partner Matthew Boulton first cast and then bored his cylinders by means of machine tools that, as we will see, were crucial for the production and reproduction of cylindrical devices.[1]

Manufacturing accuracy helped to ease the empirical contradiction inherent in the design of cylinder-piston (and other pair-closed) arrangements: on the one hand, the piston must seal the space below and above itself to utilize pressure; on the other hand, it must be able to move along the axis with as little friction as possible. The impossible space between cylinder wall and piston has to be minimized and maintained at the same time; fittingly, language-inventing engineers used Schillerian terms like *play* and *tolerance* to mark this contradiction, and in German the sealing gasket that was supposed to fill and leave open this space—rope or leather in the earliest steam engines—was even bestowed the sacred term for poetry, *Dichtung*.

All of these unexpectedly vague terms point to an area that remains understudied but is nonetheless crucial for understanding the enormous acceleration of forced motion throughout the nineteenth century: lubrication. That engines have to be lubricated to prevent catastrophic wear of their parts (and of the ears of those administering them) is a reminder of the fact that the motions of machines are always forced and that this forcing—Watt's parallel motion was only "straight," not straight—is almost always imperfect, performed by imperfectly machined parts. In the nineteenth century it had to be facilitated by materials (tallow, vegetable oil, grease) that were themselves transitory and hovered between the hard and the elastic, between the organic and the inorganic. Kinematically speaking, it is no accident that the need for lubrication decreased significantly when spherical bearings (steel spheres within a cylindrical or conical race) were introduced in the 1880s—it was, after all, another step toward pair-closure. David Landes reckons that the entire history of nineteenth-century machines (and probably that of that of the alimentation of the poor) could be written as a history of lubrication, until animal and vegetal matter was replaced by mineral and later still by synthetic products.[2] Lubrication plays a role in all parts of a machine, but the problem is exacerbated in the motor's

FIGURE 7. Outside view of the Cruquius pumping station. The main cylinder is almost four meters in diameter and is now driven, for demonstration purposes, by hydraulic power. The site has been converted into a museum, and its website (www .cruquiusmuseum.nl/englishsite/english.html) gives a full account of the history and mechanics of this engine. Photo by Robert Gisolf.

cylinder, which, having to convert pressure into motion, needs to be sealed and open at the same time.

Most of the salient features of the steam engine's cylindricality in relation to axial motion are brought into massive relief by the Cruquius engine, put into operation in 1849 to help drain the Haarlemmer Meer (fig. 7). This was a conservative engine in the sense that it was restricted to the oscillating pumping motion for which the earliest steam engines in the eighteenth century were built. Very little conversion of motion was necessary to push the eight balance beams upwards, which in turn sank eight hollow pistons into the cylindrical pump holes. What it lacked in kinematic sophistication, the Cruquius made up for in scale and cylindricality. The diameter of its piston and hence of its cylinder was 144 inches (3.66 meters)—of its outside cylinder, to be precise, since the Cruquius was a compound engine in which a smaller cylinder was nested in a larger one. The smaller cylinder received the high-pressure steam from a set of ten cylindrical boilers to push up the balancer arms and the weight trough sitting on top of the piston rod; at the top of the stroke the steam flowed into the surrounding low-pressure cylinder, where, assisted by the weight trough, it helped to push down the piston and to raise the appended pumping pistons and the water above them. The entire ensemble of cylinders was, and is still, enclosed in an imposing cylindrical structure resembling a medieval tower and flanked by a tall smokestack emerging from the boiler house.[3] Contemporaries will have remarked that this machine invalidates one of the most enduring adynata in classical rhetoric, the impossibility of exhausting the sea.

The most visible, audible, and, in the first half of its century, successful and revolutionary piston-cylinder combination was the **steam locomotive.** Unlike the Cruquius pump, it was very much concerned with the translation of motion and carried a version of Watt's parallel motion, translating the oscillation of the piston into the rotation of the driving wheel, visibly on the outside of its wheels.[4] Indeed, the locomotive's "product" was nothing but the translation of motion; it was, to speak paradoxically, a transmission tool. Franz Reuleaux was perhaps the first to recognize that the rails had to be understood as belonging to the locomotive (but neglected to mention that, like the tarmac that is part of the automobile, they were the products of cylindrical rolling).[5] Kinematically, then, the rails could be conceived as forming an enclosure of infinite diameter around the wheels, a "force-closure" (in Reuleaux's terms) that broke down every time the gravitational pull of the train overwhelmed the push of its engine: at the start or, more dangerously, when the gradient was too steep. Hence the need for tunnels, themselves products of screwing cylinders, or for an additional "cylinder chain" to link the engine more firmly to the rails, like the rack and pinion of Swiss Alpine trains.

Once the steam locomotive was able to run in a functional network of support, its dependence on cylindrical shapes broadened: its massive boiler, of course, was cylindrical, and so were the flues within the boiler through which the steam was heated and superheated; above the boiler the smokestack and below it the main cylinder, often paired on

FIGURE 8. O. Winston Link, *Cranes Lower Engine and Drive Wheels of Y-6 No. 2180 into Position*, 1958. Visible in the foreground is the frame with the (double) cylinders that drive one axle by means of a connecting rod and the others by means of coupling rods—a horizontal and simplified version of Watt's parallel-motion linkage. Suspended is the cylindrical boiler containing tubes to superheat the steam, and the various steam valves and the chimney. Link was the great photographic elegist of North American steam locomotives. © W. Conway Link.

each side, completed the ensemble (fig. 8). But like the rails, the cylindrical water towers and water cranes feeding the engine belonged to the locomotive, as did the silos that were used to load granular and liquid matter into the (often cylindrical) freight cars, and the conveyor belts that loaded and emptied them.

The steam locomotive, because of its size and the visibility of its kinematic gear, became the most passionately admired and maligned engine of the nineteenth century, the one phenomenon that embodied most succinctly what had become of the sublime in the nineteenth century—a sublime that rushed by with great speed, inevitability, and noise but also one that could be entered.[6] Zola spoke of "all that logic and all that certitude that make up the sovereign beauty of metallic beings, the precision in the power,"[7] and he devoted some of his most

FIGURE 9. An automobile traction machine outfitted for threshing (flywheel on the far side), ca. 1878. Reprinted from Thurston (1902, 355).

magnificent descriptions to the onrush and the passing of a locomotive, in particular as it shoots out of a tunnel (itself a cylinder to the locomotive's piston). Equally transformative and—*sit venia verbo*—cylindrifying was the journey within the train, where the speed with which the images rushed by the square of the compartment window at first caused nausea for those travelers who still concentrated on a vanishing point. The eye had to learn to stop focusing on a single point in which all lines converged and instead to find the line of the horizon that separated fast- from slow-moving image fields. Cultural historians have amply shown that this new experience of "seeing at speed" was intimately linked to the modes of representing images in the large panoramas of the epoch and that it trained, so to speak, spectators for the coming visual experience of the cinema.[8]

Reuleaux had still doubted the possibility of true automobiles, which could take their traction, the force-closure between wheel and surface, with them; only the emergence of rubber tires and the concomitant rolling of streets would make this kinematic compromise possible. But he did witness the widespread use of **traction engines** in agriculture: steam engines that transported themselves—however slowly—to fields and to farms to dispense rotation. Working in pairs on either side of a field and each outfitted with a horizontal drum, traction engines could be connected by a rope on which a plow or a cultivator was pulled. Alternatively, the flywheel of a traction engine could be connected through a belt to a threshing machine—or, on holidays, to the drive train of a carousel. While the silo and its miniature descendant, the tin can, led to the homogenization of time in agriculture, the traction engine provided the power to accelerate and greatly expand it and to break its complex hand movements into smaller, repetitive segments (fig. 9).[9]

CHAPTER 5

The Cylinder as Tool

In the labor theories of value that dominate economic thought of the nineteenth century, machines are treated summarily as tools used by human workers whose labor generates the value of commodities in the marketplace.[1] This view, critically important as it undoubtedly is, does not take into account that these tools are restricted to the motions delivered by the transmissions and are allowed only the freedoms allowed them by the cylinder. This does not falsify the labor theory of value but complicates it, since the characteristic motion of these cylindrical tools—rolling, reeling, transitive, intransitive, and passive turning—are not human motions. They are not quantitatively different, as were the motions of machines in early manufactories that simply multiplied and accelerated the motion of hand-held tools, but qualitatively discontinuous with the motion of the human body. Nothing in the human body turns continuously around an axis—this is such a visceral truth that film designers need only give a figure 360-plus-degree motion in any body part (preferably the neck) to confer on it alien or horror status. The concluding section on the machine lathe tries to address this in-humanity in the technological thought of Karl Marx.

ROLLING

Reuleaux's joyous pronouncement that "everything rolls" was based on his study of the intransitive rolling of transmissions. Cylindrical tools, however, roll something; they produce and then transform amorphous matter (iron, pulp, gravel, glass,) into shapes that bear the imprint of the cylinder's shape, not that of the worker's craft or ingenuity. To be sure, rolling may be the most important motion the cylinder executes in its various implementations in nineteenth century processes of production, extraction, inscription, and separation, but it is not the only motion. Without question the most massive implementation of cylinders occurred in successive—diachronic and synchronic—stages in the manufacture of iron and steel. By the end of the nineteenth century, an integrated iron and steel plant resembled a gigantic three-dimensional "cylinder chain" in which cylinders first crushed the iron ore, then transported it on conveyor belts into cylindrical blast furnaces capped by cylindrical dust catchers and heated by large cylindrical wind heaters.[2] The molten iron was transferred into large cylindrical ladles, which were driven to the Bessemer converters (cylindrical containers with an eccentric opening) where the purification and conversion of iron into steel took place.[3] Poured again into ladles, and then into smaller ingots, the steel was transferred to the mills for rolling. It was in the transition from the rectangular ingots to the various shapes produced by the **rolling mills** that the epochal shift in the integrated application of cylindrical devices became most visible (fig. 10).[4]

Before the widespread use of rolling mills—itself driven by the availability of rotational motion through steam engines, and by the need of steam locomotives for rails to rotate on—iron and steel products were shaped by the translational motion of the hammer and by the rotation of the work piece through the smith's hand. Pushing the ingot between the two turning cylinders of the rolling mill allowed for the seamless combination of these procedures. In a complicated sequence, the rolls grip and pull the hot metal forward while the reduction of diameter caused by the narrow opening forces parts of the material backwards. The resulting elongation and reshaping can be repeated in subsequent passes, flattening or rounding the steel for whatever purpose it will be used. Though derived from formerly separate processes, rolling is a genuinely technical, "inhuman" motion, and its main processes have remained unchanged since their industrial integration (fig. 11).[5]

Rolling was the characteristic machine motion of the nineteenth century. We have seen that the great synthesizer of kinematics, Franz Reuleaux, found that all planar motions of one body relative to another could be represented as the rolling of one body on another on an imaginary or, as is the case in the rolling mill, real cylindrical *Polbahn*.

FIGURE 10. Albert Renger-Patzsch, *Gute Hoffnungshütte Blast Furnace Works in Duisburg*, 1928. This partial view of a "cylindrified" steel plant shows, toward the left, the blast furnace with the girder work for the feeder conveyor belts; in the middle, a smokestack surrounded by four Cowper air heaters; protruding pipes to utilize the exhaust gases; and a train to carry away waste. © 2011 Albert Renger-Patzsch Archiv / Ann u. JürgenWilde, Zülpich / Artists Rights Society (ARS), New York.

In the rolling mill, the abstract kinematic relation was brought to bear dynamically on the relative formlessness of hot or cold steel.[6] In German, this led to the linguistic transformation from intransitive *rollen* and *wälzen* into the transitive *walzen*—a transformation that allowed Karl Marx to use the concept of *Umwälzung* to evoke the aura of technical inevitability in political change.[7]

Unlike eighteenth-century manufacturing, where the division of labor followed the logic of segmentation and acceleration, the sequence of steps in iron and steel production was guided by the temperature

FIGURE 11. Albert Renger-Patzsch, *Rolling Mill*, 1928. In this two-high rolling mill, the profile of the two work rolls allows for the reduction in width and height of the workpiece in subsequent passes. © 2011 Albert Renger-Patzsch Archiv / Ann u. Jürgen Wilde, Zülpich / Artists Rights Society (ARS), New York.

of the raw material. Just when the investigators of thermodynamics began to formulate its second law, according to which the change from hot to cold is not equivalent to that from cold to hot, manufacturers of steel and iron realized that the various phases of production, from the tapping of the liquid pig iron to its final rolling into sheets or rails or I-beams, were associated with specific speeds and danger levels of work. When the material was hottest, work had to be fastest, and a momentary misstep could lead to catastrophe. Further down the line, as the material cooled, the process slowed down, but the forces involved became greater. It is important to recognize—in particular for theoreticians of alienation—that the demand for quick and circumspect work issued from the material itself, whereas in later assembly-line work—the true successor of nineteenth-century manufacturing—speed was dictated by economic and ergonomic considerations.

By kinematic necessity there was a limited variety of shapes into which steel was rolled.[8] Those pieces that were not used as they came out of the mill—like rails and I-beams—were either flat or long, and if long were either round or square. From this basic grammar much of the structural and infrastructural language of the nineteenth century was made up.

In some instances, the originating rolled shape for a particular product changed over time, or allowed for variety, as was the case with one of the most important products to come out of the mills: iron and steel pipes. Prompted by the development of gas lighting and domestic water supply (and of pneumatic delivery systems), the high demand for iron and steel pipes required mechanized manufacturing processes, and the first successful method involved wrapping rolled sheets around a cylinder and welding the seam; when higher pressure resistance became important, a solid round billet would be either drawn over a mandrel or pierced by a cylindrical drill.[9]

The inverse product to tubing—and the cylinder with the smallest diameter in the arsenal of the nineteenth century—is **wire**. It is produced by drawing metal—typically in the form of a long rod—through a series of dies. In Reuleaux's basic grammar, machines for wire drawing are concatenations of a revolute joint with a prism followed by another revolute joint, until the desired diameter is reached. The originating rod is coiled around the so-called payoff reel, pulled through a precisely aligned die of harder material, and coiled again on a cylindrical take-up block (which is the driven part of the machine).[10]

If tubes were the gargantuan arterial and digestive system of the nineteenth century, wires were its sinews and its nerves. **Wire rope** (strands of steel wire twisted around a cylindrical core) allowed for the continuous unidirectional transmission of translational and rotational forces, for example in cranes, winding towers, suspension bridges, cable cars, and mining shafts; they replaced the digital (and potentially catastrophic) system of chains, as well as the use of natural rope (fig. 12).

Alternatively, wire was (and is) used as conductor of electrical charges, first for the transmission of telegraphic signals and later for the delivery of electric current.[11] The underwater cable inverted the principle of the wire rope: here, a core of copper wires was surrounded and insulated by natural material, such as gutta-percha or tarred hemp. It may serve as an example of the interconnectedness and evolution of cylindrical phenomena that the first successful transatlantic cable was laid in 1866 by the SS *Great Eastern,* the first large iron ship outfitted with a steam-driven screw-propeller, built by the legendary Isambard Kingdom Brunel.[12]

FIGURE 12. Piet Zwart, *Wire Drawing*, 1930s. In this photo showing the manufacture of wire rope, individual wires are twisted around a core of twisted wire that is fed through the central cylinder. Six or more of the resulting strands are then twisted around a core of steel or of natural fiber. Wire rope is critically important for two of the great innovations of the nineteenth century, suspension bridges and elevators. © 2011 Artists Rights Society (ARS), New York / c/o Pictoright Amsterdam.

If this account of nineteenth-century machines were to focus on the personalities that put these machines to work rather than on their formal logic, the gloriously named Isambard Kingdom Brunel would certainly figure prominently. His father, Marc Isambard Brunel, had organized in the first years of the nineteenth century, with the help of Samuel Bentham and Henry Maudslay, the first fully interconnected factory in which steam engines powered rolling mills, circular saws, and assembly lines; it produced blocks for the Royal Navy and became a national and international attraction from which Babbage, among others, took his ideas of mechanical reproducibility.[13] Kingdom built railways, locomotives, and suspension bridges, dug tunnels, and in 1848 hatched one of the many ill-fated pneumatic tube schemes: he wanted to "suck" trains from Exeter to Plymouth. Rats ate the tube's tallow-covered leather seals, and that was the end of that. In photographs, Brunel proudly displayed the two iconic cylinders of Victorian masculinity, the top hat and the cigar.[14]

FIGURE 13. Albert Renger-Patzsch, *Steam Roller*,
1930. © 2011 Albert Renger-Patzsch Archiv / Ann u.
Jürgen Wilde, Zülpich / Artists Rights Society (ARS),
New York.

Not to be forgotten as both factual and metaphorical rolling equip-
ment is the **steamroller**. Reuleaux showed that roads, like rails, have to
be understood as static cylinders with infinite diameter on which the
wheel of automobiles roll.[15] To smooth these surfaces, stones had to be
crushed with rolling stone crushers, and later asphalt had to be laid and
rolled with steam-driven or hand-pulled rollers (fig. 13). By the 1850s
asphalt-covered streets and, more importantly, sidewalks in London,
Paris, and Hamburg allowed men and women to walk in the city without muddying their shoes.[16]

The kinematics of transitive rolling played a crucial role in other
emerging industries; they, too, produced and shaped materials that
were rendered amorphous by rolling and whose subsequent states
depended on their temperature. Portland **cement**, which had one of
its first uses in Brunel's Thames tunnel, was produced by crushing

FIGURE 14. Albert Renger-Patzsch, *Rotating Furnace for Cement Production*, 1930.
© 2011 Albert Renger-Patzsch Archiv / Ann u. Jürgen Wilde, Zülpich / Artists Rights
Society (ARS), New York.

limestone and other elements between toothed-roll crushers into fine
powder, then burning it into clinker in large cylindrical kilns, and finally grinding it again in a cement mill into the final product (fig. 14).
In between these steps the material was stored in silos, so that cement
production followed an alternating sequence of horizontal and vertical
cylinders.[17]

An analogous process took place in the paper industry of the early
to mid–nineteenth century. The scarcity of paper had led to serious
shortages at a time when the reading public and government bureaucracies were vastly expanding. Making paper from rags was always
dominated by the translational motion of pounding, then scooping
and pressing rectangular sheets of paper. When the use of wood as the
source for cellulose proved to be practical, the **papermaking** process
became progressively cylindrical, as grinders, pulp beaters, and centrifuges prepared the pulp, and the couch roll took it up, sent it around
the innumerable press rolls, then around the drying cylinders, to the
calender rolls and finally to the reel where the paper itself formed an
(often gigantic) cylinder (fig. 15).[18]

FIGURE 15. Margaret Bourke-White, *Revolving Steam-Heated Cylinders Dry Liquid Paper Which Is Then Cooled by Cold Rollers Which Give the Paper a Smooth Surface*, at the International Paper Co, 1937. Margaret Bourke-White / Time & Life Pictures / Getty Images.

In most paper machines, this dizzying array of rolling cylinders was preceded by the "wire" on which the pulp was first spread out on tiny rectangles and shaken from side to side—an obvious reminder that the surface of the cylinder was flat and could therefore be used for rolling, printing, and helical inscription.[19] The endless paper that emerged at the end of this process would soon be fed into the rotary printing presses and into the various recording devices that began to alter the practice and theory of experimental physiology.

The deep cultural significance of the **printing press** and of movable type since the fifteenth century can hardly be overestimated; along with central perspective, it was a key element in the emergence of motion along straight lines and right angles as paradigms of rationality. These motions now became continuous, rotational, and thereby faster, as all participants—printers, papermakers, publisher, writers, and readers—realized that the oscillating motion of even the most advanced printing presses of the early nineteenth century (for example, of the Stanhope presses invoked in the first sentence of Balzac's *Les illusions perdues*) could not produce enough copies for an ever-expanding market in which daily newspapers, weekly and monthly reviews, and cheap books competed for readers' attention.[20]

The first process to go cylindrical was the inking of the form, which had previously been done by hand with round leather pads.[21] But real progress could only come from converting all ("digital") up-down or side-to-side motions into a fully rotational and contiguous process. This occurred in two stages: first, the form of type, still fastened in a flat rectangular frame, was put on a horizontal table. As the table moved to the left, a set of small cylindrical rollers smeared the form with ink; as it moved to the right, a larger cylinder pressed the sheet to the inked form. The limitations of this process were due to the remaining reciprocating motions: the stoppage and reversal in the motion of the table, and the motion of the two attendants who had to feed the paper and take it off the form. The next step had to reverse the hierarchy of motions and wrap the printing form around a printing cylinder (fig. 16).

The printing cylinder took advantage of the fact that the surface of a right cylinder is "extrinsically curved": unlike on the surface of a sphere, on the surface of a cylinder the shortest connection between two points is a straight line. This was the condition for the cylinder to exert uniform pressure in the process of rolling, but it was also the reason why it was possible to print from cylinders but not from spheres: a flat, rectangular printing form could be wrapped around a cylinder without the surface of the type being distorted.

This did not mean that the process of fastening type around cylinder was uncomplicated. To avoid the damage resulting from translational and centrifugal forces, the first printing cylinders were large enough in diameter to accommodate half a page of print; they were placed vertically in the middle, and a set of impression rollers pressed the (hand-fed) paper to the print.[22] Only with the perfection of stereotyping—the ability to cover a flat printing form with another of the nineteenth century's formless materials, paper-maché, and thus to take a copy of the entire page—could printing forms be copied and fastened around the cylinder. The printing cylinder moved into the horizontal, and the

FIGURE 16. Margaret Bourke-White, *Hearst.*
Newspaper Printing Rollers, 1935. Photo © Estate
of Margaret Bourke-White/Licensed by VAGA, New
York, NY.

entire process, from the unwinding of an endless paper roll to the cutting and folding of pages, was now performed by cylinders.[23]

Rotary printing presses are a marvel not only of interacting cylinders but also of linkages and gearing, since motion must be not only delivered to the various driving cylinders but timed for the cutting and folding of the sheets. By 1866, the fully cylindrical Walter Press printed six thousand sheets per hour.

If there was a bottleneck in the printing process, it was the mechanization and "cylindrification" of typesetting, which, until the advent of the linotype process late in the nineteenth century, still relied, literally, on digital skill and manipulation.[24] The main holdup was not so much mechanizing the selection and casting the type as integrating the strict demands of translationality—the justified column—with the irregularity of word length and division. The typewriter, also dependent on wrapping a sheet around a cylinder, could be successful only because this demand of the rectangular page no longer was heeded.[25]

REELING

To call the rolling of iron and steel the most massive implementation of cylindrical processes is justified in literal reference to the dimensions and weight of the machinery and to the infrastructural changes its products effected. But equally important and more immediately perceptible to nineteenth-century citizens of all classes were the spinning and weaving machines that constituted the other source of Great Britain's standing as the world's dominant industrial and colonial power. Directly connected to the economy of the slave trade, to the emergence of new regimes of division of labor, and to capitalist forms of trade and political influence, at their kinematic heart carding, spinning, and weaving machines anticipated the wire-drawing processes that were the most delicate form of iron and steel rolling. The fundamental difference consisted in the fact that rather than reducing an existing raw material to an ever-smaller diameter, the material for spinning had to be worked up from discontinuous matter in the first place. **Spinning machines** had to integrate all three cylindrical motions embodied in Reuleaux's lower pairs: the helical twisting motion by which the yarn was spun, the translational motion by which it was drawn, and the rotational motion by which it was reeled on to the spindles. For this process to flow continuously, the chaos of fibers—animal or, increasingly, vegetal—had to be cleaned and oriented by carding machines that took on the form of interlocking cylinders very much after the fashion of paper machines (fig. 17).[26] The roving that resulted from this treatment was then paid into the spinning machines, which took up the aligned fibers, twisted them into continuous yarn, drew them out by moving back and forth while spindles took up the yarn (fig. 18).

The mid-nineteenth-century textile factory can be regarded as a tripartite metamachine, in which carding occupied the position of the motor (the roving representing a fibrous sort of steam), the spinning mule that of the transmission, and the loom that of the tool. By the 1850s, enough cylinders had been built into the process that it had become almost fully self-acting and -controlling. The mechanical loom had earlier overcome the strict separation of translational motions in warp and weft by mastering the returning motion of the weft in John Kay's invention of the flying shuttle.

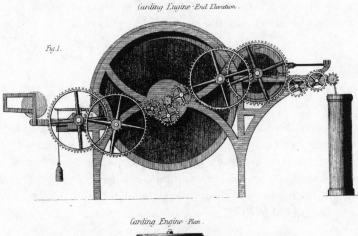

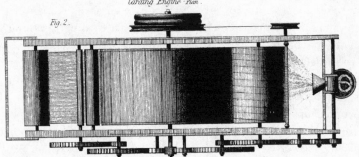

FIGURE 17. Carding machine. The design of these machines changed over time, but they essentially consisted of cylinders that combed wool or cotton repeatedly to remove clumps and align the fibers so that they were parallel with each other. Reprinted from Baines (1835).

Yarn and its metallic relative, wire, were the smallest cylinders of the nineteenth century but are not often recognized as such. Despite their size—and despite the brevity of this presentation—they were indispensable for the infrastructure of the epoch.[27]

TURNING TRANSITIVELY

The screw, as we will see later in greater detail, turns rotational into translational motion if it can move against a stationary negative version of itself—the nut. Either the nut is fixed and the screw moves through it, or the screw is fixed and the nut moves around it. Reuleaux, we have learned, called the fixed element in any mechanical ensemble the

FIGURE 18. *Platt's "Mule," International Exhibition, London 1862.* This machine performed all three of the cylindrical motions: it drew out the yarn, twisted it, and reeled it in. Driven by steam engines, the output of the machine pictured equaled that of 648 hand spinners. © Science Museum / Science & Society Picture Library—All rights reserved.

Gestell. The many fastening screws that were beginning to replace the (kinematically speaking) primitive rivets moved through the fixed nut as far as they could and then stored the energy conferred by the twist in the compression of the material. Yet a great many screws in the nineteenth century were instantaneous in the sense that the nuts through which they turned did not lend themselves to the traditional fixation as *Gestell*: as water, earth, and later air, they were amorphous and functioned as instantaneous resistance.

A striking example of this relation, and of the transition from translational to rotational and helical motion, is the ship propeller. Brunel's iconic SS *Great Eastern,* launched in 1858, began as a gigantic hybrid in which sails, paddle wheels, and screw propeller still coexisted. The sails—utilizing the translational energy of wind—could not be used together with the steam engine because cinders emanating from the funnels would set them on fire (fig. 19).[28]

The paddle wheels, although obviating the enormously difficult casting and forging of the propeller, were intended to function like a spur gear but lost ever more traction as the ship, consuming its own coal supplies, became lighter and rose out of the water. Only the screw propeller, constantly immersed, could utilize the water as a nut to derive

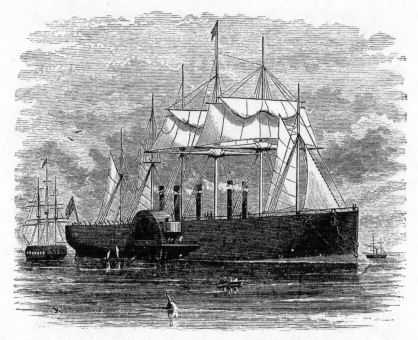

FIGURE 19. The *Great Eastern* at sea. Reprinted from Thurston (1902, 416).

continuous thrust from the rotation of its blades. The same evolution
was behind the Wright brothers' flying apparatus, as they realized that
wings could be conceived as propeller blades and vice versa, tilted at
ninety degrees.

At the other end of the density spectrum of amorphous nuts of the
nineteenth century is earth and rock. Tunneling became imperative to
lay railways at a navigable gradient, mines had to be dug deeper to
extract high-quality coal, and in the second half of the century drilling
for oil and gas gained importance.

Drilling horizontally—for tunnels and canals—provided the most
important connections to overcome geographical isolation and to build
a global infrastructure. The great tunnel projects in Europe, the United
States, and the colonies, providing a cylinder for the locomotive's and
later the automobile's piston, were constructed using hybrid kinematics.
Air was compressed in cylinders either by steam engines or by hydraulic pressure; the drills acted like piston rods shooting out straight from
a cylinder. In softer material, properly rotating drills were used, but

when tunneling through hard rock the percussive drills would open blast-holes into the rock face, which were then filled with explosives and detonated.[29] Detonation, unlike gradual combustion, was the chief phenomenon of *Auslösung* that had worried physicists because the disproportion between its seemingly minute cause (ignition) and its often-incalculable effect threatened to disrupt the analog coherence of the physical world.[30] Tunneling under water, as in Brunel's tunnel under the Thames, opened in 1843, and through mountains, as in the later tunnel underneath Mont Cenis—became a symbol both for the heroic recklessness of industrial capitalism and for the closed, cavernous and often cylindrical spaces it produced. By contrast, traditional mountain passes, like the Tremola Road up the Saint Gotthard, still exhibited (as all switchback roads do) the profile of a screw thread flattened against the slope of the mountain.

Drilling vertically for prospecting meant that the nut itself became the product of the excavation. Empty cylinders were drilled into the earth to retrieve cores for geological analysis. Where salt brine, water, oil, or gas was the object of well drilling, the debris was raised or flushed out. The derricks soon dotting the landscape from Russia to the California coast all operated under the same principle of twisting, by an assembly of steam engines and assorted linkages and gears, a drill bit into the earth that was itself connected to a system of cylindrical tubes (fig. 20).[31]

TURNING INTRANSITIVELY

A surprising number of cylinders turn in an intransitive way, not rolling on the outside of the sleeve or boring or screwing along the central axis of the cylinder but just turning "for themselves." One set of tools that use rotation exclusively are the many **centrifuges** that began their work of separating heavier from lighter substances in the scientific laboratories before they became integral to the chemical industries of the later nineteenth century, and later still to dairy production.

Centrifuges had uses beyond the scientific, however; there emerged also a pleasurable, and by some accounts addictive, use of the centrifuge in the **carousels** that appeared on fairgrounds. These fantastical and ever more elaborate mechanisms, powered by mobile steam engines and driven by bevel gears, are mechanical manifestations of the joys of rotation that were first celebrated in Goethe's description of waltzing in *The Sorrows of Young Werther.*[32]

FIGURE 20. Margaret Bourke-White, *Inside an Oil Tower*, 1937. Margaret Bourke-White / Time & Life Pictures / Getty Images.

The enigmas of rotational motion—that it diminishes toward the center, that it repeatedly passes through points on its path, that it is confined to a circumscribed form—contribute to the fascination of carousels, all the more so when they are contrasted with the up-and-down motion of the carousel's figures.[33] Combined further with the cylindrical element of the waltz—its translation onto the cylindrical rolls of mechanical organs keyed to its rhythm—the carousel provided perhaps the most vivid bodily enjoyment of the cylinder in the nineteenth century.[34]

The optical equivalent to the full-body experience of the carousel could be found in the host of cylindrical devices that reached for visual motility not through immersion but through accelerated rotation on a smaller scale: the **praxinoscope**, the **tachyscope**, the **stroboscope**, the **anorthoscope**, the **zoetrope**, the **phenakistoscope**, and the **thaumatrope**

FIGURE 21. Original zoetrope, ca. 1860s. A zoetrope is a cylinder with a series
of pictures on the inner surface that, when viewed through slits with the cylinder
rotating, give an impression of continuous motion. The idea that a sequence of
drawings should be made on a band of paper to be viewed in a rotating cylinder was
first suggested by Simon Stampfer in 1833. However, it wasn't until the 1860s, when
several patents were obtained, that the zoetrope appeared on the market. It remained
a popular parlor toy for the rest of the century. © Science Museum / Science & Society
Picture Library—All rights reserved.

all belong to this development (fig. 21). All have been identified as pre-
cursors to cinematic recording and projection devices.[35]

The linguistic version of intransitive cylindrical rotation is evident
in the **encryption devices** that also became cylindrical: whereas pre-
nineteenth-century modes of encryption were largely based on the
rectangular *tabula recta* format of commutation and substitution, the
Jefferson wheel cipher and its later reinvention, the Bazeries cylinder,
used the axis of the cylinder for the sequence and the circumference
of the disks for the selection of the letters (fig. 22).[36] This is an early
instance of the syntagmatic/paradigmatic disjunction that will govern
early twentieth-century linguistics and that, in much different dimensions, also appears in the distinction between the axis of the story and
the circumference of the plot in realist poetics.

FIGURE 22. Jefferson's "wheel cipher," later known as the Bazeries cylinder. Each disk contains the twenty-six letters of the alphabet around its edge, in scrambled order. The order of the disks is the cipher key, to be transmitted separately. Also transmitted is a cipher text; the recipient has to arrange the disks in the right order, select the cipher text, and then search on the circumference for the plaintext. The famous World War II Enigma machine is a descendant of this cylinder. Photo courtesy of the National Security Agency.

An important form of intransitive turning—an inversion, really, of the process of rolling—is the motion of the **conveyor belt.** A straight yet flexible surface is wrapped around spaced cylinders and through its movement allows the horizontal or vertical translation of material. Conveyor belts were used in coal mines, in steel and paper mills, in coking plants, and on the factory floor, soon also in a passive version where rigid products were pushed over rotating cylinders (fig. 23). One of their most significant functions was feeding the vast cylinders of blast furnaces and grain silos; in the latter case, vertical transport not only allowed for more compact storage but also charged materials with kinetic energy that could be released in the process of unloading.

TURNING PASSIVELY

In a literal sense, all cylindrical tools turn passively when an engine drives them. For some apparatuses, however, passivity is specifically

FIGURE 23. Margaret Bourke-White, *Wood Chips on Conveyor Belt after Passing through Chipper & Heading for Next Stage at Paper Mill*, 1937. Margaret Bourke-White / Time & Life Pictures / Getty Images.

focused on the homogeneity and indefiniteness of the cylinder's surface. One such device is the pin-tumbler or **Yale lock** that allows two cylinders to rotate inside one another (fig. 24).[37]

It is one of those seemingly minor cylinders on which crucial features of nineteenth-century culture depend: the ability, for example, for individuals to lock up valuables in iron safes, thereby preserving them from inspection, theft, and fire and ensuring the privacy and inviolability of the house and, ever more importantly, of the apartment. The sanctity of the *intérieur,* which Benjamin describes as central to nineteenth-century bourgeois culture, is based on the solidity of the turning cylinders of the Yale lock.[38]

A more intricate passivity characterizes the recording devices that began to dominate laboratories in the mid-1800s. Known collectively as **kymographs** (wave-writers), they all consisted of some—often

FIGURE 24. The Yale lock, invented by Linus Yale between 1860 and 1868. It has six spring-loaded pin tumblers, each in two parts, set in line with the key. The flat key is inserted, and its serrated upper edge raises each pin to the correct height so that the inner cylinder can be turned. © Science Museum / Science & Society Picture Library—All rights reserved.

gruesome—interface with the animal body and a cylindrical recording device (fig. 25). The great advantage of kymographs over previous forms of data recording was, first, that events too fleeting to be registered by human minds and hands could be recorded; second, that two parameters of events (intensity and duration) could be recorded simultaneously; and last, and most significantly, that the elimination of subjectivity from the experimental setup would allow nature to record herself. This was the unchallenged dogma of the "graphic method" that dominated experimental science in the nineteenth century until quantum physics abolished the distinction between observer and unified object or event.

The emergence, the design, and the use of kymographs, from their invention in the circle around Carl Ludwig, Hermann von Helmholtz,

FIGURE 25. A kymograph recording the blood pressure of a
dog (?). A rubber insert connects the carotid artery to a pressure
gauge; a writing implement swims in the column of blood and
records the pressure curve on endless paper wrapped around
two cylinders. Reprinted from Langendorff (1891, 206).

and Emil DuBois-Reymond to the experiments of Marey and the ergonomic applications of Taylor, are well researched, and that research
represents something like a watershed in the development of a history
of science that encompasses instruments, discursive constraints, and
deep historical investigations.[39] At issue in the present context is the
fact that kymographs reveal a relation between the shape of the cylinder and the worldview of thermodynamics that is equally present but
harder to see in other manifestations. The trust in nature recording
herself on the cylinder without fail and loss is based on the principle
of energy conservation, enunciated most clearly by Helmholtz in 1847
and fortified by results obtained from kymographs. Life, previously
a metaphysical force *(Lebenskraft),* could be made visible in a set of
continuous, varied, and periodic energy transactions; seemingly infini-
tesimal phenomena such as muscle reaction time, blood pressure, or
lung volume became recordable.[40] The two kinematic freedoms of the
cylinder linked the intensity of physiological events to their duration:

everything that happened in or to the animal body did so in measurable quantity and in measurable time. (A similar conjunction characterizes, as we will see, the relation of story and plot in realist narratives.) Vital functions and events, scratched first on soot-covered cylinders but soon inked onto endless paper rolls, became legible as curves on a surface that could be unrolled without distortion and then projected onto a coordinate system.[41] Where previously classification followed by speculation had been the norm (or vice versa, as in the case of Romantic *Naturphilosophie*), computation and comparison by overlay emerged as the standard procedure in the life sciences. This new paradigm of evidence, accelerated and broadcast by the cylindrical changes in publishing, in turn led to a new intensity of scholarly and public debate about scientific discovery and practice. To name just one example, antivivisectionism began to take shape at this time.

The original idea behind the use of kymographs—that life in all its possible manifestations could be recorded, interrogated, quantified and manipulated as a written trace in space and time—bears repeating because in retrospect we tend to focus on how dismally it has been perverted. Yet this bio-political perversion should not obscure the fact that the life recorded on the cylinder for the first time was conceived as fully immanent, fully explicable through a complex exchange of forces within the cosmos, without the intervention of transcendent agents and without imponderable matter, occult forces, or discontinuous causalities.[42]

The **phonograph** is related to the kymograph as well as to the screw-cutting lathe. Its stylus also leaves a mark on the cylinder's sleeve, but intensity and frequency are no longer separated into two dimensions as on the kymograph. In Edison's original conception, a fixed stylus engraved a helical thread around a cylinder advanced by a screw turned by a crank. Writing first onto tinfoil and then onto wax, the stylus transmitted into the groove the vibrations of sound amplified by a diaphragm (fig. 26). Later, just as in the development of the lathe, a lead screw coordinated the rotation of the cylinder with the translational motion of stylus; and later still, recording and reproducing stylus and (conical) loudspeaker were separated.[43]

The events recorded by the kymograph could be called "waves" only because a time measure, and hence a measure for the frequency of peaks and valleys, was imposed on the trace from the outside. The length of a segment of the recorded trace corresponded to a time interval measured by the clockwork driving the cylinder. In the phonograph, by contrast,

FIGURE 26. A brown wax cylinder from 1899. These were the first sound recordings produced on a widespread commercial scale. This cylinder and others—beginning with Edison's tinfoil phonograph of 1877—are collected and carefully documented by the University of California, Santa Barbara's Cylinder Preservation and Digitization Project, http://cylinders.library.ucsb.edu/index.php. Image courtesy of University of California, Santa Barbara. Davidson Library, Department of Special Collections.

as the stylus engraved the hill-and-dale dimension into the trace while the cylinder turned, time became an intrinsic part of the trace.[44] The surest indication of this switch from metered to physical time comes from the facts that the cylinder had to be rotated at the same speed during playback as during recording and that the length of the helical trace around the cylinder's axis determined the length of the recording—two minutes in the early days of Edison's phonograph.

This is as good a moment as any—given the admittedly cavalier stance toward classification of the present account—to introduce one of the most visible yet overlooked cylinders in nineteenth century architectural and mechanical design, the **rivet**. Kinematically and historically speaking a precursor to the screw, it consists of cylindrical shafts with a head on one end. Rivets were typically heated, inserted in a predrilled hole, and hammered flat on the end without the head. When welding was not yet available and bolts required the precision cutting of threads, riveting was, in spite of its labor-intensive procedure, the

FIGURE 27. Albert Renger-Patzsch, *Intersecting Traces of a Truss Bridge in Duisburg-Hochfeldt*, 1928. © 2011 Albert Renger-Patzsch Archiv / Ann u. Jürgen Wilde, Zülpich / Artists Rights Society (ARS), New York.

prevalent mode of fastening metal to metal. The great iconic metal structures of the nineteenth century—Brunel's *Great Eastern,* the Eiffel Tower, the Forth Bridge—may have looked smooth and imposing from afar but were at closer inspection covered by millions of pockmarks, the rivet heads that secured the structure against enormous stresses of wind and water. The *Great Eastern* was held by three million rivets; the Eiffel Tower is still held by two and a half million, and the Forth Bridge by seven million (fig. 27).[45]

THE MACHINE LATHE

At first sight, this tool looks nothing like a cylinder. The reason: it produces cylinders. The **lathe** is an abstract cylinder, a cylinder separated into its kinematic extremes, pure rotation and pure translation. Where the two motions meet, the lathe does its turning, honing, facing, grinding, cutting, extruding, boring, and knurling work. In its standard horizontal version, its main components are headstock, tailstock, and the carriage assembly. The headstock is set into rotational motion by a motor through a belt or any other form of transmission; the spindle at its center holds the work piece—say a steel rod—and imparts its motion to it. The tailstock supports the other end of the piece, most often through a hole in its center; it turns passively and can be moved horizontally on the axis of rotation to accommodate various lengths of work. For internal machining operations—to produce the hollow cylinder of a gun barrel, for example—it can also hold drills and reamers. Headstock and tailstock align along the central axis of the virtual cylinder constituted by the lathe (fig. 28).

The carriage assembly moves parallel to the axis of rotation; it is mounted both on a lead screw—also driven by the headstock—that advances the carriage during threading operations parallel to the axis of rotation and on a smooth feed rod that is used to guide it in facing, turning, or drilling work perpendicular to the axis of rotation. It carries the slide rest, which in turn supports the tool holder and advances the cutting tool toward the work from a range of angles.[46] Centering the rotation of the headstock and tailstock spindles on the axis of the work and calibrating the straightness of the carriage guides are of crucial importance for the accuracy of the lathe. From the combined demands of uniform rotation (of the work) and uniform translation (of the tool) in the work process it follows that the work piece itself already needs to be cylindrical.

The self-acting lathe and its many horizontal and vertical avatars are the most important tools of the machine age, and their kinematic analysis as the application of two opposed motions on a work piece can highlight how the "allegorical" interpretation of kinematics differs from the "moral" interpretation of sociology and political economy. Of course, lathes had been used for many centuries, most prominently in woodworking; writers in the sixteenth century had gone so far as to call God "the 'first wood turner,' who had created the world with such artistry."[47] What the toolmakers of the nineteenth century added was not simply steam power as a source of rotation (a lathe can be operated by hand or foot) and steel as a rigid material but the self-acting slide rest with its tool holder. Combined in this addition are two innovations: first, the tool is no longer held by the hand of a human operator, and second, the tool is advanced along the horizontal axis of the work

FIGURE 28. Model of the original screw-cutting lathe by
Henry Maudslay. This model is arranged to be driven by
hand power. The workpiece on which the screw is to be
cut is carried between head- and tailstock, with the lead
screw mounted in the lathe bed. The slide carries the tool
holder, connected to the lead screw. The depth of the cut
is controlled by a hand wheel, and a set of change wheels
allows for a range of different threads. © Science Museum /
Science & Society Picture Library—All rights reserved.

by a rigid linkage (the lead screw and its nut) at a rate identical or pro-
portionate to that at which the work is turned. Except for the initial
adjustments, human hands are no longer needed to operate this tool; it
was, as we will see, precisely this exclusion that fueled Marx's animos-
ity toward the lathe.

The push for purely technical machine tools had originated not from
capitalist desires to shrink the workforce but from the need for precise

FIGURE 29. This drawing by Mausdlay's great admirer Nasmyth shows the "slide principle" in its kinematic glory. Note that both lathes are driven by a belt attached to an unspecified power source—it is not the motor that makes the difference. Rather, the workman on the left must employ both hands and his body weight for forward pressure and his legs for lateral motion while the workman on the right needs only adjust the tool holder with two fingers. Reprinted from Buchanan (1841, 396).

and uniform engine parts at the beginning of the nineteenth century. Imprecision in the boring of steam cylinders, for example, had led to losses of energy, quick deterioration of appended linkages and tools, and the need for expensive lubrication.[48] Henry Maudslay, who was to machine tools what James Watt was to the steam engine, very clearly saw that this imprecision could be avoided only by eliminating the human body and its imprecise kinematics from the forming process.[49] The slide rest and the lead screw did exactly that (fig. 29). Maudslay's contemporaries were keenly aware that the resulting self-regulating mechanism inaugurated a new epoch in the history of tools:

> It was this holding of a tool by means of an iron hand, and constraining it to move along the surface of the work in so certain a manner, and with such definite and precise motion, which formed the great era in the history of mechanism, inasmuch as we thenceforward became possessed, by its means, of the power of operating alike on the most ponderous or delicate

pieces of machinery with a degree of minute precision, of which language cannot convey an adequate idea; and in many cases we have, through its agency, equal facility in carrying on the most perfect workmanship in the interior parts of certain machines, where neither the hand nor the eye can reach, and nevertheless we can give these parts their required form with a degree of accuracy as if we had the power of transforming ourselves into pigmy workmen, and so apply our labour to the innermost holes and corners of our machinery.[50]

Finding ways to insure accuracy, uniformity, and high output was of crucial importance to the emerging factory system, and the self-acting lathe in its many configurations was the tool to bring it about. As the actors in this unfolding drama—factory owners, philosophers, artisans, workers, government superintendents—fully knew, the lathe would subvert the traditional divisions of labor and competence, and perhaps the very nature of work.[51]

Of all the objects emerging from the lathe, the most significant was the screw. Earlier methods like filing or casting screw threads were much too cumbersome and inaccurate; at the same time, the need for screws both in machines and in precision instruments rose dramatically. Interpreted kinematically according to Reuleaux's grammar of primitive cylindrical joints, the screw is the product of the spindle's revolute joint and the carriage's prism. It completes the trinity of primitive kinematic elements (together with the prism and the revolute joint), and it is the precondition for its own production because the lead screw that advances the carriage along the workpiece is the very element that ensures the uniformity and precision of the thread it cuts. Insofar as the lead screw combines the two actions of the screw that in eighteenth-century mechanisms were still separated—moving and measuring—Maudslay can be said to have taught the screw how to reproduce itself.[52]

It was precisely this kinematic epigenesis that made the self-acting lathe so crucial and so vexing to Karl Marx as he tried to make sense of machines in the economy of capitalism. Like the majority of philosophers who incorporate questions of technology into their thought, Marx tended to view the role of machines as that of tools—an identification that, aligning the tripartite division of machines with the senses of Scripture, we have earlier called the "moral" sense of machines.[53] As readers of Das Kapital know, this is by no means a facetious alignment: Marx's exposition of the laws that govern machine-based capitalist production is shot through with explicit exhortations to overturn these laws.[54] Yet even independently of the workers' willingness to rise against the inhumanity of their working conditions, these laws, in Marx' analysis, contain "literal" contradictions that will lead to the system's undoing with the inevitability and straightness of gravitational fall. The lathe, in which straightness and revolution are isolated to the utmost, plays a crucial role in Marx's account both of capitalism's moral damnability and of its literal contradictions.

From a moral point of view, which Marx had first articulated in his *Economic-Philosophical Manuscripts* of 1844, the lathe with its self-acting slide rest represents the last step in the relentless humiliation of human labor through factory work. All protestations of anti-Idealism notwithstanding, Marx never abandoned Hegel's notion that work is the pivotal activity in the emergence of self-consciousness. Embedded in this notion is the idea—strengthened by Feuerbach and his reversal of theological concepts—that work is essentially creation, that it adds an irreducible qualitative surplus to both the work piece and the life of its maker. Although Marx would later attempt to abstract from all qualitative aspects of labor, this creationist and negentropic belief remains apparent in his ill-disguised outrage over the fact that under capitalism's rule workers have to prostitute their ability to work. The implication of this charge is that, as in the case of love, no remuneration can adequately represent the investment of vital human forces and time.[55]

Kinematic criticism shows that this outrage is sustained by the conviction that for work to be satisfying it literally must be manifest—it must be performed by the hand and its complex but imprecise motions. According to Marx's historical reconstruction of the rise of machines, the early development of motors and transmissions was driven by the need for tools, which in turn he conceived as hand tools.[56] In factory work, as the culmination of earlier tendencies for rationalization, the hand as the agent of work itself was expropriated, and the exact moment of this expropriation coincided with the advent of the self-guiding slide rest. For when it became imperative in the nineteenth century "to produce the geometrically accurate straight lines, planes, circles, cylinders, cones, and spheres," the slide rest did not imitate or amplify a specific motion of the hand; it "replaces, not some particular tool, but the hand itself."[57] The consequences of this unnatural substitution, Marx argued, reached so deeply into the social fabric that natural morality itself was destroyed: since nonmanifest work could be performed by anyone, including women and children, the male worker became the slaveholder, indeed the panderer, of his own family.[58] The dissolution of stable, patriarchal family structures and all the social problems it engendered in the newly industrialized cities were in Marx's eyes intimately linked to the emergence of the self-acting lathe and its inhuman precision.

On the other hand, in a more Kleistian vein, Marx hailed machines as providing relief from toil and advocated technological instruction for the coming communist society.[59] What he in his early writings called "abstract work" represents the element of drudgery and stultification that comes with the repetitiveness of any work and that cannot be reduced to the question of ownership of the means of production. Marx remained fascinated throughout his later writings with the inventiveness and dynamism of capitalism's drive for technical solutions to repetitiveness in production processes.

The ambivalence about the nature of work thus finds its counterpart in Marx's ambivalence about machines. The study of kinematics reveals two points that lead deeper into this vexing dilemma for Marxist thought. First, the history of kinematics shows that the lathe and similar machine tools are not necessarily linked to the dispossession and stultification of the modern worker. It is important to distinguish, in this context, between the kinematics of the self-acting lathe and the rise of work in assembly lines later in the century. It is true that the lathe helped to establish the standards of interchangeability that enabled the division of factory work into ever smaller and, ultimately, meaningless units. It is also true that Maudslay cooperated with Marc Isambart Brunel (and Samuel Bentham) on the first rationally organized factory dominated by steam power and machine tools.[60] But the precision lathe itself is not the proximate cause for the devaluation of work deplored by Marx—if indeed the toil of the pre–machine age can be called more humane or interesting than work in nineteenth-century factories. In fact, as many memoirs and treatises published at the time show, the quest for a new mechanics of precision led to unprecedented social mobility within the workshops and factories and to the rise to prominence of men whose ambitions had been suppressed in traditional guilds— Maudslay's own rise and the innovative organization of his workshop being only one instance of many.[61]

More importantly, however, kinematic analysis must dispute the claim that the lathe imitates and therefore replaces the hand.[62] There has never been continuous rotation in hand tools for the simple reason that the human skeleton neither has the ability to support it nor the strength to precisely isolate any motion. Aside from their limited range of motions, human joints are not bearings: they are wobbly and inaccurate even in their most disciplined use—they have, as kinematicists would say, too many freedoms. A screw, for example, can be handmade by means of vises and files, but it will never be accurate in the same way as the screws Maudslay produced and Nasmyth described. This is not a question of degree: the screw cut on Maudslay's lathe is the replication of another screw, the guide screw, and therefore best understood as an altogether new species.[63] Marx, by singling out the slide rest and its fistlike aspect, overlooked the guide screw as the second, irreducible component of the self-acting lathe. The same fundamental duality that Reuleaux's kinematics had identified in the motion of rolling, in the three kinematic pairs, and in the cylinder chains appears in the self-acting lathe as the duality of slide and guide. Thus it interrupts the chain of substitutions that for Marx, and other economic anthropologists, reaches back to an imaginary past in which all work was manifest, work of the hand. The replicative work of the lathe, however, introduces on the level of production the same "originary iterability" that Derrida had identified in the higher strata of Marx's value theory and commodity fetishism. What is true for the lathe is, *mutatis mutandis,* true for the steam hammer, which is not, as Marx intimates in one of his more impressive prosopopeias, a "cyclopic rebirth" of the handheld hammer, anymore than the circular saw is a "gigantic razor."[64] The monstrosity of machine tools resides not in their size but in their coupled motions.

The anthropocentric, unitary theory of tools as extensions or "projections" of human organs, to which Marx subscribed, was fully formulated by his "bourgeois" contemporary Ernst Kapp and was adopted by many later philosophers of technology; it has been at the root of much technological pessimism in the nineteenth and twentieth centuries. In whatever guise, techno-pessimists suppose an original unity of man and nature, mediated by simple tools but disrupted or fatally distorted by the intercession of machines.[65] The history of kinematics, however, reminds us that continuous rotation, as well as pure translation, is not a natural but a mechanically forced motion and that machines are apparatuses to do the forcing. From a kinematic perspective, then, the moral impetus derived from the exclusion of the human hand in the adoption of machine tools is misplaced—hands were never part of the work machine tools can do. This is not to say that working on and with machines and machine tools is not drudgery and toil, or that the private ownership of machines is just. But if the lathe with its self-acting slide rest represents a caesura in the history of tool usage, its pernicious effect on the worker cannot be attributed to the capitalist system.[66]

Failing to honor the kinematic novelty of the of self-acting lathe and its cognates, Marx arrived at a thoroughly ambivalent theory of technology in which it is never quite clear whether the nature of machines or the question of their ownership is responsible for the misery of industrial labor. We can see that he vacillates between the lathe's "literal" sense as a machine and its "moral" sense as a tool when a kinematic, "allegorical" understanding would have revealed that the intercession of machine tools represents a technological innovation—the "inhuman" separation of rotation and translation—that transcends the vision of organ projection and the "cyclopic" increase in power. A long legacy of vacillation between the Romantic adoration of unalienated handiwork and—to put it briefly—Stalinist technophilia was one of the consequences of this conflation.

Yet Marx did have the conceptual tools to tackle the lathe and the "inhumanity" that adumbrates its place in the process of production. In his mature work, his allegiance to the idea of anthropogenic work is upset by the insistence that the exchange of commodities always presupposes an inhuman supplement that confers value to them. This supplement, which, confusingly, he also calls abstract work, is not only quantitatively different from concrete effort: that is, it is not simply, as is often asserted, the average time it takes in a given economy to produce a thing. Rather, it is the name for that "ghostly objectivity" that accrues to a thing in the act of exchanging it with another—its value.[67] Outside and prior to such an act, a thing may have a use, and it may embody concrete and individual work, but only in the act of equating one product with another is its value—its commodity value—determined. Abstract work has ghostly qualities because it attaches itself to a product and because no one has actually performed it.[68]

This abstract supplement is at the heart of what Marx thought constituted the crucial difference between bourgeois and critical political economy: the analysis of the value-form of commodities. His predecessors Smith and Ricardo may have found the labor theory of value, but they—like all the other actors within capitalist economies—did not see that the exchange of commodities required a *tertium comparationis* in which their value realized itself. Abstract and retroactive, this "form of value" has no referent in actual work and thus upsets the idea of a substantive and fully represented presence of work in value.[69] One of the consequences of this analysis is Marxism's claim that capitalism, unaware of its own mechanisms of conferring value and therefore unable to rationally regulate exchange, is dangerously prone to crises and cyclical implosions.

Kinematics suggests that the lathe and its cognates function on the level of production as the same kind of "real" abstraction that Marx analyzes in the realm of exchange. They perform abstract work—not in the way the early Marx used the term, that is as disqualified and alienated work—but as the "form of work" that industrial machines allow. That form is the cylinder in the abstraction in which it is present in the lathe: as rotation, translation, and helical motion. Consumers may think that each product is shaped by the design of its inventor or the requirements of its purpose when in fact the lathe and other tools impose the ghostly presence of cylindrical forms on all industrial products. Their seeming variety derives from the ever more subtle de- and recomposition of cylindrical motions into such forms as turning, honing, facing, grinding, cutting, extruding, boring, and knurling. These motions, as we have seen, are as "inhuman" as the supplement of abstract work added to products in the process of exchange.

One must wonder whether overlooking the workings of this irreducible supplement both in machine tools and in the establishment of commodity value does not explain the pernicious ambivalence in Marx's attitude toward the role of subjective involvement in overturning capitalism. Two lines of political critique coexist in his work with little coordination, and even contradictory consequences. One is the call for a an active (over)turning, a revolution of the system because it is exploitative and dehumanizing and because it excludes the largest and most productive segment of the population from wealth and political power. This moral argument begins with the 1844 manuscripts and culminates in the *Communist Manifesto,* but we have seen that Marx continues to invoke it in his "scientific" analysis of the factory system.

The other set of arguments for the destruction of capitalism is kinematic in nature as it describes the forced motion of capitalist economy; it culminates in the "law of the tendency of the profit rate to fall," the veritable "mystery" Marx claimed to have discovered at the heart of capitalist modes of production. It states that the progressive exclusion of the human hand and its uncontrollable freedoms from the process of industrial production has an entropic effect on the entirety of capitalism's economic structure. For only humans and their hands can be exploited, only workers can be kept longer in the factory or be paid less. Whenever machines replace human workers in the factories, they decrease the contingent of "variable capital" that can be pressed for more profit. The investment in machines, in turn, is forced on the factory owner by the market, since they promise faster and initially more profitable production. But once they form part of what Marx calls "constant capital" throughout a particular industry sector, machines no longer increase the rate of profit. They cannot be kept running longer or faster than their technical specifications allow; in fact, the longer machines are in service the smaller is their contribution to the value of the commodity they produce. Competition thus forces the capitalist into a deleterious contradiction: to raise profitability, he must replace workers with machines, which diminishes the very element in the process of production that can raise his profits. This law of the tendency of the rate of profit to fall is an expression of the inherent contradictoriness of capitalist production that will be overcome only by the abolition of private ownership and competition.[70]

The Hegelian in Marx was clearly fascinated by the fact that the competition between apparently rational agents would inevitably lead to the demise of the system as a whole—that a principle of negativity could subvert even the most "scientific" of economic systems and turn it into a qualitatively new state. In Marx's succinct formulation, the negative principle at work at the heart of capitalism is called "moral attrition" *(moralischer Verschleiss),*[71] a concept by means of which he tries to capture the fact that technical innovation affords an economic advantage only so long as competitors have not caught on and leveled the playing field. Once all producers of screws, for example, used Maudslay's self-acting lathe, the increase in productivity spread over the entire sector and became the new norm.

The status of Marx's law has puzzled and agitated many exegetes because it puts the role of political activism in the destruction of capitalism into question.[72] Taken to its extremes, the argument could be interpreted in an antinomian way: working toward automation constitutes an even more efficient way of overthrowing capitalism than unionizing or striking. This would be a version of the argument Heinrich von Kleist makes in his *Marionettentheater*—that only full mechanization guarantees our way back into paradise. Indeed, unlike the more overtly moral appeals to overthrow capitalism by revolution in *Capital's* chapter on large machines, the analysis of the fall of the profit rate is reminiscent of the guiding principle and paradigmatic product of the self-acting lathe, the screw: every move forward in technological productivity results in a turn against the profitability of production, capitalism's raison d'être.

The vacillation between the moral and the kinematic reading of work, machines, and capitalist production results in a distinct slippage in Marx's vocabulary, specifically in the transitions from *Umwälzung* to *revolution* and vice versa.[73] As we have seen, *Walzen* are large cylinders used in steel, paper, glass, and cement production and, of course, in the rotary printing press; they crush and pull to produce and process a variety of formless substances that make up the raw materials of the nineteenth century. This crushing and pulling is the transitive and instrumental version of the motion that Reuleaux defined as the essential mechanical motion: rolling. Revolution, on the other hand, is the free rotation of a body around an axis unrelated to any other body. With the possible exception of the governor, nothing in machines simply rotates. While the cylinder is the optimal shape for rolling, the natural body of revolution is the sphere. When Marx speaks of *Umwälzung,* he wants his readers to imagine a contact motion that animates an entire assembly of bodies, which in their axial rotation roll something with inevitable force; when he speaks of revolution, the implications are spontaneity, identity, subjectivity, and completeness.[74]

Responsible for this conceptual slippage is the above-mentioned misinterpretation of the lathe and its cognates as substitutions for human work. The deeply problematic status (some say the demonstrable falsehood) of the "law," based as it is on the proportion of variable, human capital to constant, machine capital, lies in the kinematic incompatibility of human and mechanical work. Contrary to the stipulations of the "law," capitalists cannot replace machines with human hands if they so wish: the lathe's (and the steam roller's and the rolling mill's and the paper machine's) inhuman kinematics produces different products than the work of the hand.[75] The inability to oppose and to quantify the respective contributions of constant capital and variable capital to the rate of profit makes Marx's law fundamentally incongruent with the cylindrical kinematics and dynamics of the production process.

Whether this split between *Umwälzung* and *revolution,* between objective and subjective factors in the demise of capitalism, is fatal to Marxist analysis in general is not of interest here. It does suggest, however, that the "inhumanity" of machines should be viewed not in opposition to human creativity but as a locus of the intermixture of these two factors, as the overlapping of the human factor in machines and the machinic factor in humans. The degradation of machines to tools, and the ejection of machines from the realm of human productivity as the other of the hand lead to an inability not only to confront their impact on economic relations but also to understand them as historical and cultural agents.

CHAPTER 6

Kinematics of Narration I

Dickens and the Motion of Serialization

Before the universal availability of motive power in the steam engine, the valuation of translational and rotational motion had been predominantly a metaphysical and theological business, in which straight-line motion and its embodiments belonged to the rational and human world, rotational motion to the aesthetic and divine sphere. In the transmissions and in the machine tools of the nineteenth century this opposition was broken down into the "cylinder chains" that made up the kinematic heart of machines. Joints and linkages utilizing the axes and walls of cylinders isolated translation and rotation, converted them into all manner of intermediary motions, and transmitted them to the tools, which in turn impressed these motions on industrial products. Of interest to the engineers was not the metaphysical value or the history of motions but their use and convertibility: kinematics, an offspring of thermodynamics, was a science of conversions rather than of substance.

Yet some of the metaphysical attributes attached to motions survived even in nineteenth-century machines and their world. Throughout the century, cylindrical machines were metaphorized into revenants of ancient deities or monsters—speakers at industry conventions and world fairs were as prolific in deifying machines as Marx and his followers were in demonizing them.[1] There was the archaic association of translational up-and-down motion with crushing brute force and finality, and the equally archaic equation of rotation with wholeness, play, and continuity. The carousel, the zoetrope, the panorama played with rotation and roundness, while the steam hammer figured as the ultimate embodiment of cyclopic translational force.[2] Roulette, one of the signature inventions—and addictions—of the nineteenth century (new enough that in Balzac's *Père Goriot* it has to be explained to young Rastignac), showed rotation in its old association with the medieval wheel of fortune. Most important were the audiovisual experiences in which reciprocity and translation were slowly transformed into continuity and rotation, as in the characteristic sights and sounds of a starting locomotive when the intervals of expelling steam decreased until only a continuous sound (often topped by the whistle) accompanied the cycloids described by its running gear; or, later in the century, in the action of the film camera where the translational processes of capturing images merged with the rotation of the film reel.[3]

One of the great aesthetic innovations of the nineteenth century also partook in the kinematics of the epoch: the realist novel. In fact, many of the features that make up the problematic attribute "realistic" can be redescribed in relation to kinematic solutions in nineteenth-century machinery.[4] The purpose of such a redescription is to allow for a presentation of literary realism independent of representational claims—of the claims that by turning to social reality authors in the nineteenth century established a univocal relation between literary text and outside world—and of the formalist counterclaims—that realism is but an effect of a more or less conscious literary and rhetorical strategy.

Not the least advantage of bracketing the question of representation is that it mutes the moral overtones in the theory of realism. Realist narratives are not best understood as attempts to judge and intervene in the realities they depict and in the lives of their readers, nor do they tap, as narratologists often claim, into a timeless desire to move or be moved by storytelling. While apparently conflicting, these claims derive their justification from a common root in the rhetorical *officia*, where the task of moving an audience tended to dominate the task of delighting and educating. Without question, moving the public was the intended goal of many writers in the nineteenth century—we just need to think of Dickens or Zola; but there is a more palpable, more realistic sense of moving and motion that drives the success of realist fiction. It begins with the question: By what means do writers (and publishers) keep their readers moving their eyes in a straight line across the page, and then make them turn it over? It encompasses, furthermore, a description of the spaces in which nineteenth-century writers move their characters and envelop their readers. It finally connects with the stylistic choices by means of which writers control the motion of their narratives. This book's three chapters on the kinematics of narration, inserted in the description of cylindrical processes and phenomena, are concerned with these senses of motion.[5]

The turn to serializing novels forged the most palpable link between nineteenth-century narratives and the emerging interconnectedness of kinematic processes. Beginning in the 1830s in England and France, novels in monthly or biweekly installments became the most profitable mode of publishing and the most popular mode of consuming literature. Only with the introduction of cylinders in rotary printing presses and endless paper machines could the circulation numbers necessary for economically viable serializations be realized. Only with the establishment of a network of railroads could serials be distributed with sufficient range and speed. Only with the advent of gas lighting could they be read in the small type necessary to fit enough of a narrative on a few pages, at a time of the reader's choosing.[6] And only through the conjunction of all these factors were writers able to amass (and squander) great fortunes, become public figures, and intervene descriptively, satirically, or politically in the important debates of their times—a manifestation of literary realism (and later naturalism) that is often confused with representational fidelity.

The serialization of long narratives and the expansion of their readership forced the writing of prose to obey mechanical constraints. Subjected to the rhythm of publication, writers could neither presuppose that their readers would keep the previous installment nor be certain that they would buy the next. This loss of access to the totality of a narrative constitutes a fundamental difference to earlier conditions of literary production and consumption.[7] Romantic novels, with their foreshadowing and revelations, their radiating symbols, and their yearning for closure, had always relied on the completeness of the "volume"—on the reader's ability to peruse the text in every direction and thus to insert herself in the web of allusions. The novel's status as the most "Romantic" of literary forms, which it had gained in the aesthetics of Jena Romanticism, was predicated on its cyclical, or rather, encyclopedic form—a form that would at once be able to contain all other forms and genres and relieve narration from the obligation of linearity.[8] The *Bildungsroman* in particular embodied these ideals. Its purest incarnation, Goethe's *Wilhelm Meisters Lehrjahre* (1796), is centered on the notion that the protagonist's path will lead him to the discovery of a self that was lost in the very process of looking for it.[9] This ideal of cyclical self-recuperation was celebrated by theoreticians like Friedrich Schlegel and adopted by idealist philosophers—Hegel's *Phenomenology of the Spirit* is based on this figure, as are Schelling's systems of the early 1800s.

Gottfried Keller's *Der grüne Heinrich,* published in three volumes in 1854 (the fourth volume appeared in 1855), though a late entrant, is a *Bildungsroman* still deeply indebted to this encyclopedic ideal: the novel generates its pervasive sense of psychological and geographical nostalgia by frequent prolepses and analepses, which the reader can fully grasp only with access to the novel as a whole. The color green in the title, for example, gains its full meaning only at the end of the novel, when the green of Heinrich's childhood clothes is matched by the green of the cemetery's grass. The diegetic force that bends the narrative into its recursive form is the hero's imagination: Heinrich (like his predecessors Heinrich von Ofterdingen and Wilhelm Meister) embarks on a search for a lost unity that he imagines is concealed from him by external circumstances, in his case the ideal to live through his imagination as an artist; the course of the narration progressively deceives him of this notion by showing that the recursive, nostalgic force of the imagination is dissociated from, and indeed inimical to, the irreversibility of human life.

The contrast to a serialized *Bildungsroman* in England is instructive: Charles Dickens's *David Copperfield,* published in nineteen installments between May 1849 and November 1850, also describes a young man's development from his earliest childhood—indeed, from his birth—to maturity; it contains moments of reflection, of anticipation, and detours caused by the surfeit of imagination, but his path from poverty to comfort, from loneliness to community, and from self-indulgence to self-discipline is decidedly more forward-oriented and open-ended. David's development as a writer, unlike Heinrich Lee's struggle to be a painter, is not contained in his miserable youth, nor is it its imaginary ideal—a fact subtly underscored by his graduating seamlessly from being a copyist to being a writer of fiction. If the ideal line of Heinrich's narrated life is the circle, that of David Copperfield's, with its strong undertow of forward development retarded by occasional reflections and analepses, follows the emblematic line of the nineteenth century, the cycloid—the line traced by a point on a forward-moving wheel. It combines forward and retrograde motion and is visible to everyone as the path of the connecting rods on a locomotive's wheel.[10]

These changes in biographical writing are indicative of wider changes brought about by serial publication. In their most general form they required a fundamental realignment of a narrative's subject matter with the modes of its telling. This distinction lay dormant in Aristotle's distinction between *diegesis* and *mimesis* and developed into the relation of story and plot, *histoire* and *récit, fabula* and *sjuzhet, Erzähltem* und *Erzählung,* Form and Life, hermeneutic and proairetic code. To attempt a brief definition, *story* is the sequence of events and actions unfolding in irreversible time. In a biographical novel, for example, it is the succession of events in the life of the protagonist, regardless of the order in which they are told. The *plot* arranges and orders the telling of these events and actions through such devices as flashbacks, interspersed documents, descriptive passages, encapsulations, and interior monologues. *Narration,* finally, is the collective term for plot choices on a more general level; it encompasses such decisions as point of view, the introduction of characters, tone, and the use of dialogue.[11]

As cumbersome and as debatable as these distinctions might be, it is hard to conceive of an analysis of fictional texts that would eschew them entirely. Peter Brooks observes that the "differing status of the two terms [*story* and *plot*] by no means invalidates the distinction itself, which is central to our thinking about narrative and necessary to its analysis since it allows us to juxtapose two modes of order and in the juxtaposing to see how ordering takes place."[12] What makes the distinction between story and plot poignant for the literature of the nineteenth century are the claims of representational realism, sometimes staked out by writers themselves, sometimes by critics and readers: the claim that novels beginning in the 1830s acknowledge, and in some way "take up," social realities of their time. This belief in the ontological anteriority of the story, and in a narrative's ability to convey it, has its inverted mirror image in the argument that realism is an effect of narrative dispositions and linguistic strategies.[13] From the kinematic point of view, a third possibility comes into view: independently from all claims to fidelity in representation, serialization provides an experience of sequentiality and irreversibility that makes the distinction between story and plot "real" in the first place.

Throughout the novel's history, various narrative devices had been employed to suggest that the story occurred before and independently of its telling. Most implied a denial that plot arrangements, at least those requiring massive interventions, had taken place at all. This is the stance of the epistolary novel as well as of the "discovered manuscript" ploy that retained its popularity throughout the eighteenth century and into European Romanticism. The first edition of Goethe's *Wilhelm Meisters Lehrjahre* from 1795/96 still had on its title page "Herausgegeben von Goethe" (edited by Goethe). It is instructive to see how the novel that established serialization as the dominant mode of publishing, Charles Dickens's *Posthumous Papers of the Pickwick Club,* published between March 1836 and October 1837, overcame the limitations of these gestures.[14] Fresh over the hurdle of the first installments, Dickens declared: "Many authors entertain, not only a foolish, but a really dishonest objection to acknowledge the sources from whence they derive much valuable information. We have no such feeling. We are merely endeavouring to discharge, in an upright manner, the responsible duties of our editorial functions; and whatever ambition we might have felt under other circumstances to lay claim to the authorship of these adventures, a regard for truth forbids us to do more than claim the merit of their judicious arrangement and impartial narration."[15] By the time Dickens interjects these remarks into his narrative—a playful version of Balzac's emphatic claim to be nothing but the "secretary of his age"—it has become obvious to the reader that the univocal relation between story and plot must be one of the satirical aims of the novel: the very idea that a club as inconsequential as the Pickwickians should produce papers worthy of "judicious arrangement and impartial narration" is absurd and hilarious.

As he progressed in his writing, Dickens increased his control over all elements that projected the idea of a preexisting story. In the case of the *Pickwick Papers,* the initial plan had been that he simply annotate Robert Seymour's illustrations; the success of the first installments convinced the publisher to reverse this order, and from then on Dickens assumed a lifelong position of exacting control over the details and the placement of the illustrations in his works. He jettisoned the equally "realistic" idea of presenting loosely related sketches of modern sporting life in favor of a fully narrated frame to which each episode was related. Apart from recalibrating the relation between story and plot, these decisions betray the eagerness on the part of Dickens and his fellow writers—Balzac being perhaps the most eager of all—to distance the novelistic enterprise from the ephemeral work of the journalist, that other profiteer from cylindrical publishing practices. Moving away from journalistic immediacy (and venality) without giving up mass appeal and the claim to social relevance is one of the chief accomplishments of Dickens and the writers of his generation.[16]

Yet the self-confident rejection of naive realism did not lead novelists of the 1830s and 1840s to indulge in the two options taken by previous generations: either to invent fantastically implausible stories and present them with a gesture of editorial innocence, as the Romantics did, or to take a minimal yet plausible story, like the life and opinions of a gentleman, and sally forth on the most outlandish digressions.[17] *The Pickwick Papers* still shows the marks of these former excesses: the fantastic stories survive as interspersed tales told or read within the narration, but without any connection to the plot; and the narrative digressions are transformed into the topographical digressions taken by the wandering Pickwickians. In his later works, Dickens created some of the most memorable eccentrics in all of literature—beginning with Sam Weller but culminating in types such as Wilkins Micawber and Mr. Dick in *David Copperfield,* or Captain Cuttle and Mr. Toots in *Dombey and Son*—who allowed him to digress and repeat without disrupting the narrative's fabric. In addition, the striking characterizations served as a mnemonic bridge with which readers could connect the installments.

This progressive integration and streamlining, supported by the new capacities of cylindrical printing and distributing, engaged readers in a much more realistic relationship than the claims—often the authors' own claims—that text and audience shared the same reality. Chapters, because their limits coincided with those of the installments, became the basic unit of the novel, and readers expected that the rhythm of narrated time would match the rhythm of publication.[18] Chapters had to begin and end in such a way as to allow readers to remember the previous installment and seduce them into awaiting the next. The cliff-hanger was only the most sensational device in the overall effort to keep readers involved during the process of publication. The notion of suspense in fiction, not entirely unknown in previous epochs but never aligned with the formal partitions of the narrative, now became an integral and perfectly obvious device with which parts of the plot were joined in the real time of publication.[19]

A similar translational pull informed the introduction and stylization of a serialized novel's characters. A most revealing instance is, again, Dickens's *Pickwick Papers,* where the "boot" Sam Weller is introduced rather haphazardly in the tenth chapter. Dickens and his publisher then realized—from the reviews that appeared in the caesura between installments, but above all from the perceptible rise in sales figures—that having Sam as a Cockney counterpart to the clumsiness of Samuel Pickwick and his friends would balance out the set of characters. It was not primarily the desire to represent a real character from the lower classes that led to the prominence of "Sammy" but the feedback from real readers and the real concerns with the mechanics of the plot and the rhythm of its publication.[20] Even when in later works the introduction of characters was less experimental, it would remain linked both to the internal workings of the narration and to readers' potential for retention.[21]

Releasing parts of a novel in monthly installments and reacting to the reaction of readers may run counter to Romantic notions of inspiration and originality, but it inserts the novel into the calendar of local life. The famous Christmas chapter in *The Pickwick Papers*—some of the most joyous and good-humored pages ever to be appear in a novel—was published in December of 1836, suggesting to readers that the time of the story and the time of their lives were congruous.[22] Such synchronizations were supported by the same cylindrical processes that changed modern life on all levels: the installments were light enough to be carried along, and short enough to be read instantly, for example, on railway journeys; distribution by train created a collective of readers that consumed each installment nearly simultaneously; gaslight extended the hours in which literature could be read; and the emergence of daily newspapers created a new form of criticism that engaged with literature while it was being written and published.

There are many indications that all of these factors fostered a large virtual community and many actual communities of readers for whom discussing the events in the latest installments and speculating about their continuation became a shared and intensely experienced habit: "Once they had purchased or borrowed the latest installment, Victorians might read it aloud. This practice, in a family or neighborhood, enhanced the sense that literature in nineteenth-century England was a national event, that response was public as well as private. Moreover, reaction to the latest part could be shared and intensified. The time between installments in serial literature gave people the opportunity to review events with each other, to speculate about plot and characters, and to deepen ties to their imagined world."[23]

Precisely the communal aspect and the forced rhythm and orientation of reading distinguished these habits from the often-criticized (and highly gendered) reading addictions that had plagued the reception of sentimental novels in the latter half of the eighteenth century. Communities of interpretation would exist for the run of the print, say for two years, and then fracture and move to another author or another novel. In this way, too, novels became intertwined with the life of their readers in a nonrepresentational, nonmetaphorical manner.[24]

Constructing the plot in accordance with the requirements and the opportunities of cylindrical printing and reading made living one's life and reading literature similar in one decisive aspect: the next installment could never be known. For the first time, literature and life, existential and literary analysis became congruent. The two paradigms from which the conceptual arsenal of literary interpretation is drawn, Aristotle's *Poetics* and biblical hermeneutics, were incapable of addressing this relation. Aristotle's theory allows for an understanding of the temporality of experiencing fiction—the cleansing from pity and fear happens in time—but his discussion of tragedy and of the epic shows that this experience is caused by spatially defined performances.[25] The collective emotions provoked by Dickens's or Wilkie Collins's calculatedly terrifying serials, stretched out as they were over months and years and dispersed across the country, can hardly be described as cathartic.[26]

Biblical hermeneutics and its secular avatars that—at least in Germany—were being inserted into the university curriculum at the beginning of the nineteenth century were similarly incapable of comprehending the new mode of writing and reading. Every task of scriptural and hermeneutic interpretation—stabilizing a text's philological core, linking its parts by allegorical and typological relations, translating its message into rules of conduct—was predicated on the Book's, or a book's, totality. This did not necessarily imply formal totality or completeness: in the case of the Bible it was understood that human language and human writing only imperfectly carried the full meaning of God's Word, and in secular literature it was equally understood that the expression of subjectivity must appear externally as fragmented. Yet in both cases every interpretative step was taken within a horizon of completeness, even if interpretation itself accomplished the completion of the work.[27] Of course, nineteenth-century serial novels also eventually ended; but for the duration of their publication, interpretation—and writing—had to make do with their forced linearity and open-endedness.[28]

Shaped by their cylindrical mode of publication, serial novels may have been the first truly secular, worldly fictions in history. Without dependence on any stable external criteria, the "thrownness" of installments brought irreversibility—the crucial attribute both of life as defined by thermodynamics and of a narrative's story—to the experience of writing and reading. From these conditions resulted an openness to contingency, a porosity with regard to external forces (such as readers' reactions, the layout of journals, or the economic pressures of publishing) that culminated in a forward slant of narration, the *prorsus* of its own name. This orientation remained a defining characteristic of modern prose even when the modes of publication swung back to the traditional book format. While the historical kinematic environment lets us understand the emergence of realist modes of narration, its characteristic motion and openness are the reason why interpreters like Bakhtin, as well as a remarkable number of extra-academic writers and critics, came to appreciate the novel not just as an object of study but as a mode of being in the world.[29]

Dickens's case shows—and it similarly could be shown in the case of Balzac and other writers at the beginning of the serialization age—that the epoch of realism began not with a commitment to fidelity in the representation of an anterior reality but with a move in the opposite direction: toward the full implication of the story in the modes of its telling. Kinematic criticism shows that the attributes commonly reserved for the realist story—irreversible temporality, the inevitability and contiguity of events—instead describe the realities of serial publication and the forms of reception it generated. To say it more poignantly, we know what a literary story is—in the analytical sense of "that which is different from the plot"—only through the motion of the rotary printing press and its cylindrical avatars. But rather than introducing a mechanical alienation into the experience of reading and writing, the cylinder's motion made literature accessible on an existential level. The rotating and translating cylinders of the paper machines, the printing machines, the locomotives, the gasometers, the gas pipes: they made life literary and literature realistic.[30]

CHAPTER 7

The Cylinder as Enclosure

CONDUCTING

The steam engine has its scientific origins in seventeenth-century natural philosophy, in particular in the efforts to create and experiment with a vacuum; Robert Boyle's air pump nicely shows the cylinder-piston arrangement of the pump (driven by a crank and a rack-and-pinion linkage) coexisting with the glass sphere of the receiver, elements and functions that will wander into the steam engine and into transmissions and containing technologies of the nineteenth century.[1] In the first steam engines the piston was pulled by a vacuum, and after Watt had reconfigured the generation of power, the aptness of the cylinder for the creation and for the utilization of vacua remained of great interest to engineers. Steam engines, acting as pumps, could produce powerful vacua that, given the right cylindrical conduits, could be used to transport (cylindrical) objects.

This was the purpose of the many pneumatic **tube delivery systems** that were devised starting in the early 1800s as a means of transporting goods, people, and documents. After the failure of rather fantastical schemes for pushing or sucking passengers and things in large containers through iron tubes, the versions that succeeded and survived—in some places until today—were those that delivered written documents and smaller items in capsules.[2] Tubes were anywhere from 1½ to 3½ inches in diameter, and capsules typically had the size of a forearm. A

FIGURE 30. Men at work in the Instrument Gallery at the Central Telegraph Establishment of the General Post Office in London, 1874. In London, the post office set up a pneumatic tube system for telegraph messages in 1853; in New York City, from the 1890s, pneumatic tubes were used to carry letters between the Brooklyn and New York City post offices, a distance of 1.75 miles. Image © Science Museum Library / Science & Society Picture Library—All rights reserved.

steam engine would either create pressure at one end of the tube system and push the capsule along the tube or create a vacuum at the other end and suck it in. Such tube systems were installed within large single buildings, like department stores or hospitals, where they mostly conveyed small goods and written documents, or across towns and cities, where they became part of the postal delivery network (fig. 30). A great deal of illicit lovemaking in nineteenth-century Paris (from Maupassant's *Bel-Ami* to Proust's *Recherche*) and London (Henry James's "In the Cage") would have been impossible without the tube-delivered telegram.

Significantly, the first functioning crosstown system linked the London Stock Exchange with the offices of the International Telegraph Company. Both institutions had an increasing need for speed in communication, the stock exchange (one of the signature panoramic spaces of the epoch) because of the acceleration and extension of national and international trade, the telegraph company because the actual delivery of telegrams to their addressees proved to be the slow link in the epoch's fastest means of communication. While the transmission via telegraph was a digital process (along rolled wires, however, and captured by kymographs), the delivery of the telegram itself remained analog: the extended objects (the paper of the telegram and the hand of the addressee) needed to come in contact to complete the communication. The digitally received telegram moving in a cylinder through a rolled steel pipe is a fitting image of how, before wireless transmission, digital processes were still contained within the contraptions of analog force transmission.

Pneumatic tube systems are made up of pipes, the ubiquitous product of rolling mills in which cylinders reproduced themselves in all areas of nineteenth-century infrastructure. They are also related, however, to a species of cylinders that are consciously excluded from the present purview: the **barrels of guns and cannons.** Kinematically speaking, projectiles in barrels, like the capsules in pneumatic tubes, are pistons in conducting cylinders. Like their colleagues in civil and commercial engineering, gun makers in the nineteenth century learned to rifle the inside of the barrel to impart to the projectile a helical motion that stabilized the bullet and extended its range. But there are two crucial reasons not to include firearms in an account of kinematics: first, as the projectile exits the barrel it breaks the "pair-closure" and becomes subject to "cosmic" disturbances, particularly friction and gravitation; second, the projectile is launched, not by a controlled expansion (of steam) or the internal combustion of fuel, but by a detonation.[3] Detonations—used, as we have seen, on a large scale in the tunneling projects of the mid- to late nineteenth century—became the object of intense speculation in the second half of the nineteenth century: the disproportion between their cause (a spark) and their devastating effect seemed to unsettle the balance sheet of thermodynamic physics. Julius Robert Mayer, who developed the notion of "triggering" or "initiation" *(Auslösung)* to explain these phenomena, also extended it to psychophysical events such as the firing of nerves in muscles.[4] Intricate triggering mechanisms, often derived from the escapements of clocks, embodied these phenomena, in which the contiguity of cause and effect was purposely interrupted.[5]

If wires were the nerves of the nineteenth-century infrastructure, pipes were its bowels. Water, sewage, gas, oil, dust, and fumes were transported and evacuated through pipes; the sanitation and illumination, and hence the growth, of large cities are unthinkable without

FIGURE 31. Albert Renger-Patzsch, *Air Pipes [Rohrleitungen]*, 1936. © 2011 Albert Renger-Patzsch Archiv / Ann u. Jürgen Wilde, Zülpich / Artists Rights Society (ARS), New York.

their ubiquitous use. The elimination of typhoid and cholera, the chief scourges of large urban centers, depended on the strict separation of water and sewage in separate tunnel and pipe systems.[6] Pipes also began to deliver water to individual homes and to evacuate sewage from them. Even earlier, city streets, homes, and workplaces were illuminated by gas piped through miles upon miles of tubes (fig. 31).

Whether drawn from wrought iron, riveted together from rolled sheets of iron and steel, or, later, welded or seamlessly rolled, these cylinders served as analog conduits and containers for all varieties of the "formless" that coursed below the smooth surfaces of the nineteenth century.[7] The second Industrial Revolution is closely related to the pipe's use as a means of separation and distillation. The coking of coal as well as the production of town gas from coal had shown that the gases set free in combustion could be distilled and used in various states of refinement. Synthetic colors made from coal tar as well as lubricants and pharmaceutical products were at the heart of the emerging chemical industries. At the same time, progress in drilling for oil and in understanding its chemical composition led to the need for refineries, which began to isolate and store the derivatives of "rock oil" in various arrays of cylindrical ovens, centrifuges, and containers, all connected by pipes. Toward the end of the century refineries and chemical plants began to resemble the confused nightmare of a cylindromaniac.[8]

The need for the evacuation of noxious gases from the combustion of coal had been recognized as a problem long before the Industrial Revolution, but the enormous rise in coal burning in industrial and metropolitan centers had made the construction of tall cylindrical **chimneys** imperative.[9] Besides serving the ecological purpose of delivering gases along the chimney's axis into a stratum of high winds, the height of smokestacks was a function of an engine's power. For immobile engines, the relation between horsepower and chimney height settled at 180 feet for 250 hp, with a top diameter of 6 feet.[10] At those heights, wind resistance was an important consideration, and cylindrical smokestacks, despite the complication of building round structures with square bricks, became the norm. Smokestacks are yet another example of the interaction of multiple factors, both practical and theoretical, that converge in a cylindrical structure (fig. 32).

However, the smokestack lacked individuality and aesthetic measure, and early on it became the object not only of environmental but also of aesthetic criticism. On steamships, on locomotives, and in industrial plants, the exhausts seemed to simply flaunt the cylinder's infinite scalability. Unlike the church steeple—soon to be mourned by Proust—and the column—upon which much of Western vertical aesthetics was based—the smokestack lacked any relation to God or to the human body. Contractors and architectural firms, wherever they could, began either to relate the chimney to the column, adorning its top with capital-like flourishes, or to cover chimneys in square, campanile-style encasements.[11]

Intransitively turning devices, such as the zoetrope and the tachyscope, had used rotational motion around a central axis to trick the eye into perceiving separate images as continuous motion. At the same time, early photographic **"cameras"** used the cylinder's (and the cone's) central axis to direct light onto a circular photographic plate, dispensing with the square box behind it that repeated the camera obscura. These devices not only provided, as Benjamin said, "the first image of the encounter between man and machine" but were also instrumental in training the gaze of spectators to accept both depth of field and the aperture of cylindrical lenses as aspects of a reliable image of the world (fig. 33).[12]

FIGURE 32. Charles Sheeler, *Ford Plant, River Rouge, Power House No. 1*, 1927. Courtesy Museum of Fine Arts, Boston, the Lane Collection.

When the sensitivity and hence the speed of film, and of the camera's shutter mechanisms, exceeded that of the human eye, the recording and projection of motion, toward which the panorama and its many avatars seem to have yearned, could finally begin.[13] The emergence of cinema belongs in the trajectory of the "méthode graphique," which we have already encountered as the driving force behind the passive turning of kymograph's cylinder. If the method's inaugural instrument was the indicator that transcribed the pressure inside Watt's cylinders, its culmination came with Etienne Jules Marey's and Eadweard Muybridge's chronophotographic experiments to capture the motion of men and other animals (fig. 34).

In Walter Benjamin's analysis, the advent of cinema signifies the change from contemplation to distraction in the perception of art. In the language of kinematics and its cylindrical embodiments, cinematography begins when the translational motion of light along the axis of the lens joins the rotational motion of the film that is exposed to it.[14] Film

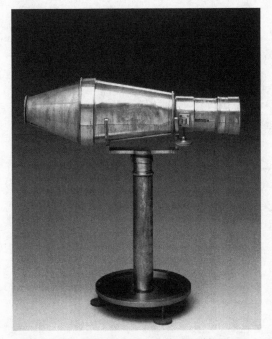

FIGURE 33. Replica of a camera designed by Peter Voigtlander in 1841. It is one of the earliest practical portrait cameras and one of the earliest cameras made of metal. The body consists of two cones, the longer of which forms the camera itself and contains the lens. The smaller cone contains the focusing screen and eyepiece. © National Media Museum / Science & Society Picture Library—All rights reserved.

cameras and projectors are light lathes that, like their metal counterparts, introduce an element of abstract "work" into the production and consumption of images.

CONTAINING

Before the panorama became a visual mass medium in the early nineteenth century, optical cylinders had long been used either as mirrors to undistort anamorphic drawings or as lenses in the magic lantern shows performed by itinerant projectionists.[15] In the large **panorama** buildings that went up all over the world—spurred on by the success of Robert Barker's panorama in London and Daguerre's diorama in

FIGURE 34. The French physiologist Etienne-Jules Marey (1830–1904) pioneered the use of photography to record and analyze movement. In 1881 he invented the photographic gun, and later he devised the first chronophotograph camera. © Science Museum / Science & Society Picture Library—All rights reserved.

Paris—these two aspects were combined and enlarged to the scale of the human body. Now the spectators themselves occupied an area surrounding the cylinder's axis, on a platform at such a height that neither the top nor the bottom of the cylinder's wall was visible. This technologically restricted aperture and disappearance of the frame relieved viewers from having to stand still and focus on a single vanishing point, as perspectival images since the Renaissance had required; instead, the images on the panorama's inner walls, created by fusing vanishing points to a horizon line, allowed spectators to turn around their body's axis on the cylinder's axis.[16] Kinematic variations on this basic constellation, where the walls moved around the platforms, or the platforms around their axis, or where the images were unrolled in front of sitting spectators, were legion and became emblematic of the epoch's addiction to visual entertainment and to replication.[17]

The panoramic closure of the visual space, where the upper and lower limits are masked and any "beyond" lies behind the horizon rather than in heaven or in hell, enforced a relation between spectator and image (and, particularly in the last quarter of the century, when panoramas increasingly exhibited patriotic and imperial themes, between spectator and history) that has variously been called "democratic" and "pathetic."[18] These two characterizations have their analogue in the peculiar conjunction of horizontal and aerial views: the flatness and uniformity of the cylindrical canvas allowed for the reproduction of a surfeit of detail, while the central axis provided a viewpoint that hovered above the represented ground. Half painting, half map, the panorama suspended the sensory ground on which human perception heretofore had taken place, and the feeling of vertigo so often reported by visitors testifies to this suspension.[19] The same masking of the frame and induced sensual disorientation became the hallmark of Wagner's opera staging—the orchestra hidden underneath the stage, the auditorium darkened, and no distinction between *aria* and *recitativo,* between rotational reflection and translational diegesis, that would allow the spectators to find their critical bearings.[20] Psychologists and historians have commented on the similarities between the experiences of viewing panoramic images, taking a railway journey, and promenading along the city boulevards and arcades, where the translational motion of the observer also fused vanishing points into a horizontal line and allowed the attention, literally, to wander.[21]

The panorama also existed in a passive incarnation, in which to be seen was more important than to see. Jeremy Bentham's **panopticon** prison was its earliest and strictest version, but the shape was quickly adopted by less overtly disciplinary institutions, such as the trading floor of stock exchanges, the café-concerts that sprang up in Paris in the second half of the nineteenth century, and other public *interieurs.*[22]

It is a truism of manufacturing that like forms tend to produce like forms. The cylinder as container, aside from its "transcendental" properties—its favorable surface-to-volume ratio, its scalability, its ability to withstand pressure—was simply easier to produce by the machine tools of the nineteenth century. The motions in rolling, drilling, turning, and planing tools, as their genealogy in the works of Reuleaux has shown, were themselves the results of complex negotiations between the linearity of straight-line motions and the continuity of rotation. Traces of these negotiations are left even on the most banal of nineteenth-century objects.

The **tin can** and the process of canning food are coeval with the cylindrical objects and practices so far mentioned. Prompted by the unique circumstances of the Napoleonic wars—wars in which very large troops could no longer rely on foraging as their means of sustenance—and further spurred on by the need of the British Empire to keep naval personnel free of scurvy and imperial agents culinarily connected to the homeland, the canning of food became central to nineteenth-century food management and preservation.

The tin can certainly was neither the first nor the only attempt to overcome the cycle of the seasons and the variability and locality of the harvest, but it was the first to impress a uniform—cylindrical—shape on all food and to involve the container in the act of preservation. Since cans were made of rolled steel (and later of aluminum) their manufacture could interface with the emerging rolling mills; they could be transported more easily than glass containers, and they could be stacked and stored for longer periods, thus contributing to the increasing homogeneity of time and space that cultural critics like Nietzsche would later bemoan.[23]

The large-scale equivalent to this disruption of natural time and of its cycle of sowing and reaping was the erection of large cylindrical storage containers. They were either parts of **grain elevators,** in which grain could be pooled, measured, stored, and shipped, and, what is more, could become the object of exchange and speculation. The means to lift the grain was the conveyor belt—a mechanism related to the belt-driven transmissions in factories and machine shops, only here used as a tool and driven by steam engines via rotating cylinders. Linked to other cylinders, notably to the locomotive and the pipe, grain elevators transformed American agriculture and with it the surface of the United States (fig. 35).[24]

The cylindrical **silos** on farms that have become iconic for states like Wisconsin or Indiana do for dairy production what the elevator does for grain: by allowing farmers to store fodder over the long winters, silos make the continuous, "unnatural" production of milk possible. While the first silos were rectangular, the cylindrical form prevailed for the same reason as it did in combustion engines: it resisted pressures and prevented air pockets that would cause the silage to ferment beyond the desired state.[25]

The **boiler** explosion was the iconic accident of the epoch and a welcome occasion for moralists to show how the daring of the engineer, the greed of the capitalist, or the somnolence of the operator was punished by the inexorable forces of nature. Once it was understood that the temperature of the water and hence the pressure of the steam were decisive factors in the measure of work, the resistance of the boiler's walls

FIGURE 35. Margaret Bourke-White, *Grain Elevators*. Margaret Bourke-White / Time & Life Pictures / Getty Images.

and seams against ever higher pressures became a focus of engineering attention. Early boilers had taken their form from brewers' kettles, and James Watt initially still used wagon-type boilers; but it turned out that only fully cylindrical vessels exhibited constant resistance to stresses, combined with optimal heat transfer and ease of manufacturing. To further distribute the pressure and facilitate the transfer of heat, the cylindrical flues in which or through which water was heated were successively multiplied, leading to the superheating boilers of the end of the century, which had essentially become huge bundles of cylindrical tubes (fig. 36).[26]

Together with the panorama, the gasholder or **gasometer** was the most visible of the urban cylinders. In its most traditional form, the wall of the cylindrical container was sunk below ground, and its roof swam on a bed of water. As gas released from burning coal was pumped underneath the roof, the structure rose, guided by a surrounding scaffold.

The weight of the structure provided the pressure necessary for the delivery of gas to streetlights, factories, and private homes, and the

FIGURE 36. Boilers for "Machinery in Motion" display, International Exhibition, London, 1862. © Science Museum Library / Science & Society Picture Library—All rights reserved.

height indicated the volume of stored gas. In this configuration, the cylinder was piston and pressure chamber at once, as was the case in unsupported structures where one section of the cylinder screwed out of the previous one pushed by the pressure of the gas (fig. 37). In alternative constructions, gasholders were built with permanent height; they used a heavy lid inside as a piston to compress the gas.[27] The gasometer was at the same time a tin can (using the cylinder's favorable surface-volume ratio), a gigantic boiler (exploiting its favorable quotient of volume and resistance to pressure), and a voluminous pipe (highlighting the cylinder's scalability). Only the last form survives in today's on-demand delivery of natural gas.[28]

REPRESENTING

All the cylinders so far encountered do something—they slide, they roll, they press, they screw, they turn, they are inscribed, they contain, they conduct—as they exploit one or another property of the form. The proliferation of cylindrical things since the early 1800s finds its explanation in their ability to isolate, transmit, and recombine rotational

FIGURE 37. Hilla and Bernd Becher, *Gas Tank Barnsley/ Sheffield, GB,* 1966. Sonnabend Gallery, New York.

and translational motions that became universally available through the steam engine, to apply these motions to a variety of formless substances and work pieces, and to enclose cylindrical spaces. Thus the cylinders of the nineteenth century all function within actual or virtual kinematic chains that produce or transmit or apply motions, and they are fully absorbed by this function.

This exhaustive functionality—part of what cultural critics at the time decried as the relentless materialism and utilitarianism of the age—left no margin for the cylinder to represent anything. The cube and its cognate polygons had a long history of signifying the presence of rationality and divine proportions in the universe; the sphere had—particularly just before and during the French Revolution—served as a symbol for equality, freedom, and perfection. Even the column, which had been at the center of so much cosmogonic, anthropological, architectural, aesthetic, and philosophical speculation from Anaximander to Heidegger, always embodied something beyond its tectonic task—the form of the earth, eternal proportions, the human body, the weight

of the world.[29] The cylinders of the nineteenth century had none of
that dignity: not only did they often have a compromising genealogy—
they started out as rectangular forms, like the smokestack or the printing press, or they really wanted to be spheres, like the tin can or the
gasometer—but they were also always busy with some kinematic,
transmissive activity. Only toward the end of the century would anthropologists and psychoanalysts seek to break through the relentless
functionality of the cylinder. Before that, a column, a cannon, or a
cigar was just a cylinder.

There were two remarkable exceptions to this functionality. The
first came from the burgeoning realm of toddler pedagogy, which tried
to extend the achievements of reformist pedagogues of the eighteenth
and early nineteenth centuries to very young children and to the objects
they encountered the world. Friedrich Froebel, the leader of this movement whose influence reaches to present day **toy** making, conceived of
geometric shapes as cosmically related. Froebel's "second gift"—his
toys were given to children in a deeply scripted sequence—consisted of
a wooden sphere, a cube, and a cylinder: "The tiny sphere is an emblem
of the 'big round world' and the planetary systems. The cube recalls the
wonderful crystals, and shows the form that men reflect in architecture
and sculpture. As for the cylinder it is Nature's special form, and God
has taught man through Nature to use it in a thousand ways, and indeed has himself fashioned man more or less in its shape." This cosmic
progression in the second gift found a slightly different representation
in the ontogenesis of the human body: "The second gift presents types
of the principal phases of human development; from the easy mobility
of the infancy and childhood,—the ball,—we pass through the half-
steady stages of boyhood and girlhood, represented in the cylinder, to
the firm character of manhood and womanhood for which the cube
furnishes the formula."[30] This integration of the cylinder has it mediate
in the stark opposition of cube and sphere that has long been a symbol
for the unpredictability of fortune. There is no better way of representing this transition than to juxtapose the monument of *agathe tyche*
(good fortune) that Goethe put into his garden in Ilmenau—a sphere
resting on a cube—with Froebel's tombstone, in which a cylinder is
interposed between a cube and a sphere.[31]

The other notable exception to kinematic functionality in the nineteenth century is the **top hat.** Although it is by no means clear what and
even whether it represents, it is obvious that it does not move and that
it does not do any work—not even the work of distinguishing between

social classes, as hats did before. Historians agree that the top hat can be traced to the hat of Quakers and antiaristocratic dissenters in the seventeenth and eighteenth centuries, that it made its re-entrance on the European scene through the sociologically novel group of the dandies at the beginning of the nineteenth century, and that it soon lost its exclusivity and spread through all strata of society. By the 1860s, the *elegants* populating the Paris opera, the brass-knuckle industrialists in England, the chimney sweeps in Germany, and a certain abolitionist president in the United States all were wearing this remarkable cylindrical extension on their heads.[32] Even women wore top hats, if only as riding gear.

There were attempts to explain this phenomenon, especially after anthropological data collected in the colonies allowed for a reverse perspective on European habits. The anthropologist Emil Selenka interpreted the top hat, along with other tribal headgear, as an "extension of existence" *(Verlängerung der Existenz);* he saw the chief virtue of its height in the fact that every current of air transmitted a slight pressure onto the wearer's scalp and thereby reminded him "of the supra-natural height of his appearance."[33] A similar fixation on the hat's axis and its exposure to wind can be found in Rudolph Hermann Lotze's *Microcosmus:* "Thus arises the pleasing delusion that we ourselves, our own life, and our strength reach up to that point, and at every step that shakes it, at every puff of wind that sets it in motion, we have quite distinctly the feeling as if a part of our own being were solemnly nodding backwards and forwards. Evidently, therefore, one feels quite differently in a cylindrical hat that encourages these emotions from what one does in a cap, the raised peak of which would perform the same office very imperfectly."[34] Whereas anthropologists and philosophers concentrated on the top hat's longitudinal axis, painters were equally concerned with its curvature. Édouard Manet, whose paintings display an extraordinary profusion of top hats, seems to have been particularly concerned with the formal implications of representing the hat's overall dimensions. It is true, of course, that the number of top hats in paintings of the nineteenth century is a consequence of painting's new commitment to "do what one sees." But this commitment implied more than simply a call for a change in subject matter; it also meant challenging the translational ideology that governed pictorial space.

The practice of linear perspective assumed that a painting is a windowpane through which our gaze travels on straight, converging

lines toward a vanishing point. The depth of space is suggested by siz-
ing and positioning objects on the canvas in receding proportions as
they appear from a singular point of view. The viewer, therefore, is
not only shackled to a specific point in front of the painting but also
excluded from the painted space.[35] Realist painting as Manet introduced it—and as Baudelaire and Mallarmé understood it—wanted to
unshackle the spectators and allow them to stroll by a canvas without
being fixated to a single point of view.[36] We have seen that the same
liberation of the spectator took place in the panoramas, only that there
it was accomplished by vastly expanding and bending the picture plane
and by fusing the vanishing points into a horizon. The realist painting
Manet had in mind would have to accomplish the same effect within
the frame of a traditional canvas.

The first prerequisite was the depiction of subjects that were no longer ordered by a vanishing point. In the case of groups of people, this
meant their representation in an unbounded physical and, at the same
time, narrative space. In contrast to a work like David's *The Oath of
the Horatii,* where the figures are represented in precise and meaningful relation to the geometry of the depicted space, thus fusing story and
plot into one imaginary whole, Manet's paintings aim to release their
figures from this geometric order and deposit them in an unstructured,
"realistic" space. In this—at the time—shocking de-rhetorization of
painting the top hat played a vital role.[37]

Manet's two most significant paintings in this regard are the *Concert at the Tuileries* (1862) and the *Masked Ball at the Opera* (1873);
cylindrical top hats appear in many more of his paintings, but not in
such numbers on a single canvas. The earlier painting caused a scan-
dal precisely because "to show people in everyday dress was an outrage against art."[38] But it is still noticeably oriented toward a vanishing
point (to the left of a conspicuously lit tree trunk in the background);
in addition, two strikingly dressed women, seated at the left front of
the group and looking straight outward, guide the beholder's gaze into
the painting. The top hats are distributed haphazardly over the entire
scene (with a dense grouping at the left), interspersed with other male
and female hats at differing heights on the picture plane, and natural-
ized, as it were, by the shape of the tree trunks.[39]

The guidance into the picture is literally masked in Manet's *Masked
Ball,* as the two women right of center looking out of the picture wear
dominoes and are absorbed, by virtue of their black dress, into the
black mass of men, all of whom wear top hats. The left, right, and top

FIGURE 38. Edouard Manet, *Masked Ball at the Opera*, 1973. National Gallery of Art, Washington, D.C.

edges of the picture planes seem to be chosen at random, cutting off figures and thus denying the composition a center (fig. 38).

The top of every single hat remains visible in a comparatively narrow band bounded by a line drawn from the lowest rim to the highest top in the foreground. The longer one concentrates on this segment, the more incongruous it becomes with a linear conception of spatial depth, as there is no, or very little, recession in this space full of cylinders. Every single one of the hats is individualized by its angle and by a highlight that indicates its height, but also its curvature and its volume. As Manet's many other top hat pictures show, the flatness and opacity of the cylinder's surface extend the highlight into a patch of paint that must itself indicate curvature.[40] These highlights persist even where the top hats are almost absorbed into the background, as in Manet's late painting *Un Bar au Folies-Bergères*.

The compact band of cylinders in the *Masked Ball,* so carefully tilted at various angles and compressed into a friezelike band with nonlinear depth, surely is an instance of what Michael Fried has called the "strikingness" in Manet's art.[41] It does away with the linear excavation of the picture plane and replaces it with a painted space that extends only as far as its objects. This space is not construed a priori and indifferent to what it contains; instead, it is the totality of all things represented. The cylindrical top hat is such a privileged object in this space because its volume is a function of its height and lateral extension. Where there is an extended highlight indicating a top hat, there must be corresponding depth. This intrinsic depth of the cylindrical form releases the viewer from having to assume a unique viewpoint; it allows him to become what he sees—a flaneur.

Julius Meier-Graefe's aptly described the scene in Manet's painting as a *Fleischbörse*, a meat market,[42] and indeed the foyer of the opera house, together with the stock exchange, the café-concerts, and the panoramas, was one of the crucial panoptic spaces in nineteenth-century cities. The opening scene of Balzac's *The Splendors and Miseries of Courtesans* describes just such a masked ball in an opera foyer. But beyond the social commentary, Manet's cylindrical conception of space proved to be influential for later views and practices of painting.

In particular Paul Cézanne extended the top hat–centered view into a general theory of perception and painting. Rather than taking the cylindrical hat simply as an indicator of convexity and hence of volume, Cézanne believed that "all things seen in space are convex," including shadows and lights.[43] The fact that we perceive things and spaces as flat, Cézanne argued, stems from the restlessness of our eyes, which constantly scan surfaces. The liberation of the viewer from the strictures of linear perspective thus would lead not to indifferent gazing, Cézanne hoped, but to a new kind of attention that would reveal things as they really are: "Everything is spherical and cylindrical."[44]

CHAPTER 8

Kinematics of Narration II

Balzac and the Cylindrical Shape of the Plot

Logically speaking, the relation between rotary printing presses and serialized narratives is that of a necessary condition. The presses do not cause these narratives—that would amount to "vulgar" materialism—nor does their presence, and that of other machines, somehow force its own literary representation—that is the metaphysical assumption behind social and anthropological theories of realism. But without the rotation of the presses there would be no serialized narrative, including all the formal consequences this entails for the conception, distribution, and consumption of realist stories. It is obvious that this is a stronger relationship than that provided by the poetic concept of mimesis or by its rhetorical cognate, metaphor. Without necessarily shouldering the metaphysical weight that comes with it, I have in this study used the notion of partaking and of implication. Narratives of the nineteenth century partake in the motion of the machines, which in turn are, as we have seen, implicated in a long, submerged, and antagonistic history of valuing motion.[1]

Authors, publishers, and readers encountered the rhythm of machines as a technical given and fell in with it in various ways. Authors overlaid the interruption between installments with the forward movement of the story in such a way that coherence and contiguous motivation were preserved. Publishers served as the interface between writers and readers through sales figures and near-simultaneous distribution of installments. Readers developed new forms of reading and reacting to an open, evolving narrative. From the interplay of these reactions emerged a virtual community for which literature partook in life and its inevitable forward slant and openness. This communally experienced and verified stratum of mechanically produced narrative is what we variously call *story, fabula, récit,* or *das Erzählte.* It is the temporal dimension in which story and life coincide.

Prose writing that sought to harness this dimension as its privileged means of generating closeness to life became increasingly popular in the nineteenth century. Reportage, sensation fiction, Edgar Allen Poe's breathless tales, and the detective story are examples of this tendency. Yet larger and more ambitious projects needed to find ways of slowing down the "eccentric rapidity" (Hölderlin) of the serialized story. The summary name for these ways is "plot," and the following pages will describe them from a kinematic point of view.

It should be clear that the distinction between story and plot is analytical only and cannot hope to completely separate these elements. Dickens's invention of the fully integrated serialized narrative shows that he achieved the forward pull of the story by throttling its motion with such interventions as strong characterizations, interspersed tales, descriptive passages, illustrations, and deftly placed chapter endings. These are all elements of plotting that would become more varied and less imperative as the paradigm of realist storytelling became the new norm. At the end of the nineteenth century, Ferdinand de Saussure likened a distinction related to that of story and plot, the distinction between linguistic sign and its referent, to the distinction between the two sides of a sheet of paper. In the age of kinematics we prefer the comparison to such characteristic nineteenth-century motions as rolling, in which translation and rotation can only be artificially separated. Engineers and writers alike sought to capture and articulate this peculiar conjunction of two motions in the analysis of the turn of the screw.

Given the ineluctable temporal dimension of the story, the devices to manipulate and contain narrative motion can be conceived as spatial. While the etymology of plot already suggests as much, spatiality should be understood at this level of analysis simply as the imposition of limits and hence of finitude on the flow of the story. We have seen that in machines measurable work is expressed in the translational motion of the tool—the downward motion of a steam hammer, say—but that in order to become utilizable this motion must be returned, inflected, rotated; it must be confined within the spatial dimensions of the machine. Similarly, the translational motion of the story must be bent and inflected so as to generate—at the very least—a beginning and an ending, and to contain them within the narrative rather than pushing them into extradiegetic space, as was the case with the epistolary novel or the "found manuscript" plot.[2]

"Can be conceived as," "similarly"—it is inevitable that in the description of plot devices a metaphorical register will gain the upper hand. Unlike the partaking relation between cylindrical machines and the emergence of the realist story, the shaping of the plot constitutes a response, a "counter-rhythmic interruption," a "transport" (Hölderlin), of kinematic forces into the realm of language and form.[3] Yet because of its constitutive function, this transport is more than a rhetorical device. Just as the history of kinematics reveals the structure of the story to consist of stronger relations than that of metonymic contiguity, so it shows the author's response to be more than elocutionary ornament. Together they create narrative tension, a quality almost unknown to previous epochs of fictional writing.

The dilemma of having to conjoin two motions—often figured as progression and digression—was well known to authors of the pre-rotational epoch, and the best, like Diderot, Fielding, Sterne, Wieland, or Jean Paul, made it an object of reflection and wit. Sterne (1986, 95) describes the predicament with the help of retarding diacritics: "For, if he [the author] begins a digression,—from that moment, I observe, his whole work stands stock still;—and if he goes on with his main work,—then there is an end of his digression."

Fielding's *Tom Jones,* heir to a long tradition of picaresque and adventure novels, confronts the problem by conceiving of the narrative as a sequence of episodes held together by the single thread of the mystery of the protagonist's parentage; the protagonist thus moves through events, localities, and experiences that are linked by temporal causality or spatial contiguity. This "moving through" is represented in the way the hero moves through physical space: he flees or searches or is exiled. Because of its involuntary nature, the trajectory of the protagonist follows that of a Newtonian body, propelled by external forces the causality of which remains opaque to him and to others. He falls horizontally through the frames of the episodes and finds rest only once all the external forces have been disentangled, deflected, and balanced.[4] While the relative strength and contingency of these frames may have made the narrative more easily digestible in larger portions, they will prove too inelastic and underdetermined to survive under the requirements of rotational printing.

The other fictional form in relation to which Dickens and Balzac unrolled their narratives had been conceived explicitly against picaresque episodicity: the Romantic *Bildungsroman,* in which every episode is nestled within another, all of them sharing as their focal point the development of the hero. There, the end comprises the beginning and the beginning presages the end in a structure that seeks to suggest the simultaneous presence of all of its parts. It is often marked by the introduction of powerful symbols and images, which radiate over the entirety of the narrative. Rather than falling, the energy that propels the hero through the world is his imagination, most often in the form of a pervasive nostalgia, following Novalis's languid dictum: "Where are we going? Always towards home."[5]

If the straight lines and flat surfaces of the picaresque novel form a polygon and the ideal of the Romantic novel is perfect sphericity such that every area of text is curved toward a center, writers of the nineteenth century, by wrapping the narration around an omniscient narrator, availed themselves of all of the advantages of the cylindrical structure.[6] The result of bending a flat surface around a central axis, the cylinder's surface is curved and holds tension, but the curvature is extrinsic, and every area on its surface is flat: points on its surface can be connected by straight lines while the surface itself is under tension. For engineers, tension is an irreducibly temporal phenomenon, as it embodies a material's memory of its original shape.

The most immediate benefit of this form is the potentially limitless scalability of a cylindrical plot—it can be augmented without distorting the integrity of the shape (as the makers of tin cans, pipes, or gas holders well knew). Dickens had already exploited this feature when he incrementally expanded the role of Sam Weller without markedly unbalancing the adventures of the Pickwickians. But to have realized the narrative potential of cylindrical scaling was the epochal insight of Honoré de Balzac.[7] Each component of his *Comédie humaine* can be read and understood on its own, as a "flat" narrative, while it also is a segment of a larger, curved surface on which characters and places can reappear and thus refer to one another. This insight allowed Balzac to bend epic linearity without abolishing temporal and causal relation: we learn, for example, of the causes of Madame de Beauséant's self-induced exile from Paris in a novel (*Le Père Goriot*) that was written after the novel that centered on her lonely fate in Normandy (*La femme abandonée*). What emerged with this procedure was the possibility of a vast and panoramic narrative in which individual works—not all of which fully qualified as novels—figured as so many scenes (of private life, of political life, of life in Paris, of life in the provinces, of manners in the country), while the prospect of completion, central to the Romantic novel, could be kept alive.

This complex reorganization of narrative space has caught the attention of many readers of Balzac's oeuvre. Here is a particularly striking insight from Hans Blumenberg, who calls "perspectival" what here is called cylindrical:

> Concerning the problem of [the representation of] reality, there is a decisive difference between the epic-linear and the perspectival recurrence of characters; a completely different consciousness of space emerges, a more subtle participation in the world on the part of the novel. The perspectival system of Balzac's novels allows for a translation of linear episodicity into simultaneity. To achieve this, more is required than simple non-contradiction of already known predicates. . . . This [simultaneity] is entirely different from the well-known simultaneous preparation of individual characters for their final encounter at the intersection of the story. Not only and not exclusively the characters in the novel move through the events of the story, but the reader too moves around the rock of imaginary reality and peruses the possibility that it offers.[8]

The scenic arrangement of plots and subplots on a vaster canvas corresponded precisely to the way the panorama had begun to tell stories once it had abandoned the practice of dazzling visitors with views of distant cities and shores. Dissolving the implicit frame around perspectival drawing, and fusing the vanishing points into a composite and continuous line, panorama painters created a *horizon,* that peculiar circle in whose center an observer stands always on the perpendicular axis.[9] The inverse cylindrical concept and implement was the focus by means of which the expanse of the horizon could be perused and navigated. Painters arranged episodes and characters in such a way that the narrative could be viewed from any direction on the central axis. Turning around one's axis, recognizing individual figures by focusing on an area, and contemplating scenes on different areas of the canvas became the way of immersing oneself in panoramic visual narratives. Balzac's project is panoramic in this same sense of creating a horizon in which focused particularity and horizontal totality can be combined in one narrative structure. A reader can contemplate Rastignac's rise in *Père Goriot* and then turn around and encounter him again in *La maison Nucingen,* or turn further and see him through the eyes of Lucien de Rubempré, or hear of him in *La peau de chagrin.* All of these appearances are contained in a homogenous temporal and spatial horizon.

Balzac thus duplicated on a macroscopic scale what Dickens had done within the frame of a single narrative: integrating the syncopation of serial publication into the overall structure of the plot. As it extends the narrative horizon beyond the boundaries of a single publication, Balzac's *Comédie humaine* brings into view the idea of an oeuvre.[10] More than a single book, more than the sum total of the books authored by a single writer, an oeuvre coheres through thematic and stylistic correspondences in much the same way as a serialized novel coheres across its installments.

Panoramic ordering allowed authors to disengage the protagonists from their environment, a key ingredient in the construction of the realistic rendering of space. Recurrence and other markers of correspondence made characters independent of the physical space in which they acted. The descriptions of London or Paris or Yonville, unprecedented in their density of historical and physical detail, served to provide a background that was recognizable for readers yet—unlike Romantic landscapes—indifferent to the individual's fate that unfolded before it. It was not Oliver's London or Rastignac's Paris or Emma's Yonville, but that of Dickens, Balzac, or Flaubert, described in minute and telling detail. This separation of background space and individual fate allowed for a reader's identification of and with space—she no longer needed to identify with the hero or heroine (say with Emma Bovary or Becky Sharp) but certainly could identify with the horrors of having to live in the provinces or the anxieties of succeeding in the city. This disengagement allowed for unsympathetic characters to become protagonists without turning narratives into outright farces or moralizing tales, and it furthered a cognitive relationship to narratives that exceeded the boundaries of empathy.[11]

Just as serialization aligned the novel with the temporal reality of its readers' (and writers') life, so did the panoramic plot recreate their experience of space. No longer focusing on a window of possibilities before (and a mountain of consequences behind) them, or any longer indulging in the fantasy of a bird's-eye view over all aspects of narrated events, the panoramic plot with its widened, yet limited point of view enacted the peculiar being-in-space of the nineteenth century. While it was first and foremost a formal innovation that enabled narrative closure and internal coherence, it also contributed to the overall sense of what was possible and what could be expected in a narrative. It was a shift from the realm of representing to that of represented space. The historical kinematics of sense perception provides a clue to the efficacy of this transition. Wolfgang Schivelbusch has shown that the railway journey, by forcing passengers' gaze to focus on the horizon rather than on the rapidity of individual scenes in the foreground or on the unchanging background, changed the perception of space and of the body within it.[12] The horizon was the line that encircled the spectator; it had no opening and therefore left no gateway through which the wholly unexpected, wondrous, or inexplicable could enter; but it also extended to behind the spectator's or actor's back and thus harbored the possibility of unobserved simultaneities.[13]

Balzac, Flaubert, and Thackeray began to describe the open countryside—the provinces—as such a finite space that surrounded protagonists fully; but the most prominent figurations of this being in space were located in, and often as, the city. These either were panoramic spaces in the proper sense of the term (i.e., they allowed for visual access that was restricted only by the front-back dissymmetry of the human body) or were panoptic and allowed for the—observed or unobservable—observation of the protagonist from all sides. In the arc of a narrative, the same space could turn from one configuration to the other, and this transition was indicative of the hero's changed fortunes.

A typical instance is the auditorium of an opera house or a theater: the young hero—for example, Eugène de Rastignac in *Père Goriot,* or Lucien de Rubempré in Balzac's novels concerned with his fate—is introduced into this space by a benefactress and is shown—and shown to—the important members of a city's society in their boxes. He returns later to observe the behavior of a lover whom he suspects of betrayal, and finally becomes the object of the gleeful or scornful looks of the circle from which he is being ostracized. The debtors' prison in Dickens novels fulfill the same function, only the other way around: the protagonist enters under the disdainful or curious looks of the inmates and leaves, if all goes well, under their cheers and admiration.[14] The stock exchange, the public gardens (which were often centered by a rotating cylindrical bandstand), and later in the century the great *café-concerts* are further examples of settings in which the transactions typical of panoramic spaces took place.

All of these spaces were products and, at the same time, condensations of the modern city that grew to unimagined size and complexity within a very short time beginning in the early decades of the century. Much of the kinematic activity outlined in the earlier chapters had taken place in and shaped the city—streets were rolled, gasometers and pipes delivered gas, the products of paper machines and printing presses were in everybody's hands, and much of heavy industry was still within city limits. For authors like Balzac, Stendhal, Thackeray, and Dickens, the city itself became a potentially closed, "horizontal" space that oscillated between panorama and panopticon. In the second half of the century, panoramic sight lines were cut into cities with the construction of boulevards and the elimination of medieval asymmetries that had still been important to the narratives of authors like Victor Hugo and Eugène Sue.

This cylindrical spatiality sheathed the most significant motivating force in nineteenth-century protagonists: ambition. Literally, *amb-ire* means to walk around—not in the sense of the picaresque hero who traverses the spaces of his adventures without belonging in them, or in the sense of the Romantic wanderer who goes out only to come back and find himself, but in the manner of the visitor to a panorama, who walks and turns around his own axis to observe and experience the space that makes up his horizon. Ambition is the desire to dominate or "own" this space, to have access to it at all levels and over its entire circumference, and to be appreciated, envied, or feared in turn.[15] The ambitious subject is threatened and driven by what is behind him and is constantly turning and moving to occupy the central axis of his chosen space, and to maintain control and receive attention. Sociology later in the century will systematize the concept of milieu to designate this panoramic quality of social spaces.[16]

CHAPTER 9

Gears and Screws

The linkages in which Reuleaux's analysis of machines found its fulcrum were, by virtue of their arrangements of cylindrical axes, forced to transmit motion across a two-dimensional plane, and all deviation from this plane was perceived by the machine and its designers as "cosmic" interference. Looking at the first implementation of the parallel-motion linkage in steam engines with working beams, we can see how the plane of motion is limited to the rectangular area that reaches from the cylinder to the working end of the beam; in a similar, if more expansive way, the plane of motion of a locomotive is restricted to the area bounded by the rails. The fact that motion must be forced into this plane to allow for its continuity and repetition limits the design of machines and, as we have seen, the shape of products machine tools are able to form. One could say that the success of nineteenth-century machine designers consisted in their embracing this constraint of (kinematic) freedoms, their ingenuity in finding ever-new ways of using cylindrical parts to produce, transmit, and apply motion.

A good way to visualize the historical and cultural boundaries of this productive period for plane kinematics is to remember the antecedents and successors of nineteenth-century machines. At the beginning of the epoch we encounter the fantasies of fully movable, unrestrained puppets and automata, such as Olympia in E. T. A. Hoffmann's wildly popular story (and Offenbach's even more popular operetta), and their dark siblings, Frankenstein's and others' monsters who wander about the world with too much of the freedom of organisms carrying their artificial soul.[1] These figures, some of which—the automata—were built and exhibited, still embody the eighteenth-century antagonism between the (beautiful) freedom of organic beings and the mindless repetitiveness of clocks and other mechanisms. Kleist's anecdote, with which we began the history of kinematics, had shown that this opposition was dubious and highly ideological.[2]

At the far end of the epoch, toward the beginning of the twentieth century, we see the progressive integration of human motion into the process of production in such phenomena as Taylorism: the measurement of the worker's movement on the factory floor, its registration, segmentation, optimization, and final adaptation to the motion of machines.[3] Assembly-line work was one of its consequences. The other approach to overcoming the planar limitation of machines was to build machines that defied cosmic interference and moved through all six freedoms to which rigid bodies were entitled: robots. This required not only new designs and materials but also new, nonmechanical forms of motion control. Modern-day factories—for example, a car plant— show the convergence of these two postkinematic, postcylindrical tendencies: minutely timed human motions interact with the freedoms of robot arms.

One of the arguments that runs through the present analysis of kinematic and literary phenomena alike interprets the adaptation to the restraint imposed by the finitude of planar motion as a characteristic strength of nineteenth-century culture. Neither wanting to imitate organic totality nor aiming to burst through the dimensions of mechanisms, but accepting in the midst of its processes of production an unnatural, "inhuman" breakdown and recombination of translational and rotational motion: this seems in retrospective a remarkable stance. Unlike earlier and later epochs of employing machines, it confronts "the human" and "the technical" in rare starkness. In narratives, the resulting "inhuman" voice—to name one example, the experience of narrative suspense—can be heard in many of the narratives that are shaped by and in turn shape the epoch.

However, since machines needed to be compact and motion to be diverted and apportioned, there existed kinematic means to break open the kinematic plane. They were cognate yet distinct, they were, in a sense, limit cases of one another: **gears and screws**. A gear is a screw whose pitch angle is parallel to the cylinder's axis; a screw is a gear with a pitch so large that one tooth wraps around the entirety of the cylinder. Their differences and points of intersection are in evidence in the so-called worm gear, in which a screw drives a gear, but not vice versa.[4]

Like screws, gears require at least one negative of themselves to perform their task and are often assembled into trains of four, five, or more.[5] With one exception, however, no gear is the other's *Gestell*. In geared transmissions, each of the gears has to be able to rotate (engaged or idle). The exception, the rack-and-pinion arrangement, is at the same time an illustration of Reuleaux's principle of pair-closure over force-closure. The meshing of gear teeth, in which translational and rotational forces are compounded, results in mechanical efficiency significantly higher than that of two rolling cylinders, which are always threatened by slippage. An already mentioned example is that of trains in the Swiss Alps. Their wheels and the rails can be conceived as two cylinders rolling on one another (the latter having an extremely large diameter). As soon as the gradient becomes so steep that gravitational forces exceed frictional forces, the wheels would begin to slip—were it not for the spur gear that engages a rack laid into the middle of the track to hold the train in place. The rack, and ultimately the earth, serves as the *Gestell*.

By displacing and translating rotation from one axis to another— parallel or through a range of degrees—the interconnection of gears brings home like no other arrangement the relation between torque and rotational speed, the conceptualization of which was one of the inaugural achievements of post-Newtonian mechanics. If a small gear drives another gear twice its size, it completes one revolution in half the time of the driven gear—it is twice as fast. But it takes twice the expenditure of force to turn the larger gear once around, and if the larger gear were to turn with the same velocity as the smaller gear, the force it released—the torque—would be twice that of the small gear. Torque is dependent on the diameter of the gear, which means that it cannot be reduced to a mathematical point, that it always involves extended bodies.

Like screws, gears of all kinds have existed for a long time—all mills translate the rotation of the waterwheel to the grindstones by a set of gears—but only with the convergence of three interrelated factors (the availability of motive power, the emergence of industries hungry for that power, and the manufacture of durable iron and steel) do gears come into their own.[6] Unlike rolling mills, which produce something from the interaction of translation and rotation, gears only transmit motion. That is why they could become symbols for the ineluctability and futility of motion—for example, in bureaucracies.

The screw, however, was honored with its own theory, and for a reason. The cylinder of the nineteenth century was able to constrain motion so successfully that movement along its inside axis became the standard of translation, while cylindrical rolling exemplified a new form of engaged, analog rotation. We have seen that these two motions have behind them a long and controversial history concerning their metaphysical and physical valuation. Averse to all transcendental arguments, the engineers of the nineteenth century transformed these debates into practical conventions that set standards for precision, reproducibility, and variability.[7] But the screw truly united these historically antagonistic forces in a single motion. The helical incision on a cylindrical shaft makes the two motions interact with an inevitability and lack of play that composite mechanisms such as linkages could never achieve. In Franz Reuleaux's taxonomy, the screw and the environment into which it turns—the "female" nut, or an undifferentiated medium of resistance like wood, earth, metal, water, or air, or another screw—constitutes the negentropic ideal of "pair-closure." For every turn about the shaft there is a movement along the axis, and vice versa. This immediate, undialectical yoking of opposites—technically speaking, the twist—has made the screw such a powerful agent in the mechanical and philosophical history leading up to the nineteenth century. And once its properties were defined expansively—as is the case in screw theory emerging in the 1860s—it would show a way to break through the limitation of the kinematic plane (fig. 39).

Of course there were screws before the nineteenth century. The screw, after all, is one of the six simple machines, those mechanical elements to which traditionally all complex mechanisms can be reduced in both technical and historical analyses.[8] Looking at the other five machines—the lever, the incline plane, the wedge, the wheel-and-axle, and the pulley—we see that the first three transmit forces along straight lines and the others through rotation but that only the screw turns one into the other. In the grammar of simple machines, the screw is an incline wrapped around a cylindrical shaft. Given that the incline is a variant of the lever and the wedge, and the wheel and the pulley are variants of the cylinder, we may say that the screw is indeed the most primitive of all machines.[9] Reuleaux, who established the screw-nut pair as the basic form of all pair-closure, pioneered this reduction and made it fundamental for the project of kinematics.

FIGURE 39. Peter Keetman, *Schraubenpumpe,*
1960. This image shows, among other things, the
proximity of gear and screw; if in this assembly one
screw were driving the other, this would be a simple
geared transmission (although transmitting motion in
a 1:1 ratio is most often pointless). This is, however,
a screw pump: two screws with massive threads
turning in synchrony to transport a liquid along
their common axis. In operation they are encased
in a cylindrical housing with an inlet and an outlet.
© F. C. Gundlach Foundation, Hamburg (Germany).

While theoretical understanding of the screw and its motions—and
the technical intricacies of its manufacture on the lathe—belongs in
the nineteenth century, the history of the screw stretches far back in
time. In antiquity, the most visible of all screws was the so-called screw
of Archimedes, a large contraption consisting of a tree trunk around
which a helical thread was glued and then covered by a cylindrical
sleeve; Vitruvius described in great detail its manufacture and its employment as a means to raise water.[10] It was often entered into the debate about *perpetua mobilia,* machines that could raise as least as much

energy as they consumed. Other helical devices made use of the screw's ability to produce translational force if twisted into a solid medium, whether soil or wood or, if repetition was needed, a nut carved with the negative of the screw's thread that would function as the screw's *Gestell*. Olive and wine presses were the most archaic of these mechanisms; later they were adapted to crush or dry other matter, including paper, wool, and, alas, the bones of victims of the Inquisition. The first printing presses utilized screws as a means of exerting and spreading pressure. Inversely, the screw could also be used to lift or force things apart or jack them up, notably defensive structures such as heavy doors or walls. When *engineer* still meant "military technician," the screw belonged to the arsenal of structure-busting implements.

In all of these applications, screws were open-ended bolts and produced their effect through motion; yet there was also the large class of screws used as fastening devices that turned into a mating surface, either wood or the precut thread in a metal body. Screw fasteners had their main areas of application in clock, gun, and furniture making, where connections between metal parts were needed that, unlike those achieved by gluing, forging, or soldering, could be reversed. Strong metals were necessary, and great skill was required for filing the thread of each individual screw. Precision instrument makers used metal screws in astronomical, nautical, and military instruments to index and to fasten positions, using the screw's ability to measure translational advancement.[11] We have already seen how the need for precision and standardization in screw cutting became the principal driver in the development of the self-acting lathe.

At the same time as its use in instruments and machines became more widespread and the question of its standardization more pressing, thinking about the screw played an important, if undervalued, role in the development of modern concepts of motion and space. In fact, one would not far overstate the case by saying that the development of modern, critical philosophy in the writings of Immanuel Kant is driven by his thinking about screws. In one of his precritical essays, "Von dem ersten Grunde des Unterschieds der Gegenden im Raume" (On the Ultimate Foundation of the Differentiation of Regions in Space) (1768), Immanuel Kant had remarked that screw threads bore no intrinsic markers that would allow an observer, including God, to make the distinction between a left-handed and a right-handed screw: "A screw thread which is wrapped around its shaft from left to right will never fit into a nut whose threads run from right to left even if the diameter of the shaft and the number and pitch of its threads are identical."[12] If the first item of creation had been a screw, God himself would not have been able to tell whether next he would have to design a left- or a right-handed nut. Kant took this to mean that space itself must be oriented and contain the *Gegenden* against which thread orientation can be determined. Insofar as space is independent from the objects containing it (the essay was directed explicitly against "the illustrious Leibniz"), Kant concluded that the enantiomorphic directionality of the screw and of other screwlike objects was a decisive argument in favor of Newton's concept of absolute space.[13]

Only two years later, in his breakthrough *Inaugural Dissertation* of 1770, Kant used the screw argument again, but this time to support a radically new hypothesis. Now the inability to tell the difference between a left- and a right-handed screw was used to show that there is an irreducible difference between our sensible experience (which leads us to find the right nut eventually) and our ability to conceptualize and articulate phenomena such as handedness.[14] This distinction between sensibility and intelligibility, between intuitions and concepts, became *the* critical distinction in Kant's philosophy.

Kant used the example of the screw and its handedness repeatedly in his critical philosophy to blunt any attempts at drawing direct inference from sensory experience or from the analysis of concepts alone.[15] Handedness, Kant insisted, is one of those problems that cannot be "solved" in the eighteenth-century manner of finding definitive solutions to geometric or astronomical questions. The direction of a screw's thread can be determined only "ethically": by a conventional reference to the human hand, which, as Kant pointed out in his essay on orientation, is itself spatially unmarked and needs to be identified by reference to "the feeling of left and right."[16] The nineteenth century would take this Kantian idea of conventions seriously: industrial production required the interchangeability and standardization of, for example, screw threads and their orientation across countries and continents. The Metre Convention of 1875 and its various standard measurements were the culmination of this long process.[17]

The spatial relation between the screw's two motions has a temporal dimension. It is only through turning in time that the spatiality of the screw's thread—its pitch—is revealed. This is not the case with Reuleaux's two other primitive joints, the revolute joint and the prism, both of which are fully determined independently of their being set in motion. The relationship between pitch and time was remarkable enough that one of the early modern historians of machines, Jacob Leupold, claimed in 1724: "Most often it is the case that people know that something big can be manipulated with it [i.e., the screw], but not how and in what way it is connected to time, and that untold time, and finally such force of machines, wheels, and shafts is necessary as cannot be produced nor be had."[18] Leupold here seeks to rebuff those who believe that with the help of screws—for example, in jacks—any resistance at all can be overcome. Theoretically they are right, but in the real world any increase in force has to be paid for by an increase in time (of revolution). The finer the pitch of a screw, the less force need be applied to turn it; but to cover the same lifting distance as a screw with twice as coarse a pitch, one has to turn the screw twice as often. It all comes back to the fact that simple machines do not generate but only convert force, and that every increase in force costs time: "The open-ended screw is one of the most powerful and versatile lifting tools, because through it a small apparatus can develop untold force. . . . However, in relation to time and force not a hair's breadth is actually gained."[19] It is worth dwelling on the phenomenology of the screw because its embodiment of opposites—translation and rotation, space and time—resonated widely with idealist philosophers of the early nineteenth century. Eager to overcome the underlying dualities in Kant's critical philosophy—the schism between intuitions and concepts first revealed in the screw's ambiguous orientation—thinkers such as Hegel and Hölderlin maintained that any complete philosophical system would have to be built on the identity of identity and difference. Otherwise, they argued, the search for first principles would lead to an infinite regress that could be stopped only by a fiat issuing from outside the system. This necessity led Hegel, as mentioned, to envisage the path of logic—the most abstract of the many ways in which spirit manifests itself—as a coil in which end and beginning were fused, a "circle entwined around itself."[20] Friedrich Hölderlin, in his epistolary novel *Hyperion,* quotes Heraclitus's enigmatic phrase "the one that is differentiated within itself" as an instance of such a complex principle.[21] One example Heraclitus gives is the screw in which "the straight and the crooked path," translation and rotation, are "one and the same";[22] for Hölderlin it is this tension between opposing forces that produces beauty.

No one put the image of the screw to greater use than Goethe, however. His essay "On the Spiral Tendency of Vegetation" takes up the botanical examples that Kant used to illustrate the qualities of handedness and fashions from them a "fundamental law of life."[23] Intent on proving that all forms of organic growth are driven by the same forces—and therefore do not require a special creation to explain their variety—Goethe identifies a "vertical system" that consolidates "longitudinal fibers" into a "spiritual staff," around which the "spiral tendency" wraps nourishment and variation. Everything that grows moves by turning around a straight line. A tree is a macroscopic example of these translational and rotational "tendencies": the trunk's verticality is twisted by the spiral outgrowth of the branches. It is only because growth is so slow that we no longer perceive the helical motion in the plant.

Goethe conceives of the spiral tendency as a substantive, not simply as a formal, law. Translational and rotational motions, he argues, are embodiments of male and female forces respectively, their polarity and combination an expression of vitality as such. In the earlier "Essay on Meteorology" he had proposed to understand the changes in seasons and other recurring atmospheric phenomena as the result of a spiral motion of the globe. The earth not only turns around its axis but also contracts and expands in semidiurnal rhythm and thereby creates itself the motion of the atmosphere around it. "This moving force contracts twice and rises twice in twenty-four hours . . . and we best imagine it as living spiral, as an animate screw without end."[24] The spiral tendency of plants and animals is in the last instance driven by the spiral motion of the earth.

When screw theory in the technical sense emerged in the mid–nineteenth century its goal was not speculation but generalization. Perhaps the philosophical mysteries and natural occurrences of helical motions had an influence in its rise; doubtless the universal availability of screws in the wake of Maudslay's screw-cutting lathe and the increasing use of screws as propellers and drills did.[25] First and foremost, however, treatises such as Sir Robert Ball's *Theory of the Screw* sought to overcome the restrictions of their kinematic predecessors, notably Reulaux's kinematics of linkages. Linkages force the transmission of motion across the two dimensions of a plane—that is why the isolation of translation and of rotation is so crucial to its success, and why Reuleaux dreamed of machines that were entirely composed of "pair-closed" links. For as soon as a revolute joint's rotation, for example, is afflicted by translation, or a link's translational motion by rotation, as soon as a linkage moves outside its constraints and behaves like a "normal" body in three-dimensional space, the kinematics of linkages breaks down, either immediately or with the wear and tear of long use. From a three-dimensional point of view, the kinematics of linkage is an overly abstract, even "a degenerate science": "When we seek to write a coherent and comprehensive theory about the nature of the freedoms and constraints in machinery whose actions and motions are held to be only two-dimensional, we write a degenerate science. The science contains many exceptions and hardly any rules; and we find that many call it, not the science of the kinetostatics of planar mechanisms or some such respectable thing, but, more simply and quite derogatorily, linkages and all that."[26] Similarly (if less angrily) motivated, screw theory seeks to overcome the abstractions and limitations of planar kinematics by generalizing the laws of motion of all rigid bodies. It states that "any given displacement of a rigid body can be effected by a rotation about an axis combined with a translation parallel to that axis."[27] This statement, which is not original to Ball, summarizes a long process of simplifying and standardizing the description of motion in space.[28] The seemingly infinite possibilities, or "freedoms," of unextended point masses to move about in absolute space—the two parameters inherited from Newton's theoretical mechanics—are reduced for rigid bodies to six freedoms: the translations along the three axes that can intersect at ninety-degree angles, and the rotations around them. Screw theory presupposes that rigid bodies—defined by at least three points that do not lie on the same plane and whose distance from one another does not change—are restricted to these freedoms and then reduces their possible motions to two, rotation and translation.[29]

We know that these reductions had their mechanical parallel in the reduction of Reuleaux's three primitive joints to the screw-nut pair. However, when Ball and the screw theorists speak of screws, they no longer mean actual cylindrical objects with helical threads cut into them but the possible motion of any body whatsoever, including that of the screw independently of the nut. The motion of the screw is not dependent on the forcing by the nut (or by any medium into which the screw might be drilled); rather, the notion of "instantaneous screw" implies that as soon as a body moves it initiates a screwlike motion. It may be that the pitch of that screw is infinite—as would be the case in a purely translational motion—or that it is zero—as would be the case in a purely rotational motion—or, most likely, a combination of the two; but it is a screw even at the smallest increment. The elimination of the nut from the consideration of the screw amounts, in the language of

Reuleaux that Heidegger had tacitly adopted, to the elimination of the *Gestell*: for screw theorists, the whole world is a *Gestell*.

Since it opens up into three-dimensional space, screw theory also does away with the radical and, in the end, unworkable abstraction from forces in kinematics. Ball cites Poinsot's discovery "that any system of forces which act upon a rigid body can be replaced by a single force, and a couple in a plane perpendicular to the force."[30] As we have seen, a couple of forces acting in opposite directions initiates the rotation of a rigid body. The distance between these forces—best imagined as, and termed, a "wrench"—multiplied by their product gives the measure by which torque is calculated. (The single force perpendicular to the rotating lever is the inertial translation of a body.)

To complete the conceptual arsenal of screw theory, Ball defines as pitch "the rectilinear distance through which the nut is translated parallel to the axis of the screw while the nut is rotated through the angular unit of circular measure," which leads to the redefinition of a screw as the "straight line with which a definite linear magnitude termed the pitch is associated."[31] Ball also gives a definition of twist ("A body is said to receive a twist about a screw when it is rotated uniformly about the screw while it is translated uniformly parallel to the screw"), and this culminates in the fundamental definition of the motion of all rigid bodies: "The canonical form to which the displacement of a rigid body can be reduced is a twist about a screw."[32] As to the forces involved, he concludes that the "canonical form to which a system of forces acting on a rigid body can be reduced is a wrench on a screw."[33]

The implications and the applications of screw theory are far too complex to be followed here. Its conceptual importance for the end of the epoch of the cylinder is more easily grasped. The focus on the planar kinematics of the nineteenth century revealed that one way of understanding the rise and the logic of machines, and of the products, processes, spaces, and cultures they engendered, was to understand them as constraints on freedoms—as the elimination of what Heinrich von Kleist in his epochal essay of 1810 called the *Ziererei*, the affectation of freedom. Reuleaux's *Kinematics of Machinery* had attempted to base these processes of elimination on an embodied grammar in which the cylinder and its properties were the most rudimentary conjunctions that co- and subordinated motions. The centrodes and the geometry of rolling, the prismatic and the revolute joint, and the combined "cylinder chains" in the various linkages that he sought to systematize all served the purpose of eliminating unwanted kinematic freedoms and their noxious manifestations, such as friction, noise, heat, and vibration.

Screw theory generalizes the insights of Reuleaux's *Kinematik,* but in doing so it abolishes its fundamental tenets and hopes. It is not a theory to guide the construction of transmissions toward the goal of ultimate pair-closure of all of its elements but a description of the possible motions of any rigid body whatsoever. It does not provide a grammar to constrain freedoms; rather, it abolishes the distinction between freedom and constraint altogether. It no longer accepts the categorical difference between mechanical and "cosmic" motion, between machines and their environment. The objects of applied screw theory will be a new class of artifacts whose goal is controlled motion through all six freedoms: robots.[34] Screw theory in its technical form—rather than in the speculative form of Kant or Goethe—ends the epoch of the cylinder by infinitely extending its kinematics.

The potentially dark vision that there is no fundamental difference between the motion of mechanical and organic bodies—which to uphold may be the ultimate purpose of modern dance—did not necessarily depress the writers of the nineteenth century, who cheerfully called their own productions "machines" (Trollope) and saw themselves as machinists of sorts. Rather, as the following pages seek to show, the peculiar conjunction of motions in the movement of the screw and its universalization held the promise of a new way of constructing narratives. If, to put it starkly, the cylinder as motor and as tool affected the way stories were conceived and understood, and if the cylinder as spatial enclosure bent the narrative horizon of the realist plot, the screw provided a template for conjoining these two aspects into a single narrative motion. What was being told and how it was being told became the other of each other in the helical figure of free indirect discourse. It is not by accident that the critique of this construction at the end of the nineteenth century would be delivered in a novel with the title *The Turn of the Screw.*

CHAPTER 10

Kinematics of Narration III

Henry James and the Turn of the Screw

If the rolling cylinders in the various machines that contribute to the acceleration of writing, publishing, and reading in the nineteenth century are implied in the temporal sequence of the story, the cylinder's particular curvature and scalability provide the model for bending this sequence into a finite, legible, and memorable shape. We have associated these two aspects with the predominance of translational and rotational motion respectively and have paired them with their rhetorical cognates metonymy and metaphor, which in turn affords us a kinematically focused view of the history and rhetoric of the novel. Analytically productive though these dichotomies may be, they are, just like the concepts of story and plot, necessary abstractions that fail fully to capture the complexities of nineteenth-century narratives, which are never just stories and never just narrative reflections. Only modernist narratives in the twentieth century will attempt to reach for such purity.

It helps in this context to remember that neither pure translation nor rotation "exists" anywhere in the natural world: that, after all, is the brute fact behind the need for tools and machines. The task of isolating, transmitting, and applying these apparently exclusive motions fell to the "cylinder chains" of the nineteenth century. We have also seen that in the wake of the widespread emergence of new transmissions kinematicists of the second half of the nineteenth century began to theorize that the dichotomy between the two motions might be resolved in the more general concept of the screw: every motion of a rigid body is a combination of translational and rotational displacements even if one parameter approaches zero. This theoretical (in the terms of screw theory, instantaneous) screw articulates the underlying commonality but also the common limitation of all motion. "Everything moves like a screw" also means that there is no "free" motion beyond the motions that potentially can be embodied in machines—kinematically speaking, the whole world is a machine.

At the same time as the insight into the common ground of rotation and translation was first formulated among designers of machines, writers of long prose works also began to reflect on the kinematics of their trade. There had been intense debates about the representational complexities and paradoxes of realist prose, notably in the 1850s during the "battle of realism" that brought the work of Flaubert, Baudelaire, and Sue into conflict with the courts.[1] But there also had been discussions among writers and reviewers about the technical peculiarities of writing prose under the new regime of serial publication, instantaneous review, and mass circulation. How could form and content, plot and story, suspense and truth be integrated in one seamless motion?[2] The exclusion of digression through the speed of the rotary printing press as well as the elimination of miracles and pure contingencies through the closure of narrative space brought forth the ideal of a narrative in which story and plot were conjoined in much the same way as in a screw translation and rotation were joined into one motion. Nothing—such was the tacit formula for this ideal—should happen in a narrative that was not accounted for in the plot, neither a miracle issuing from an instance beyond the plane of narration nor an accident that had no relation to any of the events preceding it. This narrative recuperation of both transcendence and raw contingency had been explored and problematized by the most advanced novelists of the eighteenth century—Sterne and Wieland come to mind—only to become the undisputed basis for the realists of the nineteenth century.[3] Inversely, nothing would be told that did not have bearing on the development of the story—no digressions would derail the progress of the story, no description would be unrelated to the development of a character or the setting of a mood, no symbol would unduly absorb the reader's attention. Whatever happens has to be told, whatever is told has to happen—this is the most succinct formula of the realist helix that emerged as the ideal motion of nineteenth-century narrative prose.[4]

As with all ideals, it is questionable whether this formula was ever fully enacted. In Dickens, as we have seen, digressions survive in the multitude of eccentric characters whose state of mind is, more often than not, digression from purposeful action. Balzac, whose portrait of Mme. Vauquer at the beginning of *Père Goriot* became famous for replacing idle ecphrasis with functional description, still luxuriates in straight-out moralizing or political pamphleteering.[5] The recurrence of characters in his work might alleviate the suspicion of contingency, but an encounter like the meeting of Lucien and Abbé Herrera/Vautrin/ Collin at the end of *Les illusions perdues* still feels contrived, even if we know that the criminal mastermind has been seen in other cir- cumstances. The creation of a criminal mastermind who manipulates events within the narrative—as in *Splendeurs et misères* or in *Histoire des Treize*—is another way for Balzac to justify fantastical sequences of events without breaking their relation to narrative explanation.

Flaubert, however, might have come very close to the helical ideal. The shock *Madame Bovary* imparted (and continues to impart) to readers judicial and private alike can be articulated in the kinematics of a fully integrated narrative screw. Every description, from Charles Bovary's cap to Emma Bovary's death, at the same time serves as a commentary and moves the story along. The seduction scene at the agricultural fair only brings to the surface this intertwining of narrative rotation (in the description of the fair) and translation (in Rodolphe's seduction of Emma). Flaubert's great stylistic tool, the fully sustained *discours indirect libre,* generates a sense of universal oppressiveness not so much through ambivalence as through the simultaneity of inner and outer perspective, of description and interpretation, of moving the story forward and reflecting on it.[6] Just as the human skeleton does not allow for continuous rotational and translational motion, the human conscience does not allow for a position in which inside and outside, interpretation and description, empathy and criticism are conjoined. In this sense, free indirect speech is as inhuman as the motions of indus- trial machines.[7]

No one writer thought and wrote more about the kinematics involved in the conjunction of story and plot than Henry James. He mercilessly criticized Flaubert for the dreariness of his subjects, but equally for his stylistic machinations.[8] Having himself written perfectly integrated novels, such as *Roderick Hudson* and *The Princess Casamassima* (which, in addition, are linked Balzac-style through the employment of a recurring character), he became increasingly interested in the "craft of fiction," in the way he and his fellow writers "excavated" their sub- ject matter and handled the design of their narratives. He experimented

with extravagant plot devices, such as the perspective of the uncompre-
hending child in *What Maisie Knew* or the forced theatrical unity of
space in the late *The Outcry*. His great late novels have in common the
investment of an inordinate amount of descriptive energy and psychological analysis in characters who suddenly, in a moment of dramatic
recognition, glimpse into the abyss of the story: such is the case when
Lambert Strether accidentally encounters Chad and Mme. de Vionnet in
The Ambassadors, or when Milly Theale understands Kate's and Den-
sher's plan in *The Wings of the Dove,* or when the shopkeeper informs
Maggie of Charlotte's and the Prince's visit in *The Golden Bowl,* or
when—in *Portrait of a Lady,* an earlier work, it is true—Isabel Archer
sees her husband in conversation with Mme Merle.

The contingency of these events—regardless of whether they can be
anticipated by the reader *(The Wings of the Dove, The Golden Bowl)*—
destroys the integration of logical and psychological developments that
the narrative expends such efforts to construe. All that immersing and
reflecting—all that lyrical rotation—comes to naught in the sudden
lurching forward—in the dramatic translation—of the anagnorisis: the
violence of the motion is such that in their remainder these narratives
must struggle to regain a semblance of regular pace. This seeming ir-
ruption of ancient tragedy into the fabric of the modern novel is in fact
prepared for by James's interest in the nineteenth-century avatars of
tragedy: the ghost story, the detective story, the horrific *Tales of the
Grotesque and Arabesque* that Edgar Allan Poe had published in 1839
and that Baudelaire had hailed as truly modern narratives.[9]

In these tales, all energy was focused on the story and on the sequence and verisimilitude of events; their brevity allowed an author to
counter the pull of serial publication and to "write backwards," knowing that readers could read them in one sitting. With their extreme
concern with the "wheels and pinions" of the story, these narratives
threatened to coarsen the profile of the realist helix into a narrative
prism that would lose all ability to turn and reflect, complicate, retard
and suspend.[10] Against this threat to the narrative achievements of the
nineteenth century—and against the unchecked belief in ghostly phenomena so prevalent in the second half of the century—Henry James
set his own "ghost stories."[11] Yet his fullest exploration of the tensions
between the verisimilitude of a storyline and a fully motivated plot
came in a serialized novel appropriately titled *The Turn of the Screw.*

The story moves forward with all the force of one of Poe's tales
and with none of the retardations and stoppages that slow down the

pace in James's large-scale works. But unlike in Poe, "where the . . . phenomena evoked, the moving accidents, coming straight, as I say, are immediate and flat," the tale's vanishing point is the question of its own representational realism:[12] whether the figures of the two deceased servants can be seen by anyone but the governess who is narrating the events, and, if so, whether they are actually seen or only imagined by her. At first it seems that the core story of James's short novel (the governess's engagement and subsequent sojourn at Bly, the exposure to the apparitions, the sequence of events that culminate in Miles's death) and the framing of its plot (the recuperation of and the reading from a first-person account in a manuscript) turn within one another the way a bolt turns in a nut. Every slide toward the culmination of the story is joined to a turn in the plot: nothing happens that escapes the frantic interpretation and reflection of the anxious first-person narrator; everything she does as a result of her reflections is designed to bring the story to an end. This assembly is driven, as many critics have observed, by couples of diegetic forces: Mrs. Grose and the governess, Miles and Flora, Peter Quint and Miss Jessel, the inside and the outside of the house, the two towers. And these in turn are driven by a para- and extradiegetic couple that seeks to expand the fiction of realism outward: the anonymous narrator of the frame, and Douglas, the owner and reader of the governess's manuscript.

The narrative frame elaborately stages the proof of the story's philological authenticity: the manuscript, retrieved from a safe and read at a country house party, is declared to be in the governess's handwriting. By establishing an uninterrupted, "analog" sequence of hands ending in Douglas's hand, which holds the manuscript while reading it aloud, James seeks to focus the (intradiegetic) listeners' attention in the same direction as the protagonist's, only once removed: they wonder whether her experiences are realistic in the traditional sense of transcribing sense experiences or whether her unconscious desires—love for her master, envy of her predecessors, passion for the children—generated the images of the deceased servants. The same concern animates most contemporary criticism, even if it is on the more general and theoretically more sophisticated level of psychoanalysis and trauma studies.[13] Forcing attention this way is the first turn of James's narrative screw.

Looking more closely at this forced orientation of interpretive scholarship, James seems to intimate that one of the signature disciplines of the early nineteenth century, textual criticism, sets the stage for its psychological counterpart, psychoanalysis, surely the most "realistic" form of hermeneutics. The narratological purpose of staging is the claim that there is at least one instance—the manuscript—that allows us to determine that the screw is turning, not the bolt. This is, of course, a classic *metabasis eis allo genos,* although one that has more importance for our understanding of realism than is usually acknowledged.[14] James suggests—successfully, if we look at the bulk of criticism concerning this tale—that the manuscript in the narrative is (in the language of textual criticism) the "archetype" of the narrative, and that therefore we can train our sights on the realism of the narrated experiences.

By stepping back from free indirect discourse and its suggestion of narrative totality toward its narratological ancestor, the "found manuscript," James disassembles, as it were, the continuous screw of Flaubertian realism into its constituent parts of story and plot, while at the same time making it impossible to weigh their relation as one of priority or dependence. Fixated though the governess may be on discovering the truth (and her interpreters on understanding her psyche), the narrative frame—*qua* element of the narration—is not an external *Gestell,* as Reuleaux would say, that could support the distinction between the truth of what is being told and the consistency of its telling. Rather, by exposing the framelessness of its construction, the tale is a demonstration of how narratives work, not how they mean. Needlessly subjected to the "counter-rhythmical interruption" of serialization—the story can easily be read in one sitting, although it was published in installments—the tale is, as James himself admitted, a "very mechanical matter," a "machine for reading" in much the same way as Picasso claimed that his cubist paintings were "machines for seeing."[15]

The mechanical nature of the tale is evident not only in the groundlessness of its outer frame but also in the hollowness of its core. If the apparitions of the ghosts—the apparent truth content of the story—had been submitted to the governess's, and consequently to the readers', judgment, they would have required a mode of representation that actually suspended indications of their existence in space and time. Yet at each instance we are alerted to the ghosts' presence by statements like "She rose . . . and, within a dozen feet of me, stood there as my vile predecessor" or simply "Miss Jessel stood before us on the opposite bank exactly as she had stood the other time."[16] This unwillingness to attempt the representation of visual ghostliness—exacerbated by James's decision to abandon free indirect discourse in favor of first-person narration—is joined with the factual omission of representing the linguistic signs that convince even Mrs. Grose of the continued presence of the servants: the children's "appalling language."[17] This omission—veiled though it may be by concerns over decency and censorship—shows that while James designed the narrative mechanism to put us, the readers, into the position of worrying with and about the unnamed governess, we are in fact in the position of Mrs. Grose: we could be convinced of the presence of the ghosts and of their vileness if the language that made the housekeeper and the principal of Miles's school recoil were not made, literally, obscene to us. For the minimal level of literary realism is surely the ability of language to repeat itself, to quote.

By denying the existence, or at least the literary representability, of this minimal level of realism at the very heart of the narrative, James repeats the gesture with which he has dismantled its outer frame. Not only is the analog transmission of the manuscript a deceptive attempt to quote the governess, but the quotable proof of the event's reality is withheld from the reader's judgment. There is, as a consequence, deep uncertainty about how the story is told as well as about whether there is a story to be told. With these maneuvers James unbraids plot and story, uncoils the narrative helix, and thus derealizes the mode of storytelling that Dickens first mastered in the 1830s. This proves to be portentous, for it not only sheds additional light on the disruptive moments of anagnorisis in James's own late novels, which all carry more than just an intimation of unspeakable obscenity, but also points to the bifurcation in the road just ahead for the novel as a genre. Some of the modernist experiments right after James will go down the path of breaking James's reticence and tell "obscene" stories—stories that are sexually explicit, concerned with crime, luxury, and transgression, or simply too private or too pointless; in James's English D.H. Lawrence and Thomas Hardy, in French Joris-Karl Huysmans and André Gide come to mind, but also the rising tide of pulp and detective literature that sloshes underneath the pier of "high" literature. Other, formal experiments, will jettison the task of telling stories in favor of approximating in their mode of presentation the disaggregate acoustics and visuality that characterize modern life; John Dos Passos, James Joyce, Virginia Woolf, and others move in this direction. The pressures emanating from the competing media of photography, film, radio, and phonography further accelerate the dismantling of the smoothly running novel-machine of the nineteenth century.[18] Perhaps the most radical moment in the dismantling of cylindrical prose was reached in

1970 when Samuel Beckett set a short narrative inside a gigantic rubber cylinder in which two hundred naked individuals were engaging in startlingly meaningless and repetitive activities.[19]

It must be repeated that a kinematic analysis of nineteenth-century narratives does not preclude other avenues of interpretation. It would be absurd, to cite just one example, to neglect the ethical fearlessness and originality in the representation of human unhappiness in Eliot's *Middlemarch* in favor of concentrating on its braiding of plotlines, its spatial arrangements, or the history of its publication. The point is simply that the narrative conventions that allowed this fearlessness and originality to manifest itself can be described as a manipulation of motions; that the isolation and integration of these motions, rather than representing a timeless attitude of humanity toward narration, or a diffusedly felt sentiment peculiar to writers in the nineteenth century, is, literally and analogically, driven by the development of industrial machines and transmissions that rely on the kinematics of the cylinder; and that these narrative conventions are "realistic" through their implication in this epochal management of motions. The kinematic viewpoint suggests that the metaphysical description of literary realism—fictions are realistic because they represent the world as it is—can be more firmly written in functional and historical terms—fictions are realistic because they are produced and consumed in the same motions in which the machines of the epoch move.

Epilogue

It is hard to say exactly when the epoch of the cylinder was over, and with it the epoch in which visible transmission of motion by contact was the technical and cultural norm. Epochs—in the sense that the notion is used in these pages—are not simply temporal extensions; they often overlap or are separated by elapsed chronological time.[1] Their characteristic achievements and practices, of course, live on even if newer paradigms garner more attention: steel is still being rolled (even if largely outside the eyes of Western consumers), cars are still being driven by cylindrical engines and helical gears (even though with much less enthusiasm), papers and books are still being printed on rotary presses (even though an end of this practice is clearly visible). Yet the focus of technological, economic, and cultural attention has long wandered to other processes and developments, notably those that are powered by electrical energy and that allow for the digital transmission of motion and information.

Historically, the end of kinematics came first from the Romantic natural philosopher Hans Christian Oersted, and then from experimenters and theoreticians in England, Michael Faraday and later James Clerk Maxwell in particular. Kinematically speaking, the discovery of electromagnetism and the idea of convertibility it entailed can be based on the observation, as early as 1821, of the rotation of an electromagnetic wire around its axis.[2] This incident of "natural" rotation, fully exploited, would later obviate the forced rotation of kinematics and lead to the development of electric generators that leaped over the contact transmissions of steam engines.

With the exception of telegraphy, most electrical applications remained in the background throughout most of the century. Perhaps the Electrical Exhibition in Paris 1881 was the moment where the discontinuous and invisible culture of electricity finally asserted itself publicly: "Henri de Parville, who wrote a detailed account of this groundbreaking exposition, noted a curious and disturbing side effect. 'For the first time, the public was confronted with many machines, whose appearance did not express their function. We are not yet in the habit of observing machines that function without any apparent cause. Their occult workings baffle us. The secret of their existence escapes us.' The mechanism of a steam engine had been obvious from the movement of its parts. An electrical generator, however, hid the sources, causes, and actions of its seemingly magical power."[3] Henry Adams, in his famous chapter on *The Dynamo and the Virgin,* takes the World Exhibition of 1900 in Paris as the cutoff date when the analog world and the visibility of its kinematics came to an end and were overwhelmed by the ubiquity of electricity and the use of invisible radiation:

> Between the dynamo and the engine-house outside, the break of
> continuity amounted to an abysmal fracture for a historian's objects.
> No more relation could he discover between the steam and the electric
> current than between the Cross and the cathedral. The forces were
> interchangeable if not reversible, but he could see only an absolute *fiat* in
> electricity as in faith. . . . Langley [Adam's guide, a physicist] seemed to
> be worried by the same trouble. For he constantly repeated that the new
> forces were anarchical, and especially that he was not responsible for the
> new rays, that were little short of parricidal in their wicked spirit towards
> science. His own rays, with which he had doubled the solar spectrum,
> were altogether harmless and beneficent; but Radium denied its God,—
> or, what was to Langley the same thing, denied the truths of his Science.
> The force was wholly new. . . . Thus it happened that, after ten years'
> pursuit, he [Adams] found himself lying in the Gallery of Machines at the
> Great Exhibition of 1900, with his historical neck broken by the sudden
> irruption of force totally new.[4]

Aby Warburg, finally, unleashed the full torrent of his hatred against the men he held responsible for the modern ubiquity of electrical and discontinuous culture: "Franklin and the Wright brothers, who invented the dirigible airplane, are precisely those ominous destroyers of the sense of distance, who threaten to lead the planet back into chaos.

Telegram and telephone destroy the cosmos. Mythical and symbolic thinking strive to form spiritual bonds between humanity and the surrounding world, shaping distance into the space required for devotion and reflection: the distance undone by the instantaneous electric connection."[5] The disappearance and withdrawal of contact motion, the emergence of immeasurable forces, velocities, scales, and quantities, the growing role of chemical industries and their integration into the processes of heavy industries, and of course the deployment of all these energies in the design of ever more powerful and deadly weapons quite unmetaphorically led to the destruction of the cosmos, at the latest in the Great War.

Beyond and beneath these cosmic events were smaller developments that also testified to the disappearance of the cylinder. The new panoramas that were being exhibited at the beginning of the twentieth century no longer invited the spectator inside to contemplate the painted surfaces but made them look in from the outside onto stereoscopic images. The pictorial canvas no longer contained the cylindricality and sphericity of objects within a coherent field of representation, as it did in the works of Manet and Cézanne, but—in the work of Picasso, and of Fernand Leger in particular—set them free in their own space. Marcel Duchamp's *Bicycle Wheel* readymade exhibited rotation for no purpose whatsoever. Edison's rolls were flattened into disks and lost their strict time limit. Rubber tires established a hybrid of force- and pair-closure between wheel and road. Cars no longer had to be started by initial rotation but were equipped with a "self-starter."[6]

Walter Benjamin is the chronicler of the effects this "fury of disappearance" (Hegel) had on the mentality of European cultures. His practice of extreme attention to the seemingly insignificant consequences of this withdrawal of visibility, palpability, and panoramic accessibility stands in significant contrast to the wholesale condemnation of "technology" or "technics" that became fashionable with the works of Spengler, F. G. Jünger, and Heidegger.

In a penetrating analysis of the intellectual sources of contemporary writing on technology, Mark Hansen has shown to what extent twentieth-century techno-criticism remained wedded to the idea that machines were first and foremost sediment of intention and subjectivity.[7] Inversely, the works of Georges Canguilhem, and in particular that of Gilbert Simondon have shown how kinematic necessities and the forces of technological milieus drive the development of actual technical objects to such a degree that it is perfectly productive to describe them using the "natural" concepts of speciation, individuation, and evolution.[8]

In the field of literary studies nothing really compares to these openings to mixed "modes of existence": to an acceptance of narratives as intermixture of intentional and technical factors and to an understanding of its historical manifestations.[9] Yet we have seen in the discussion of Dickens's work how the concept of story, and attendant attributes such as characterization and suspense, develop in an analogous and linked relationship to the movements of nineteenth-century machines; how the constructions of plots in individual works, and the idea of a comprehensive oeuvre in Balzac, follow in the wake of the emergence of panoramic and horizontal spaces; and how in Flaubert the intertwining of subjective and objective, diegetic and descriptive strands creates a mode of narrative that in its ineluctable progress follows the helix of a screw thread. While in these three aspects we can detect a progressive detachment from the bare facts of forced motion, each stands in a relation to the kinematics of the age that is more than intentional. That relation, rather than the professed will to capture the realities of the time, provides a reliable basis for addressing nineteenth-century prose as "realistic."

Other factors besides habitual technophobia work against the reading of nineteenth-century novels as techno-human hybrids within a kinematic culture. They have to do with the institutional history of literary scholarship as much as with attempts to reclaim literature as the pure expression of intentionality.

One is embedded in the history of aesthetics and the flow of national traditions; it is the continued persistence, even in the most refined deconstructive readings, of an idealist legacy and its preferred literary paradigms, poetry and tragedy. This legacy has its origins in Germany in the late eighteenth and early nineteenth centuries; its survival and current expansion as the global parlance of critical theory have historical and sociological reasons that exceed the present frame. A brief look at its intellectual genealogy, however, has the double advantage of bringing us back, fittingly by means of an anecdote, to the beginning of our investigation into the rise of kinematics, and of helping to explain a glaring anomaly: the absence of German entrants into the cohort of kinematically realist writers.

In a coincidence of names and places almost too rich to believe, Heinrich von Kleist in 1801 fell into conversation with a traveler named Christian Gottlieb Hölder in the Swiss town of Unterseen. Their paths

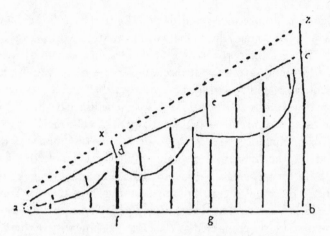

FIGURE 40. Kleist's model of the tragic mechanism. a—b is the extension of life, the contiguity of fate; b—c is the intensity of the hero's character; the "parabolic lines" indicate the necessary deviations to make the hero's path interesting to the spectator. Reprinted from Hölder (1803–4, 174).

had crossed while they were hiking in the surrounding mountains, which for both men were sanctified by the poems and descriptions they had suggested to the young Goethe on his first journey to Switzerland in 1775. The two men's common reverence for Goethe led to a "conversation in the mountains" about the principles of tragedy. Kleist proceeded to explain his theory, more precisely, his "rules," of tragedy by carving an image into the table, shown in figure 40.

The line a—b, Kleist explained, represents the temporal extension of the hero's life, the events that structure it and the purposes he sets for himself, in short his fate; it is divided into the three segments a—f, f—g, and g—b, which correspond to the exposition, the rising action, and the catastrophe. The line c—b represents the intensity of the hero's character, the force with which he wants to counter the onward push of fate. If the difference of fate and character were of linear value, the action would follow the straight line a—c until the hero was crushed at point c. Such a linear unfolding of the conflict, however, would be uninteresting for the spectator (who looks on from point a); the poet therefore has to introduce deviations ("undulations") in which the hero seems to succumb to his fate before he rises again at the end of each act (d, e, c). The whole design can be scaled at will such that b—c can be increased to z to give the action a steeper gradient.[10]

Much would have to be said of this. Remarkable is the conviction with which the young Kleist—he was at the time working on his first tragedy, *Robert Guiskard,* which he would burn shortly thereafter—claimed he could give a set of mechanical rules that would guide the construction of flawless tragedies. Remarkable, but not singular: at the very time of this conversation, F. W. J. Schelling gave his lectures on the philosophy of art, in which he spoke of Greek tragedy as a "geometric or arithmetic problem that can be solved completely, without remainder," and his former roommate Friedrich Hölderlin was hard at work on formulating a "calculable law" designed to make writing tragedies a mechanical craft among others.[11] These theories conceived of tragedy as a collision of straight-line forces that resulted in the annihilation of the force embodied by the hero. The linearity of this conception is evident from the images Hölderlin and Kleist use to visualize it: Hölderlin sees the tragic conflict as a lever where one of the two arms has to be weighted in order to achieve balance;[12] Kleist, as his carving shows, conceives of tragedy as a wedge driven between fate and character.[13] Lever and wedge are part of the set of "primitive machines" that since antiquity were seen—and used—to transmit and convert force.

The linearity of these poetic machines has its limits in the desire of the audience for variation. Hölderlin therefore urges poets to interrupt the flow of action with what he called "caesura, the pure word," and to use it as a movable fulcrum in such a way that the arms of the lever are balanced. If most of the weight of the action is toward the beginning, the fulcrum also has to move toward the beginning to counteract the relative lightness at the end, and vice versa. The drawings in the notes to the translation of Sophocles' *Antigone,* with its (reversed and) inclined fulcrum, show that Hölderlin already saw the beginnings of a linkage in his construction.[14] Kleist tried to countervail the threat of boring the audience by including the parabolic lines that deviate from the "character line" a—c. It easy to see that integrating, rather than just superimposing, these lines into the design would have turned the tragic wedge into a screw.

Highlighting the presence of technical thinking in Schelling's, Hölderlin's, and Kleist's poetics provides a glimpse of nineteenth-century literary kinematics *in statu nascendi;* it shows the concepts and conflicts we have encountered as instrumental in defining serialized "realistic" prose, namely story (fate) and plot (character), in an as yet static relation that has as its only solution a catastrophic collision. The motion of the cylindrical press will concretize and mobilize these

concepts: the caesura is transformed into the interval between installments, the counter-rhythmical interruptions into the plot devices that
structure the onrush of representations, the tragic wedge into the narrative screw of inhuman, free and indirect observation.

If they were there to be used, why did German authors of the nineteenth century not avail themselves of these concepts, and the insights
they contained, for the writing of prose? It is a startling fact, after all,
that a nation that prided itself in having woven literature into the very
fabric of its institutions, and whose renown in the literary world was
unrivaled by the time of Goethe's death in 1832, would not contribute
a single remarkable entrant into the canon of realist novels until that
canon fell apart at the end of the nineteenth century.[15]

To be sure, many extrinsic factors help explain this absence. There
was the heavy censorship that weighed on German countries after 1819
and that, interestingly, pushed political pamphleteering into novels because publications above "20 Bogen" were exempt from scrutiny; there
was the lag in industrialization, itself related to the lag in political uni-
fication; there was the absence of an urban center in which serialized
novels could grow. And there was the shadow of Goethe, whose attempt to guide his protagonist Wilhelm Meister into narrative modernity had ended in resignation, isolation, and formal dissolution.

From the standpoint of narrative kinematics, however, the most powerful obstacle to the development of realist modes of narration came
from the fixation on tragedy as the superior art form. This dominance,
too, was fueled by various extranarratological factors: by a fixation on
ancient Greece as the sacred fount of all art (and the methodological
dominance of classical philology in the universities); by the importance
of tragedy in idealist and postidealist systems of philosophy; by the
hope of poets in the early decades of the nineteenth century to effect a
cathartic "patriotic turn" in the fractured German polity.

Yet at the heart of the decision in favor of tragedy stood the belief that the difference between the freedom to shape a story and the
ineluctable pull of the story itself is directly indicative of the conflict
between character and fate in the broadest and hence the most real
sense possible. Tragedies, in the understanding of Hegel, Schelling,
Kleist, Hölderlin, and others are realistic because they make visible
the primordial conflict between the translational pull of being and the
arresting power of human beings; they neither are simply products of
an author's imagination nor are fully subject to an author's manipula-
tions. As Kleist's drawing shows, the relation between character and

fate *is* the relation between plot and story: character is tragedy's plot, as fate is its story. This coincidence changes the task of the poet fundamentally: it becomes a vocation, a *Beruf,* in the most powerful way imaginable. For if indeed at the root of the German word *Dichtung* is the Latin *dictare,* then the tragic poet takes dictation from being itself. Many German authors of the post-Goethe era—Christian Dietrich Grabbe, Friedrich Hebbel, even Heinrich Heine—tried to answer this call, particularly when fate came to be perceived as national destiny rather than just as individual life. In Richard Wagner and in the early writings of Friedrich Nietzsche this German "Pan-Tragism" reached its nineteenth-century apogee.[16]

The strange attractor tragedy, then, promised a kind of transcendental mechanics that, joined with the potential of national relevance, pulled German literature and its most ambitious authors away from the heteroglossia of serialized narratives, from their compromises, their improvisations, and their dependence on embodied technicality.[17] As we have seen, to the common origin and linear divergence of character and fate in the tragic wedge the novel opposes their prosaic equidistance, and to the perpendicular welding of story to plot their intertwining in the narrative helix. When German authors in the 1850s and 1860s joined their European contemporaries in writing long and often serialized prose, they still did so with tragic and nationalist ambitions. The anti-Semitism that poisons the works of Wilhelm Raabe and Gustav Freytag is, in contrast to the lapses of Dickens and Balzac, an avatar of the tragic conflict, and as such essential to their narratives.[18] Even where "only" the fate of German national unity is at stake, as in Friedrich Spielhagen, the novels never gain the integrated forward momentum that comes from allowing the futurity and contingency of serialization to shape the narration. When with Theodor Fontane a confirmed Anglophile and admirer of Dickens came onto the Prussian scene in the 1870s, his writings, compared with those of his European and American contemporaries, already seemed quaint and formally unadventurous. Forty lost years in an artistic revolution are not easily made up.[19]

The lack of German contributions to the realist canon would remain an interesting, yet decidedly regional problem, were it not for the fact that the language of contemporary literary criticism was largely forged in the hearth of German tragic theory. This is the second factor that works against an acceptance of novels as semitechnical objects. Lukacs's early theory of the novel, Benjamin's hope for a pure language, Heidegger's *Auslegung,* and Gadamer's hermeneutics are the tributaries to a practice of criticism that even in its Marxist and postcolonial version is searching for some way of uncovering the pure word, of interrupting the text and revealing what is below or beyond it. Few, it is true, believe that outside the domain of law and politics a pure word can ever be heard as such—it appears always as a trope, both in the narrow rhetorical and in the wider narratological sense of the term. Still, the task of the interpreter, in this view, is quite literally to ex-tort, to untwist the helix of the text. The very great majority of academic writings on nineteenth-century narrative conform to this imperative of extortion.

Apart from the fact that the singularity of the pure word stands to be engulfed by the "Nile of language" that is the novel, interpretation-as-extortion misunderstands the fundamental incongruence between tragic criticism and realist texts. It consists in the fact that the *entire* project of realist writing, publishing, and reading functions, as we have seen, as a trope, as a forward-slanted, intertwined motion of fate and character, story and plot, that no act of interpretation can wrench to a standstill. There is no proposition, object, or instance in the stories of Lucien de Rubempré, or Pip, or Emma Bovary that would decisively interrupt the sequence of representation—in the first and last case, not even their more or less tragic deaths. There is no word or phrase, even if obsessively repeated, that would serve as more than as a marker of recognition. Even when authors begin to incorporate the interruption of tragic anagnorisis, as in Henry James, or the poetic recurrence of a "petite phrase," as in Proust, these do not function as truths that could derail the narrative vehicle.

One of the unspoken motivations in the search for an uncontorted story behind or around nineteenth-century novels is the institutional and often the personal need to teach the novel. Ever since secular hermeneutics made its way into the university curriculum in the nineteenth century, novels have been subjected to exegetical treatments that aim at extracting at least a minimal moral message from them. At times this practice closely hews to the procedures of scriptural readings, and novels take the place of a Passion from which personal meaning can be culled; at other times, the reconstruction of a novel's social context serves to exemplify the distance between historical and ideal circumstances. While such approaches may help to guide students toward reading, they are bound to disappoint in the long run. For the most part, nineteenth-century novels are either patently obvious about their message (Dickens is a case in point, but so is Balzac), they delight in paradoxical constructions, like Flaubert's advice to not follow the advice in books, or their ostensible message is vexingly vapid, like James's "Live all you can."

The primary pleasure in and of modern novels is not moral or hermeneutic, it is not even—this was the purpose behind showing narratives in their kinematic context—entirely human. Rather, it comes from a protointellectual abandonment to motions that were cosmic antagonists before the cylinders of the nineteenth century brought them to earth and forced them into a relation of convertibility. The pleasure of being pulled along while being able to reflect on that pulling, of falling in with a rhythm that is at once propulsive and retarding, and of immersing and distancing oneself at the same time is at the basis of a reading that is as much a relation to the world of machines as it is to the temporality of human life.

Despite the withdrawal of nineteenth-century kinematics from our life-world, this pleasure seems to have survived perfectly well the transition to different media. Radio plays in the 1930s and 1940s, and recently the emergence of sophisticated television shows such as *The Wire* and *Mad Men,* have elicited a reaction that repeats the relation between Dickens or Sue and their audience in astonishing detail. The persistence of this pleasure does not mean that this mode of constructing and appreciating narratives is the right one or the only one; the writers of the twentieth century who sought to arrest the literary machine with small parables, with anamorphic writing, with Mennipean mixtures, or with fractured stories have added immeasurably to the experience of literature. But as Federico Ferrari and Jean Luc Nancy have shown in their portrait of the novelistic enterprise, the prose that arises with the cylinders of the nineteenth century makes a peculiar experience of finitude available:

> From one page to the next, the prosaic [il prosaico] goes on, is constantly in the act of passing, whereas the poetic interrupts itself. The novel is exactly this impossibility to arrest itself, to enclose the infinite in the page. Not the endless search for a bad infinitude, not the infinite search for a meaning that is in itself complete and absolute, but the very experience, on the surface of the page, of the experience of the finitude of meaning. In the body of the novel, on the skin of its pages, the finite and fragile sense of daily existence is at stake, the quotidian passing among other bodies, which in their turn are finite and perfect. There is no beginning and no end in the finite writing of the novel because there is no absolute meaning of the story outside of itself, and because every body exposes on its skin, at the limits of its existence, all the meaning there is.[20]

Just as this prose incorporates the mechanical, so do the machines of the nineteenth century incorporate the "spiritual." We have seen how even in their most massive concretions as locomotives and steel mills they contain an inalienable core of history and of metaphysics, and how this core, through innumerable cylindrical processes and products, remained present in an epoch that professed to champion pure functionality.

Rescuing and articulating this core of meaning in mechanisms may prove to be an even more urgent task than saving and enjoying a kinematic mode of reading. The focus on motors and tools that has obscured the logic and history of transmissions always implied not only that the thermodynamic flow of energy on a cosmic scale was irreversible but also that the direction of this flow through machines would make transmissions necessarily subservient and inherently devoid of information. This focus has, in due course, led to the despoliation of energy sources and their environment, and the task now before engineers is to reevaluate this focus and its technical implications. "Alternative energy" generated by mechanical means involves rethinking and repositioning the function of transmissions. Not only have the accuracy and smoothness of transmissions become an ecological imperative, as Reuleaux predicted, but a contraption like the wind turbine actually represents an alternative to the hierarchy of machine parts. In contrast to a motor driving a transmission and storing its energy in the rotation of a flywheel, now the flywheel itself drives a motor to produce, rather than consume, energy. Again, it is a cylindrical bearing through which this reverse flow is transmitted. "For in the cylinder alone are certitudes to be found and without nothing but mystery."[21]

Notes

1. INTRODUCTION

1. This point will be recalled at various junctures in the following pages. Suffice it here to quote two sources. Hugo Horwitz (1933–34, 121): "The advanced technology of rotation has to be regarded as one of the most remarkable phenomena ever produced in human material culture. Without any precedents in nature, it is an original creation of the human mind. . . . It is the principle of modern technology to convert all reciprocal motion into rotational motion. The immense number of machines that are characteristic of today's industry, modern means of transport, and many household appliances would be impossible without the technical elements of one cylinder rotating in another." Hans Blumenberg (2001a, 44): "There is a hiatus between Lilienthal and the Brothers Wright: the flying machine is an original invention because it frees itself from the old dream of imitating the flight of birds and solves the problem with a new principle. The combustion engine (which also is an original invention) is in this case not as crucial and characteristic as the use of a propeller, for rotating elements are purely technical; they cannot be derived from *imitatio* or *perfectio* because nature knows no rotating organs. Is it too daring to claim that the airplane is so much part of the immanent technological process that the day of Kitty Hawk would have come even if never a bird had populated the skies?"

2. Kleist (1997b, 49–55); the critical German version is in Kleist (1997a, 317–31). For the philological commentary, see Kleist (1990, 1137–47). The secondary literature on this short text is vast; for an overview, see Oschmann (2007, 206–13) and Ruprecht (2006, 19–55).

3. For the important aesthetic implications of the genre of anecdotes, see Fenves (2001, 152–73). For the police reports that make up much of the *Berliner Abendblätter* and contributed largely to its initial popularity, see Barnert

(1997); see Wild (2002) for a specific account of the censorship imposed on the *Abendblätter*. For a chronicle of the events surrounding the publication and eventual demise of the paper, see Staengle (1997), particularly the discussion of Kleist's letters (404–10).

4. Incidentally, the order served as the title for a 1852 novel by "the German Walter Scott" Willibald Alexis, who is often credited with having connected German literature to European realism.

5. See Fox (1990).

6. Georg Büchner's drama *Dantons Tod* exploits to the utmost this coincidence of rationality, mechanics, and terror; see Müller-Sievers (2003, 118–27).

7. Schiller (1967); see also Behler (1995) and Berghahn (2004).

8. With his notion that "Sympathie" had to accompany graceful motion, Schiller revived a concept that had preoccupied him since his first, failed, medical dissertation in 1779. See Neubauer (1982) on the relation of medicine and aesthetics in early Schiller; Riedel (1985) has shown how the medical and anthropological concerns of Schiller's years at the Karlsschule carried over into the mature, "ideological" writings of the late 1790s and early 1800s.

9. "Grazie ist immer nur die Schönheit der durch Freyheit bewegten Gestalt" [Grace is always only the beauty of the physique that freedom sets in motion] (Schiller 1962, 265; trans., 2005, 134). On Schiller's concepts of grace and dignity, see Beiser (2005, 101–18); on his aesthetics of motion, see Oschmann (2007, 149–200). Strangely, von Wiese (1967, 211) claims that "it is highly unlikely that Kleist thought of Schiller's essay 'On Gracefulness and Dignity'" (Es ist kaum anzunehmen, dass Kleist bei seiner Schrift an Schillers Aufsatz "Über Anmut und Würde" gedacht hat).

10. Wild (2002) shows how Kleist's comedy *Der zerbrochene Krug*, which had its premiere under Goethe's direction in Weimar in 1808, tried to raise the same question of the fundamental difference between original sin and aesthetic education. See also Wild (2003).

11. Bredekamp (1993) shows how automata before 1800 were part of a quite different context of imitating motion than the industrial machines that followed them. See also von Matt (1971) and the first two pages of von Helmholtz's "On the Interaction of Natural Forces" (1854) in Helmholtz (1995, 18–45).

12. The "Marionettentheater" has been a touchstone in the development of literary theory for the last twenty-five years, particularly since de Man's essay "Aesthetic Formalization: Kleist's Über das Marionettentheater" (1984, 263–90), which interprets Kleist's anti-Schillerean polemics as a conflict, within the text, between mimetic and performative strategies of reading and writing. On the "realist" end of the spectrum is Berger (2000), who interviews puppeteers and adduces a great deal of Newtonian physics and mathematics.

13. "Dagegen sei diese Linie wieder, von einer anderen Seite, etwas sehr Geheimnißvolles. Denn sie wäre nichts anders, als der Weg der Seele des Tänzers" (Kleist 1997a, 319). "Jede Bewegung, sagte er, hätte einen Schwerpunct; es wäre genug, diesen, im Innern der Figur, zu regieren; die Glieder, welche nichts als Pendel wären, folgten, ohne irgendein Zuthun, auf eine mechanische Weise von selbst" [Every movement, he said, had a center of gravity; it was enough to control this, at the interior of the figure; the limbs, which were nothing

but pendulums, followed by themselves mechanically, without any assistance] (Kleist 1997a, 318; trans., Kleist 1997b, 50).

14. "Die Bewegungen seiner Finger [verhalten sich] zur Bewegung der daran befestigten Puppen ziemlich künstlich, etwa wie die Zahlen zu ihren Logarithmen oder die Asymptote zur Hyperbel" [An important subtext to Kleist's use of the mathematical graph as a trace of grace is Hogarth's praise of the undulating, "serpentine" line of civilized dance] (Kleist 1997a, 319; trans., 1997b, 50–51). See Hogarth (1997, 111).

15. For the complicated history of the distinction between metaphor and catachresis, see Parker (1990).

16. For the notion that Newtonian physics can be called imaginary as opposed to the "real" quality of Aristotelian physics and the "symbolic" quality of quantum physics, see Kassung (2001, 20–47).

17. See Gillispie (1990, 144–50).

18. One way of understanding this real-world insufficiency of Newtonian mechanics is to chart the role of friction in machines. In the demonstration devices of the Newtonians it was a negligible factor, to be analyzed away; in the emerging industrial waterwheels it became a crucial element of their construction, and the production and dissipation of heat through friction became a first step toward a comprehensive theory of thermodynamics. One iconic instance in this transition is brilliantly retold in Schaffer (1994, esp. 172–78).

19. One of the few interpreters to see this goal in Kleist is Ruprecht (2006, 36): "In Kleist, absolute dancerly grace is a non-human quality. . . . A crank figures as the superlative puppeteer."

20. See Rheinberger (1997, 1–23) and the succinct summary in Rheinberger (2005).

21. A splendid epistemic history of the pendulum can be found in Kassung (2007). Kassung describes the story of the pendulum as determined by the concepts "number" and "circle." Though Kassung often calls the pendulum a "machine," there is little reflection in his text on the difference between kinetics and kinematics, between the staged free fall of the pendulum and the forced rotation of the crank. The point of contact between the two would be the cycloid—the forced pendulum curve that Huygens discovered to be truly isochronous and brachistochrone. It is identical to the curve on a moving crank, like that of a driven locomotive wheel.

22. For the epochal significance of the crank, see White (1966, 114–15): "Students of applied mechanics are agreed that the technical advance which characterizes specifically the modern age is that from reciprocating motions to rotary motions. . . . Continuous rotary motion is typical of inorganic matter, whereas reciprocating motion is the sole form of motion found in living things. The crank connects these kinds of motion; therefore we who are organic find that crank motion does not come easily to us. . . . To use a crank, our tendons and muscles must relate themselves to the motion of galaxies and electrons. From this inhuman adventure our race long recoiled."

23. The patent for the parallel-motion linkage dates from 1784. See Watt's letter to Boulton on June 30, 1784: "I think it a very probable thing to succeed, and one of the most ingenious simple pieces of mechanism I have contrived."

In a letter to his son James from 1808, he writes: "Though I am not over anxious after fame, yet I am more proud of the parallel motion than of any other mechanical invention I have ever made." Quoted in Dickinson and Jenkins (1919/1989, 141, 142). The patent expired in 1800.

24. "Eine Gruppe von vier Bauern, die nach einem raschen Takt die Ronde tanzte, hätte von Tenier nicht hübscher gemalt werden können" (Kleist 1990, 556; translation, 1997b, 49).

25. For a contemporary definition of the *Reihen* dance, see Adelung (1811, 1051–52). For an analysis of Newton's "bucket experiment," in which a bucket full of water, suspended by a rope, is alternately made to rotate and then stopped to show the effect of centrifugal forces even in the absence of direct contact, see Ghins (1990).

26. Kleist (1990, 406, modified; trans., 1997c, 538). On the mechanical nature of tropes, see de Man (1984, 285–88).

27. Building on Friedrich Gottlieb Klopstock's reflections on the German hexameter and Karl Philipp Moritz's *Versuch einer deutschen Prosodie* of 1786, these projects culminate in Friedrich Hölderlin's call for a "reliable," mechanical art of tragedy making, a lawlike calculus ("gesetzlicher Kalkul"; Hölderlin 1998, 309) that will take poeticizing away from enthusiasts and put it in the hands of poetic engineers. See the "Epilogue" below.

28. See, for example, Rühlmann (1875, 1:1).

29. The canonical work on the history of scriptural exegesis is De Lubac (1998); on the emergence of secular from theological hermeneutics, see Dyck (1977). For the parallel procedure in the Jewish tradition, known by the acronym PaRDeS, see Theissen (2007, n. 7).

30. For the insistent return of images of falling and its opposite, re-surrection, see Schneider (2000).

31. The story of this differentiation is told in Martínez (2009, 1–37).

32. See Heidegger (2009, 307) (recently published preparatory notes for the "Technics" essay): "In what sense is 'continuous rotation the soul of technics'? Roll, wheel (the rotating, in such a way, that at the same time the center moves forward—car wheel)." [Inwiefern ist die "unausgesetzte Drehbewegung die Seele der Technik"? Walze, Rad (das Drehende, so zwar, dass sich zugleich der Mittelpunkt fortbewegt—Wagenrad).] The internal quotation is most likely from Reuleaux, whom Heidegger was reading at the time.

33. Blumenberg (2009) and (2010). See also the important collection of explanatory essays in Haverkamp and Mende (2009).

34. The relation between these two thinkers and their approaches is the subject of Zumbusch (2004). Coincidentally, Benjamin's maternal great-uncle was the eminent mathematician Arthur Moritz Schoenflies, who wrote (1901–8) the summary and retrospective entry "Kinematik" in Felix Klein's encyclopedia of applied mathematics. It contains (269) a succinct appreciation and analysis of Reuleaux's key terms.

35. This is by necessity an abbreviated argument that focuses on Benjamin's vocabulary in his later writings on the culture of the nineteenth century. Samuel Weber (2008, 53–94) shows that in Benjamin's earlier speculations on the

nature of language there emerges a concept of incessant translation as a means of rescuing language from the bonds of signification.

2. THE RISE OF KINEMATICS

1. Mayer (1876, 104). On the change in the understanding of causality that accompanied the rise of thermodynamics, see Kassung (2001, 160–64). The rise of thermodynamics itself has been recounted many times; three of the most insightful accounts are Smith (1998), Brush (1978), and Cardwell (1971).

2. The insistence on the analog world of motion transmission is meant to counterbalance, not contradict, recent emphasis on the archaeology of digital processes. Perhaps the most penetrating of these archaeologies is Siegert (2003). The focus of this extraordinary book is on the physiological and mathematical logic of these developments, which at times outpaced innovations in engineering and machine design—and which therefore gives the impression of running parallel to the kinematic history here told. For an immanent description of the change between eighteenth- and nineteenth-century conceptions of physics, see Maxwell (1876, preface): "Physical Science, which up to the end of the eighteenth century had been fully occupied in forming a conception of natural phenomena as the result of forces acting between one body and another, has now fairly entered on the next stage of progress—that in which the energy of a material system is conceived as determined by the configuration and motion of that system, and in which the ideas of configuration, motion, and force are generalised to the utmost extent warranted by their physical definitions."

3. On the emergence of "convertibility" from the thought of German and English natural philosophy, see Heimann (1974); see also Smith (1998, 126–49) and Rabinbach (1992, 45–64). The most authoritative formulation of the first law came from Hermann von Helmholtz (1847). It encompassed—in fact was partly proven by the aid of—the "machine" of the animal body that no longer was governed by imponderable forces. Helmholtz, like many of the great nineteenth-century scientists, was a brilliant and engaged popularizer of scientific discoveries who felt obligated to make the work in his and other laboratories transparent to the public. See his lecture "On the Conservation of Force" (1862–63), in Helmholtz (1995), and the shorter Königsberg lecture "The Interaction of Natural Forces," also in Helmholtz (1995). This sense of obligation to the general public, including workers and women, is characteristic of European science of the epoch. In the German context, the tradition of public scientific lectures was founded by Alexander von Humboldt with his pathbreaking *Kosmos-Vorlesungen* of 1827–28; in London, Faraday's lectures at the Royal Institution were immensely popular, and in France the lectures of François Arago, Auguste Comte, and the Saint-Simonians drew large crowds.

4. Harrison's fourth chronometer, the crowning achievement of eighteenth-century mechanics, needed to be sheltered from the environment so that its (self-) measurement would remain reliable; see L. Brown (1998, 233–48), Bredekamp (1993, 11–17), and Pynchon (1997, 316–26) for a description of how the chronometer continues to tick even when it's swallowed. See also

Zimmerman (1962, 3): "A watch mechanism . . . is not designed to transmit energy. The proper movement of its hand is its sole function. The energy stored in the spring is used only to overcome the frictional resistances encountered by the members of the mechanism." See Mumford (1967, 84): "If the invention of the mechanical clock heralded the new will-to-order, the use of the cannon in the fourteenth century enlarged the will-to-power; and the machine as we know it represents the convergence and the systematic embodiment of these two prime elements."

5. The "discovery" of the conservation of force is, as Kuhn (1959) has shown, a celebrated example of simultaneous discovery. One of the factors producing the simultaneity was the experimental work done in the machine shops. For a discussion and criticism of Kuhn, see Bevilacqua (1993).

6. Cournot, quoted, among others, in Canguilhem (2006, 131).

7. See Lowell (1971), who, alas, pays scant attention to kinematics; on the impact of the law of entropy on historiography and culture in the latter half of the nineteenth century, see Brush (1978).

8. See Thurston (1884, 441): "It may be asserted, as a general and fundamental principle, that, in all good engineering, the sole cause of waste of mechanical energy is friction."

9. For a Whiggish history of modern kinematics, see Reuleaux (1875, 3–27; trans., 1876, 1–25); see also Moon (2007), which provides an ample bibliography. There is such a thing as medieval kinematics, as Clagett (1959, 199–219) shows. Much like nineteenth-century kinematics, it was conceived as the science of the effects, rather than the causes, of motion, the difference being that the neglect of causes was entirely theoretical at the time.

10. Quoted in Willis (1870, viii).

11. See Hartenberg and Denavit (164, 7). See also Poinsot (1834, 23): "From the simple idea of a mere motion of translation, which carries forward at every instant all the equal molecules of the body through small equal and parallel lines in space, and from the simple idea of the rotation of the body about an axis, which remains immovable during this instant, results the complex idea of the most general motion of which a body is capable in absolute space. Nothing is more clear than this resolution of any kind of motion into two others which we can conceive perfectly, and which we may consider separately, since they are such that, if at every instant they were executed one after the other, every point in the body would be brought to the same place at which it arrives, by its natural motion, at the instant of which we are speaking." This is at the same time the founding principle of screw theory; see chapter 9 of this book.

12. "In kinematic analysis both the motions of particles and those of rigid bodies are of interest. The motion of a particle is necessarily linear, since it is not meaningful to speak of the rotation of a point. If a particle is moving on a straight line, it is said to have rectilinear motion; otherwise it has curvilinear motion. When a rigid body moves in such a way that each particle has the same motion, the motion is called translation. If each particle is, in addition, moving in a straight line, it is rectilinear translation; otherwise it is curvilinear translation. The type of motion most frequently of interest in mechanism study is plane motion. A body is said to have plane motion when its particles move in parallel

or coincident planes. If a body has plane motion, it may be translation, rotation, or a combination of the two. In plane rotation the path of each particle is a circle whose center is on a fixed axis perpendicular to the plane of rotation" (Zimmerman 1962, 16).

13. Poinsot (1837/1877, 34–35): "Pour abréger le discours, nous appelerons *couple* l'ensemble de deux forces, telle que P et –P, égales, parallèles et contraires, mais non appliqués au même point. La perpendiculaire commune AB, menée entre les directions des deux forces, sera *le bras de levier* du couple, et le produit P × AB de l'une des forces par le bras de levier en sera nommé *le moment.*" The saying among car racers is "Horsepower sells cars, torque wins races." For Michel Serres (1975; 1992; 1974, 173), Poinsot's discovery of an irreducible spatiality and temporality in rotation—or rather its conception as irreducible difference—is the decisive step toward modernity, which he defines as the epoch of the motor. Motors for Serres are "differential engines" insofar as they draw energy from a difference (in heat). The importance of the concept of "couple" and of Poinsot's statics and dynamics for Serres—perhaps the only contemporary philosopher with equal metaphysical and physical competence— cannot be overestimated.

14. This was the title for the 1876 English translation of the volume published just one year earlier by Reuleaux in German as *Theoretische Kinematik.* A second volume with a more practical bent followed in 1900. As there was, and is, considerable variability in the use of the terms *kinematics, kinetics,* and *dynamics,* here is the definition by Hunt (1978, 2) that guides the present account: "*Kinematics . . .* is that branch of dynamics that deals with motion on its own in isolation from the forces associated with motion. . . . The other branch of dynamics, *kinetics,* involves itself with forces, energy, momentum, inertia, dynamic stability, and equilibrium, and the like; kinetics is outside of the scope of this book, though it is of course important in the functioning of many mechanisms, sometimes of central importance."

15. Ampère (1834/1856, 48–49): "Elle [la science] doit d'abord s'occuper de toutes les considerations relatives aux espaces parcourus dans les différents mouvements, aux temps employés à les parcourir, à la determination des vitesses d'après les diverses relations qui peuvent exister entre ces espaces et ces temps. Elle doit ensuite étudier les différents instruments à l'aide desquels on peut changer un mouvement en un autre; ensorte qu'en comprenant, comme c'est l'usage, ces instruments sous le nom de machines, il faudra définir une machine, non pas comme on le fait ordinairement, *un instrument à l'aide duquel on peut changer la direction et l'intensité d'une force donnée, mais bien un instrument à l'aide duquel on peut changer la direction et la vitesse d'un mouvement donné.*" The first half of the translation is from Hartenberg and Denavit (1964, 15), who significantly leave out the second part. See also Smith and Wise (1989, 199) and the excellent account by Martínez (2009).

16. See Ferguson (1962, 195–97); Reuleaux (1875, 5–8) takes Watt's mechanism to be the foundational invention of modern kinematics. On the importance of patents in the early days of the Industrial Revolution, see Robinson (1972). Interestingly, Robinson quotes from an unpublished letter from Small to Watt concerning the first patent in 1769 for the separate condenser; at that

time, Small believed that two separate classes of machines were necessary, one "class for producing reciprocal motions, and another for producing motions round axes" (120).

It can be—and has been—argued that other inventions of Watt were as important as the parallel motion, notably the indicator diagram by which the internal state of a cylinder could be checked (see Dickinson 1963; Chadarevian 1993; Brain and Wise 1994) and the governor (see Koschorke 2000). The latter is crucial for the history of cybernetics; the former, as we will see, for the emergence of self-inscribing machines. Forbes (1958, 153–54) voices the kinematic consensus when he states: "Indeed, the steam-engine would have remained an accessory to the water-mill, pumping up water that worked the wheel, had not Watt by his invention of the 'sun-and-planet motion' and his 'parallel motion' solved the problem of converting the oscillation of the beam into rotary motion." This is not quite right. The sun-and-planet gear was used on the working end of the beam, where it drove a wheel that would then impart rotational motion. But as long as the motor end of the beam was only pulled and not pushed, that motion was jerky and could not be used, for example, to drive spinning machines.

17. See Thurston (1902, 110–11).

18. The science of lubrication is called tribology, and a tribological history of the Industrial Revolution would result in an entirely probable and promising narrative. Both tribology and kinematics are negentropic enterprises, with kinematics counting on the power of mathematical abstraction while tribology used first animal, then mineral, and now synthetic substances to guarantee adhesion and to reduce friction. In contrast to the inventors of phonography, telephony, and similar media of the late nineteenth century, who initially used entire animal and even human organs as interfaces (see Siegert 1998, 82), early tribologists experimented with formless animal substances such as lard and tallow and used leather rings as seals. This difference between formless animal substances and whole organs seems to be gruesomely significant for the distinction between machines and media. Animal fat and tallow are part of the "formless" that, like steam, cement, pulp, asphalt, iron, water, glass, and excrement, is produced by—or runs through—the cylindrical machines of the nineteenth century. For a brief definition and introduction to tribology, see Buckley (1985, 3–20).

19. Boulton promised to deliver to Watt engines "with as great a difference of accuracy as there is between the blacksmith and the mathematical instrument maker" (quoted in Ferguson 1962, 189). On the difficulties of boring cylinders with sufficient accuracy, and the subsequent rise of machine tools, see Paulinyi (1997, 319–52).

20. James Watt, quoted in Routledge (1989, 8) and Carnegie (1905, 110). In a letter to Boulton quoted in Muirhead (1859, 289), he more lightly calls it "a new hare." For a discussion of the change in the modes of scientific discovery at the turn of the nineteenth century, see Schaffer (1986).

21. Stephenson's link motion, by means of which the direction of rotation is "changed" (i.e., translated in different directions), is perhaps the second most important linkage in the early nineteenth century. See Routledge (1989, 16–17). After his retirement from business, Watt occupied himself with further

developments of linkages: he perfected a perspective-drawing pantograph and invented another linkage that could copy sculptures in three dimensions (see Carnegie 1905, 129–31).

22. See Willis (1870, 27): "The path-motion of a rotating piece may be considered as unlimited in extent in either direction, since the piece may go on performing any number of revolutions in the same direction. But a piece that travels in a right line is necessarily limited in its motion either way, to the length of that line." Aristotle deduced from this limitation that translation was an imperfect motion (see chapter 3). Cardwell (1972, 90–91) shows that Watt, like many of his successors, had imagined a "direct rotative engine," consisting of two concentric cylinders, the inner one outfitted with a blade. The difficulties in building such a contraption were overcome in the turbines of the 1880s. The Wankel motor is a direct rotative engine, built on a principle discovered by Reuleaux.

23. The difference between kinematics and dynamics (or kinetics, in Hunt's terminology) is well exemplified in the analysis of the slider-crank linkage. For the kinematicist it does not matter whether the linkage is driven at the rotating end through a crank or at the slider end through some form of straight-acting force (as is the case in combustion engines). From a dynamic point of view, however, it is important to recognize that every oscillating motion has a dead point that needs to be overcome—for example, through the inertial motion of a flywheel—to keep motion "alive." No locomotive could start if its linkages were aligned in a straight line.

24. Reuleaux (1875, 256–57). Heidegger (2009, 309), reading and citing Reuleaux, comes very close to deriving his notion of *Gestell* from the "technical" term of fixing one of the links of a linkage. Linkages without *Gestell* are often the subject of kinetic sculpture.

25. One set of Reuleaux's models was sold to Cornell University and is now part of a brilliant site called Kinematic Models for Design Digital Library (KMODDL; http://kmoddl.library.cornell.edu/), where many of them can be viewed in motion. The site also makes available some of the most important books on the history and practice of kinematics. I owe the *spiritus rector* of the Cornell group, Frank Moon, a great debt of gratitude.

One of the more astonishing products of kinematic scholarship, published just before the dominance of digital design programs, is Hrones and Nelson's gigantic *Analysis of the Four-Bar Linkage* (1951); on more than seven hundred pages it shows various configurations of linkages and the coupler-point curves they produce—another evidence for the grace and surprising unpredictability of forced motion.

Theo Jansen's "strandbeasts," finally, are large and complex linkages made from discarded plastic tubing; they are propelled by wind and have primitive (analog) sensors that turn them away from the water. Some have "lived" unguided for more than two weeks. They can be seen at www.strandbeest.com/index.php, and on various YouTube videos.

26. On the political stakes in the rise of physiology in the German universities, see Lenoir (1992); in an obvious effort to ingratiate kinematics to physiologists, Reuleaux (1900, 728–77) appended a "Kinematik im Thierreich"

(Kinematics in the Animal Kingdom) that demonstrates the continuity between physiological and kinematic descriptions of animal motion. For a comparative history of engineering education in France, Great Britain, Germany, and the United States in the nineteenth century, see König (1999, 167–232), and on the tensions between universities and the various institutes training mechanical engineers, see Radkau (2008, 169–84, 144): only when the Kaiser intervened in 1899 were polytechnic institutes given the right to award doctorates.

27. See the collection in Helmholtz (1995).

28. Reuleaux (1876, 22; Ger., 1875, 26): "The question is to make the science of machinery deductive." For an appreciation of Reuleaux's work, see Weihe (1925) and Moon (2003). Moon (2007), which gives a biographical sketch (47–58), is the first comprehensive discussion of Reuleaux's kinematics in English. Reuleaux became important for readers of Deleuze and Guattari (1998), perhaps the last great work of modernist machine philosophy in the vein of Giedeon (1948) and Mumford (1967), and for scholars who tried to work out the implications of Jacques Lacan's theory that the symbolic order resembles a machine. By far the most penetrating attempt in this respect is Berz (2001). It tells a counterstory to the present account of kinematics in that it concentrates on mechanisms that interrupt motion (like escapements in clocks). Reuleaux pays considerable attention to these elements (which he calls *Sperrgetriebe*), and Berz develops a fully convincing logic of interruption and its usage in firing mechanisms. The vanishing point of his analysis is the machine gun, in which the interruption of motion causes its continuation. Berz places this development against a background of standardization and militarization in the latter half of the nineteenth century and the beginning of the twentieth to paint a truly impressive (and depressing) picture of weapons technology. This brilliant and exhaustive book is the reason why the present attempt can dispense with a discussion of weapons as cylindrical phenomena.

29. "Every motion which occurs in the machine thus connects itself with one leading idea, of which the single propositions considered contain special applications. Just as the old philosopher compared the constant gradual alteration of things to a flowing, and condensed it into the sentence: 'Everything flows'; so we may express the numberless motions in that wonderful production of the human brain which we call a machine in one word, 'Everything rolls.' Through the whole machine, hidden or apparent, the same fundamental law of rolling applies to the mutual motions of the parts" (Reuleaux 1876, 84; Ger., 1875, 87). It is of considerable importance for the discussion of Marx's social kinematics that Reuleaux (1875, 67), in the first mentioning of rolling, hesitates between two words, *rollen* and *wälzen* (rendered as "rolling" and "turning" in Reuleaux [1876, 65]). Marx's notion of *Umwälzung*—in contrast to "revolution"—must be read in this kinematic context.

30. Reuleaux (1875, 67; trans., 1876, 64).

31. "All relative motions of con-plane figures may be considered to be rolling motions, and the motion of any points in them can be determined so soon as the centroids of the figures are known" (Reuleaux 1876, 64; Ger., 1875, 67). See also Moon (2007, 71–72; 003, 266–67).

32. "A machine is a combination of resistant bodies so arranged that by their means the mechanical forces of nature can be compelled to do work accompanied by certain determinate motions" (Reuleaux 1876, 35; Ger., 1875, 38). This is the definition quoted by Deleuze and Guattari (1998, 141).

33. Here is a modern definition of rolling (Harrisberger 1961, 53): "Rolling contact is a special case of motion transmission by direct contact. . . . The criteria for rolling contact are: 1. A point on one element cannot successively contact more than one point on the other element. 2. The relative velocity of the coincident points must be zero. . . . 3. The point of contact . . . *must* lie on the line of centers."

34. Reuleaux (1876, 65; Ger., 1875, 68).

35. Heidegger (2009, 307): "The roll, the wheel (the rotating [das Drehende] in such a way that at the same time its center moves forward—the wagon wheel." The most expansive discussion of cycloids in Reuleaux is in Reuleaux (1900, 3–140).

36. See Reuleaux (1900, 5–7), as well as Berz (2001, 84–92) and Kassung (2007, 185–217).

37. Reuleaux (1900, 97–99): "the reciprocity of rolling" (die Gegenseitigkeit der Rollung).

38. Reuleaux (1875, 90; trans., 1876, 87).

39. Reuleaux (1876, 91; Ger., 1875, 94).

40. Reuleaux (1900, 165).

41. See also Berz (2001, 98–104), who concentrates on the "Schloss" (lock) as the crucial element in weapon design.

42. This striving for generality was also behind Reuleaux's ill-fated attempt to devise a logical notation that would transfer the design of machines from the machine shop to the logician's desk. See Reuleaux (1875, 243–71; trans., 1876, 273–74). Reuleaux invested equal energy in the invention of words for machine parts. The naming of machine parts is a remarkable example of Adamic language, as these objects were unnatural, nameless inventions. While the English words *crank, coupler, follower, governor,* and *guide* seem to be taken from the characters of a Drury Lane comedy, the German enacts the (equally hilarious) propensity for agglutination: *Druckkraftorgan, Schubkurbelkette, Kurbelkapselwerk,* to say nothing of *Stellhemmwerk* and *Kapselräderwerk.* Once his kinematics was internationally accepted (in particular after Kennedy's English translation of 1876), Reuleaux became concerned with the translation and standardization of kinematic terminology; see Reuleaux (1900, 7–13).

43. Reuleaux (1876, 87; Ger., 1875, 597 n.). Ducati, the Italian motorcycle manufacturer, builds its engines with a "desmodromic" valve design. Closing and opening of the valve are actuated by a rigid link rather than by springs in an effort to eliminate "valve float" at high rpms. This is a pleasing example of replacing a "force-closure," where "cosmic" forces such as gravity and elasticity still play a role, with a "pair-closure," where one element encloses the other. The disadvantage is that such linkages require extremely precise machining and strong materials.

44. Reuleaux (1876, 226; Ger., 1875, 222).

45. The chapter covers pages 201–46 in the 1876 translation and pages 195–242 in the original German edition.

46 . Reuleaux (1876, 244; Ger., 1875, 240).

47. Reuleaux (1876, 235–36; Ger., 1875, 231).

48. Reuleaux (1876, 235–36; Ger., 1875, 231).

49. Reuleaux (Ger., 1875, 514). This portion of the text is not included in Kennedy's English translation of 1876, which merely summarizes the chapter on the social impact of machines (Reuleaux 1875, 514–30), citing the hope (610) that it may receive independent publication.

3. THE VALUATION OF MOTIONS

1. The strongest arguments for the importance of these relations come from Canguilhem (1975) and even more from his student Simondon (1958, 85–112), who show how the neglect of kinematic logic artificially built up the unbridgeable opposition between man and machine, which in turn has distorted Western thinking about the "Question of Technology."

2. See Schild (1967, 116).

3. This view, then, adds a crucial dimension of formal and technical constraint to Heidegger's view that bridges are not themselves technical implements but things that gather essential aspects of being human; see Heidegger (2004, 146–56) ("Bauen, Wohnen, Denken").

4. On Benjamin, see Weigel (1997, 1–23). The fraught notion of "epoch," whose use ranges from historical division to phenomenological "bracketing," is literally linked to the suspension of motion; see the volume edited by Herzog and Koselleck (1987). See also Blumenberg (1983, 468): "What does one expect to see when the question of a change of epoch is posed? Since all history is composed of changes, the 'epoch-making' movements must be assumed to be both copious and rapid but also to move in a single, unambiguous direction and to be structurally interconnected, mutually dependent. He who speaks of the reality of a change of epoch takes on the burden of demonstrating that something is definitively decided. It must be possible to show that something is present that cannot be disposed of again, that an irreversible change has been produced."

5. See Siegert (1999, 166–85).

6. See Schivelbusch (1988, 64–69) and Benjamin (2006b, 81–82).

7. Spengler (1923, 1189): "Ihr Körper wird immer geistiger, immer verschwiegener. Diese Räder, Walzen und Hebel reden nicht mehr. Alles, was entscheidend ist, zieht sich ins Innere zurück." Benjamin (2006b, 190–91): "This development is taking place in many areas. A case in point is the telephone, where the lifting of a receiver has taken the place of the steady movement that used to be required to crank the older models. With regard to countless movements of switching, inserting, pressing, and the like, the 'snapping' by the photographer had the greatest consequences. . . . Baudelaire speaks of a man who plunges into the crowd as into a reservoir of electric energy." For a criticism of Benjamin's view of the urban experience as a series of shocks, see Moretti (2005, 114–29). On the enthusiasm for communication with ghosts, see Andriopoulos (2006).

8. The following should be read as a kinematically focused version of Hans Blumenberg's metaphorological investigations into the paradigms "Organic and Mechanical Background Metaphorics" and "Geometric Symbolism und Metaphorics" in Blumenberg (2010, 62–76 and 115–32).

9. Plato, *Nomoi* 893a–895b, and *Timaios* 34a (trans., Plato 2003). For good measure, Plato adds: "And as this circular movement required no feet, the universe was created without legs and without feet." For a commentary, see Gauss (1961, 216–21). Oliver (2005a, 14) unfortunately does not distinguish between circular and rotational motion. On the function of sphericity as a metaphor (not a symbol) of perfection, see Blumenberg (1987, 169).

10. Kepler (1981).

11. Aristotle, *Physics* 8.5–10 (Aristotle 1984, 427–46). See also Aristotle, *On the Heavens*, chs. 3–7 (Aristotle 1984, 472–76). It is remarkable that even such deeply penetrating texts as Bröcker (1964, 49), which claims that "the disquieting mystery that Aristotle's philosophy seeks to solve and that keeps it out of breath [is]: the mystery of motion as the being of non-being" (das beunruhigende Rätsel, das die arist. Philosophie lösen will und das sie in Atem hält: das Rätsel der Bewegung als des Seins des Nichtseienden), do not attend to Aristotle's distinction between (perfect) rotation and (imperfect) translation.

12. On the difference between Plato and Aristotle with regard to motion— the difference between imitation and causation, roughly speaking—see Berti (1985); for a reading of the last chapters of book 8 as the culmination of Aristotle's vision of change and eternity, see Sachs (1995, 227–31). Bachelard (1994, 236) sensualizes this theological predicament disarmingly: "Everything round invites a caress."

13. Dante Alighieri, *La divina commedia* 33.127–45. Kinematically speaking, both the *inferno* and the *purgatorio* are screws, and traces of the theology of the screwing motion will find their way into the novel of the nineteenth century. Beckett (1974, 21–22) was well aware of this genealogy.

14. Aquinas, *Summa contra Gentiles* 3.3.82 (1934, 207): "For there is no contrary to the circular movements of the heavenly bodies, so that there can be nothing violent in them: whereas there are movements contrary to that of the lower bodies; for instance downward movement is contrary to upward movement." See also Oliver (2005a, 153): "The celestial motion is an embodiment of creative and sustaining intellective motion: if we could 'see' thought, it would look like celestial rotation. Therefore, on Aquinas' view, one looks for an explanation of celestial motion that encompasses the spheres' exalted cosmological status and points directly to an immaterial source of being which is imparted via the heavens' motion." On the circularity of incarnation, see Oliver (2005b, 67). On the secular tradition of medieval kinematics, in particular the distinction between a science of motion that investigates causes (dynamics) and a science of motion that is concerned only with the description of effects (kinematics), see Clagett (1959, 205–19).

15. See Nicholas of Cusa, *De ludo globi* 1.8–22 (in Nicholas of Cusa 2001, 1185–92) and Blumenberg (2001b), who draws from this dialogue the most momentous consequences.

16. See Frautschi et al. (2008, 60–62).

17. The emergence of central perspective obviously is a much more complex story than can be presented here. For a sophisticated overview of the impact of perspectival painting and thinking, see Field (1997, 20–61), Damisch (1994, 3–55) (plus the important critique of Damisch by Davis 1996b), and Summers (2007, 43–77). Their common text of reference is Panofsky (1994). Panofsky argues that the human eye—more specifically its mobile sphericity—is excluded from the flat constructions of linear perspective. On the ancient sources of the intromission-extramission debate, see Bartsch (2006, 58–67); on the importance of the kinematics of vision, see Crone (1999, 35–71); for a particularly striking example, see L. Steinberg (1987) and Edgerton (1987).

18. See Alberti (1988, 7). Fundamental for Alberti is Grafton (2000); see also Chastel (1991).

19. See Wittkower (1953).

20. See Biagioli (2003).

21. On the art of memory, see Yates (1966, 118, fig. 3). For an example of how memory houses were actually employed in the fifteenth century, see Kent (2002).

22. See Ong (1958, 53–91). Two examples, reproduced in Ong's book, can now be seen in the digital catalog of the Bibliothèque Nationale: one is from Celaya (1525, screen 140, http://gallica.bnf.fr/ark:/12148/bpt6k109374h/f140.image), and one from Tartaret (1493, screen 117, http://gallica.bnf.fr/ark:/12148/bpt6k52888x/f117.image). Both represent images of syllogistic linearity before that, too, was taken over by the algebra of mnemonic names.

23. See Ray (1682), Müller-Wille (1999), and Barsanti (1992).

24. See Pacioli (1980, 23). On the Platonic solids, see Kemp (1990, 63–64) and Vesely (2004, 155–56). On universal languages, see Slaughter (1982, vii); for a strictly perspectival treatment of the alphabet, see the images from Hans Lencker's *Perspectiva literaria* (1567) in "Perspectiva Literaria," January 30, 2004, www.spamula.net/blog/archives/000292.html.

25. See Ficino (1576/1959, 1461), as well as Leinkauf (2005) and Hankins (2005), who chart the reception of the *Timaios* in the Renaissance and early modernity. The *Timaios* would again become a central text of reference for German *Naturphilosophie*, beginning with Schelling's own commentary in 1794.

26. See Kepler (1938, 26), and Copernicus, *On the Revolutions* 1.1 (1995): "In the beginning we should remark that the world is globe-shaped; whether because this figure is the most perfect of all, as it is an integral whole and needs no joints; or because this figure is the one having the greatest volume and thus is especially suitable for that which is going to comprehend and conserve all things; or even because the separate parts of the world, i.e., the sun, moon, and stars are viewed under such a form; or because everything in the world tends to be delimited by this form, as is apparent in the case of drops of water and other liquid bodies, when they become delimited of themselves. And so no one would hesitate to say that this form belongs to the heavenly bodies."

What is being summarized here in near-criminal brevity has been the subject of Hans Blumenberg's most exciting book, *The Genesis of the Copernican World* (1987). Blumenberg is interested in circumscribing the scientific and theological space in which Copernicus's *De revolutionibus* could appear (and be dedicated to the pope, without immediate repercussions), and in understanding what parts of Copernicus's claim were taken up by later interpreters. At the heart of Corpernicus's proposal, and of Blumenberg's book, is a distinction that also appears in the present context: the distinction between the earth's diurnal motion (its axial rotation) and its eccentric orbit (its curvilinear motion). Blumenberg sometimes puts great emphasis on this difference and sometimes elides it. It would be very rewarding indeed to read Blumenberg's book, and the many texts that prepare and echo it, in light of the shifting importance of this distinction.

27. On the homogeneity of space, see Damisch (1994, 58), Panofsky (1994), and Koyré (1957, 58–109). Koyré (1965, 74) cites Descartes's *Le monde* with this explanation of translational motion: "God conserves everything by one continuous action, and consequently, does not conserve it as it may have been some time previously, but precisely as it is at the very instant in which He conserves it. But of all movements, it is only right-line motion that is entirely simple, and whose whole nature is comprised in an instant. For, to conceive right-line motion, it is sufficient to think that a body is in action to move to a certain side, which is something that is found in each of the instants that can be determined during the time that it moves. Whereas, in order to conceive of circular motion, or any other that may occur, one needs to consider at least two of its instants, and the relation that there is between them."

28. See Kanitschneider (1984, 112). Early in the first day of the *Dialogues,* Galileo praises Plato for the theory that "these world bodies, after their creation and the establishment of the whole, were for a certain time set in straight motion by their Maker. Then later, reaching certain definite places, they were set in rotation one by one, passing from straight to circular motion, and have ever since been preserved and maintained in this. A sublime concept, and worthy indeed of Plato." Koyré (1965, 201–20; the Galileo quote is on 213) tries to make sense of this spurious attribution to Plato. Remarkable in this as in many other discussions is the slippage from rotational to circular motion—it is the geometric fixation on the solar system as a whole that makes it possible. See para. 30 of Descartes's *Principles of Philosophy* (Descartes 1991, 96).

29. See Gillispie (1990, 144–50) and Koyré (1965, 3–24). Newton's own intense theological concerns, in particular his defense of Arianism, did impinge on the formation of his philosophy; see Oliver (2005a, 157–62). But the eighteenth century was able to disregard these concerns and take the emphasis on mathematical objectivity as an antitheological commitment. On the flattening of hierarchies of motion, see Oliver (2005a, 171): "Newton therefore describes not a hierarchy of motions which can stretch up to participate qualitatively in a transcendent source of motion, but rather a flattened, extended, quantified and monadic universe of discrete objects whose motion does not require any explanations by reference to other beings."

30. See Jammer (1997, 59–84). Cohen (1980, 52–154) sees in Newton's ability to abstract from phenomena, to work out the mathematical consequences of a system, and then to reapply his results to physical bodies the central elements of his "style."

31. See Newton (1995, 333–35); see also Oliver (2005a, 156–57) and Kant (1968b, 264).

32. Newton (1995, 335). The exchange with Bentley is amply discussed in Koyré (1965, 201–20). For a reminder of the difference between orbital and rotational motion, see Schell (1870, 11): "If the earth, for example, did not possess axial rotation, its annual motion around the sun would consist in a curvilinear translation, by virtue of which all of its points would describe parallel and congruent ellipses." (Würde die Erde z.B. keine Axendrehung besitzen so bestände ihre jährliche Bewegung um die Sonne in einer krummlinigen Translation, vermöge welcher alle ihre Punkte parallele und congruente Ellipsen beschreiben würden.)

33. Of course Newton was perfectly aware of the dynamics of rotational motion; among many others, the second example for his first law of motion is a "spinning hoop" (Newton 1995, 233), and the solar system as a whole can be conceived as a rotating body with the sun as its center. His famous bucket experiment (see Ghins 1990, 29–50) is designed to show the absoluteness of rotational motion. What is at stake in the transition from Newtonian dynamics to machine kinematics is the origin, measure, and dominance of rigid body rotation.

A similar argument as that made here looking forward to the dominance of the machine paradigm could be made looking backward on Newton's dispute with the Cartesians, who maintained that the circular motion of the planets resulted from the rotation of dense vortices. For Descartes and Newton's contemporary Huygens, the idea of a force acting instantaneously across the empty skies was philosophically so repellent that they instead assumed the "System of the World" to be an analog machine in which motion was transmitted by contiguity. See Koyré (1965, 53–138).

34. I am using the excellent new web-based translation by Ian Johnston (2008); the German is in Kant (1968a, 234–35). It is remarkable that Kant exemplifies the repulsive force with exactly that phenomenon that will drive the Industrial Revolution: the "expansive force" of steam ("vapours"). Kant is not unjustified in imputing to Newton the proposition of a repulsive force. Analyzing the consequences of Boyle's law that the pressure of a gas is inversely proportional to its volume—yet another important relation for the conception of steam engines—Newton conceived of a force that makes particles repel each other. But this microscopic force is not on the same level of importance and certainty as gravitational force and certainly was not conceived by Newton as playing a role in the configuration of the solar system. See Cohen (1980, 75–78); see also Koyré (1965, 19 n. 1): "It seems to me quite certain that Newton arrived at the conclusion that a purely mechanical explanation of attraction was perfectly impossible because, in order to do so, he had to postulate another—less awkward, yet still non-mechanical—power, namely, that of repulsion."

35. Kant (2008; Ger., 1968a, 263, 264).

36. Kant (2008; Ger., 1968a, 264).

37. See Lalla (2003), Kant (2005, 147–207), and Müller-Sievers (2009). For a discussion of the treatise in the history of Copernican revolutions (which Kant would later invoke in his *Critique of Pure Reason*), see Blumenberg (1987, 573–94).

38. Kant (1968a, 263, 264).

39. Kant (2008; Ger., 1968a, 286).

40. Kant (1968a, 287). The essay's full title (quoting the prize question of the Berlin Academy of Science) is "Untersuchung der Frage, ob die Erde in ihrer Umdrehung um die Achse, wodurch sie die Abwechslung des Tages und der Nacht hervorbringt, einige Veränderung seit den ersten Zeiten ihres Ursprungs erlitten habe und woraus man sich versichern könnte welche von der Königl. Akademie der Wissenschaften zu Berlin zum Preise für das jetztlaufende Jahr aufgegeben worden" (Kant 1968c, 1:183–91).

41. The same assumption is carried over into Kant's epistemological and critical philosophy, which is equally characterized by oppositional forces such as intuition and concept, sensibility and understanding, duty and inclination, machine and organism, and so forth. German idealism and Romantic aesthetics are fueled to a large degree by the desire to overcome these oppositions. See Müller-Sievers (1997, 65–89); one of the best accounts of the importance of Kant's natural philosophy for Hegel is still Horstmann (1990).

42. Schelling (2000, 77; 2001, 150).

43. Oken (1847, 33).

44. See Hegel (1986, 101 (§270).

45. Goethe (1999, 47 (#391). A simile from Goethe's admirer George Eliot (2000, 27) shows how potent the notion of rotation was: "In short, woman was a problem which, since Mr. Brooke's mind felt blank before it, could be hardly less complicated than the revolutions of an irregular solid."

46. See Osten (2002, 213–29).

47. It must be recalled that even though translational motion as inertial motion is posited as "natural" in the Newtonian worldview, it does not exist as such unless it is forced: "Postulating a world in which pure inertial motion, uniform and rectilinear, [exists], is utterly impossible" (Koyré 1965, 69; see also Kassung [2001, 40–47], for whom this fact is proof that classical, Newtonian physics is, in the Lacanian sense, imaginary).

48. Baudelaire (1995, 40).

49. Ferguson (1962, 205). See also Sylvester's own witty account in Sylvester (1875).

50. Becker (1875, 45).

51. Kempe (1877).

4. THE CYLINDER AS MOTOR

1. See "The Machine Lathe," in chapter 5 below. For Boulton's Soho works, see Dickinson (1958, 183–85). Hawkins (1904, 39) gives these somewhat circuitous reasons for the superiority of the cylinder in his *New Catechism of the Steam Engine*: "*Ques.* Why is the cylinder the most approved form for its office of transforming energy of combustion into work? *Ans.* Because, 1st, the circular form is the strongest; 2nd, it is easier to make and repair; and 3rd, it is best adapted to fit the round form of the piston." The fact that a perfect circle can be drawn by means of a compass whereas a straight line always requires a straight line as ruler is at the basis of this preference for the cylinder from the point of view of manufacturability. See Kempe (1877).

2. See Landes (2003, 298–99). This book has been a major source of inspiration for the present account. Piet Bertema kindly consulted the Cruquius engine's logbook and found that in 1868 the cylinder consumed twelve pounds of tallow per twenty-four hours as lubrication material.

3. On the practice of hiding large steam engines in elaborate architectural structures to diminish their uncanniness, see Wise (1999).

4. Properly speaking, the transformation of motion in locomotives occurs by means of a crosshead, which accomplishes its task mainly by virtue of its material strength and its precision. Interestingly, Watt had taken out a patent for the crosshead joint as well but had decided against it because the available steel was not strong enough and its surfaces could not be planed without the aid of precision machine tools; see Paulinyi (1997, 334–35).

5. Reuleaux (1875, 231; trans., 1876, 235).

6. For a rather imaginative account of the eroticism of locomotives, see Asendorf (1993, 105): "Of the locomotive's three forms of motion—the up and down of the pistons [?], the circular motion of the wheels, and the movement forward through space—it was particularly the first whose up and down suggested the back and forth of the legs in human and animal mobility (and the thought of sexual intercourse)." For a more sober account, see W. Weber (1997, 171–214); see also the opening pages of Sternberger (1955).

7. The full quote from *La bête humaine* (Zola 1966, 1127–28): "C'était une de ces machines d'express, à deux essieux couplés, d'une elegance fine et géante, avec ses grandes roues légères reunites par des bras d'acier, son pontrail large, ses reins allongés et puissantes, toute cette logique et toute cette certitude qui font la beauté souveraine des êtres de métal, la precision dans la force."

8. See Sternberger (1955) and Schivelbusch (1986). On the "invention" of the horizon, see Koschorke (1990).

9. See Giedion (1948, 130–68) and W. Weber (1997, 133–37). Traction engines are objects of intense veneration and nostalgia in Great Britain, and their conservators have built up impressive web-based archives. See, e.g., the University of Reading's "Victorian Farming" website, www.reading.ac.uk/merl/nof/victorianfarming/index.php, as well as the photo archive of surviving traction engines at www.steamscenes.org.uk/.

5. THE CYLINDER AS TOOL

1. See the classic account by Foucault (2002, 240–45) and the imaginative reinterpretation by Vogl (2002, 335–46).

2. See Bashforth (1957, 137–39). For a graphic overview of the entire process of pig iron manufacture, see Camp and Francis (1951, 283).

3. See Bashforth (1959, 16–89). On the Bessemer and later open-hearth process, see Rolt (1970, 178–87). Open-hearth furnaces are rectangular; nonetheless, cylindrical shapes dominate every blast furnace assembly. Aside from the elements mentioned above, there are the smokestacks, the calcination kilns, the hot-blast stoves, and the various pipes and containers that catch and clean the escaping gases, to say nothing of the innumerable ovens, pumps, tanks, and

miles of connecting pipe with which chemicals released in the coking process are recovered; see Camp and Francis (1951, 233).

4. This precise moment of transition is depicted in Adolph Menzel's painting *Iron Rolling Mill* (1872–75). Michael Fried's interpretation (2002, 118–24) that the introduction of the red-hot ingot between the rollers represents an "offense to vision," needs to be augmented by this kinematic dimension.

5. See Paulinyi (1997, 403): "The often misunderstood central importance of rolling consists in the fact that in contrast to forging with the hammer it is a machine-tool technique. In both cases, form is changed through pressure; but in the case of forging the result is in the hands of the man who holds and guides the workpiece on the anvil. . . . [In rolling] the results of the transformation—which forms can be rolled with what precision—are due, not to the personal abilities of the steel worker, but predominantly to the error-free functioning of the rolling mill." (Die sehr oft verkannt zentrale Bedeutung des Walzens liegt darin, dass es im Unterschied zum Schmieden mit dem Hammerwerk eine Maschinen-Werkzeug-Technik ist. In beiden Fällen geht es um eine Druckumformung, aber beim Schmieden liegt das Ergebnis in den Händen des Mannes, der auf dem Amboß das Werkstück hält und führt. . . . Das Ergebnis des Umformens—die Möglichkeiten, welche Formen mit welcher Präzision gewalzt werden können—bestimmten nicht die persönlichen Fähigkeiten der Walzarbeiter, sondern vorrangig die Konstruktion und das fehlerfreie Funktionieren der Walzstrecke.)

6. The nomenclature of the process, with its "angles of bite," "vertical force," "radial thrust," and "point of no-slip," varies in the literature and between countries. For a detailed description, see Bashforth (1962, 67–100, esp. 79).

7. See below, and Magdanz (2006) for the additional relation between rolling and waltzing *(walzen)*.

8. For an overview of shapes and the sequence of rolling, see Bashforth (1962, 87). The collective name for these products is "semifinished materials," in German *Halbzeug*. This latter notion has gained considerable weight in recent discussions about the work and status of absolute metaphors as they are conceived by Hans Blumenberg. His archaeology of preconceptual processes treats absolute metaphors as "semifinished materials" that are finished only when a more stable language coalesces around them. See Campe (2009, 1).

9. See Camp and Francis (1951, 1120–95).

10. For a history of wire drawing and a description of its nineteenth- and twentieth-century machinery, see Camp and Francis (1951, 1037–82).

11. Telegraph lines were laid along railway lines, partly to benefit from the cleared path and partly to transmit traffic signals; see Crump (2007, 167–85).

12. See Rudyard Kipling's memorable opening lines from "The Deep-Sea Cables" (quoted in Otis 2002, 104): "The wrecks dissolve above us; their dust drops down from afar— / Down to the dark, to the utter dark, where the blind white sea-snakes are. / There is no sound, no echo of sound, in the deserts of the deep, / Or the grey level plains of ooze where the shell-burred cables creep."

13. Babbage (1989b, 1–13); see Paulinyi (1997, 332).

14. For Brunel's biography, see Rolt (1959). Brunel University's website shows a video with images from Brunel's career: (www.brunel.ac.uk/about/ history/isambard-kingdom-brunel).

15. Reuleaux (1876, 235–36; Ger., 1875, 231).

16. See Frost (1910, 154–88). See also Martin (1855). How crucial this development was in eliminating social distinctions shows in the episode of Rastignac's first visit to Madame de Restaud, where, too poor to afford a cab, he is mortified to arrive with mud-splattered shoes; Balzac (1994, 43–44).

17. See Sabin (1904, 10–22) and Reid (1877, 182–206 [crushers] and 239–61 [kilns]).

18. The patent for the first paper machine, the Foudrinier machine, dating from July 24, 1806, specifies: "A vessel or trough from which the paper stuff . . . is caused to flow upon the moulds. . . . A set of cylinders, upon which is passed, in the manner of a jack towel, an endless web of felting. There is a third cylinder in contact with one of these cylinders, and this third cylinder communicates by means of another web of felt with an additional pair of pressing cylinders." The illustrations in Sindall (1920) and Henderson (1941) show how the arrangement of cylinders progressed over the nineteenth century and into the twentieth. For a local account of a German paper factory in 1828, see Barnikel (1965, 315–404); the owner of this factory, Friedrich Koenig, was the same man who had built the first steam-powered cylindrical printing press for the *Times* in London. He also furnished the publisher Cotta with a printing machine on which the "Cotta Edition" of Friedrich Schiller's collected works was printed.

19. The "Cylinder machine," however, a rival process to the Foudrinier machine, dispensed with the wire: " This machine differs somewhat . . . in the method of forming the web of paper. A cylinder covered with a woven metal wire screen, and half immersed, revolves in a vat of pulp, and by means of a vacuum within the cylinder, the pulp is made to adhere to the screen on the periphery of the cylinder, thereby forming the paper, which is then detached and passed on to a cylinder with felting" (Hunter 1978, 350).

20. Balzac (2001, 3). The novel revolves around the mechanization of papermaking, as one of the protagonists searches for new raw materials to produce endless paper while the other, a vain and venal journalist, is more concerned with covering it with ink.

21. See S. Steinberg (1996, 9).

22. See Routledge (1989, 226–27).

23. For an authoritative account of this process, see Gerhardt (1975, 104–30).

24. See McKitterick (2003, 210–16) for Babbage's thought on copying type.

25. For the history of typesetting, see J. Thompson (1904). It is important to remember that justification was not—as it is now on a word processor—an aesthetic choice but a necessity of keeping type securely fastened in the frame; see Ringwalt (1981, 261). For the typewriter, see the legendary account in Kittler (1999, 183–263).

26. See R. Marsden (1888, 108–45). For an account of the history of mechanization in textile manufacturing, see Cardwell (1972, 75–78).

27. The rise of textile industry and its machines has been the subject of many penetrating studies. As Marx has shown, this process predates by a few decades

the nineteenth century, but only in the nineteenth century does its full integration turn it into a "factory system." For a detailed account of the process of
mechanization, see Paulinyi (1997, 280–328).

28. See Routledge (1989, 92–106). On the development of marine propellers,
see Gutsche (1937).

29. For a history of tunneling and rock-drilling machines and an exhaustive
description of the main tunneling projects in Europe and the United States, see
Drinker (1878, 1–300).

30. See Mayer (1876).

31. For the history of well drilling, see Brantly (1971, 1–220).

32. On the emergence of the waltz and other rotary dances within a general
destruction of linear practices in the history of playing, building, fencing, and
exercising, see Eichberg (1980).

33. See Benjamin (1981b ["Berliner Kindheit um Neunzehnhundert"], 268)
for an impression from the child's point of view.

34. See Magdanz (2006). On the carousel, see also F. Fried (1964) and of
course Rilke's poem "The Merry-Go-Round" ("All this goes by and hastens to
its ending / and turns and circles, aimless in its run"). The inversion of the carousel, the rotating drum against whose walls the fairground visitors are pressed
while the floor recedes, also has its origin at this time. It reappears in Truffaut's
Les 400 coups as a not-too-veiled allusion to the process of filmmaking. On
the variety of nineteenth-century fairground rides, see (the unfortunately very
Anglo-centric) Braithwaite (1976).

35. See Crary (1990, 97–136) and, for images of these devices, Nekes (2002,
340–53). On the birth of cinema from the graphic method of Marey, see Mannoni (2002).

36. For Jefferson's own description of the device, see Kahn (1967, 193–94).

37. See B. Phillips (2005, 10–11), as well as this description by Giedion (1948,
64): "We have: the fixed cylindrical lock case, or escutcheon; the smaller, eccen-
trically placed cylinder, or plug (both cylinders having corresponding holes);
and fitting vertically onto these holes, five round pins, each in two sections. . . .
Constantly pressing the pin tumbler downward are five small spiral springs set
into the uppermost part of the holes." For Giedion, the Yale lock is a key element in the progress from manufacture (of wrought-iron locks) to mechanical
devices. The cylindrical form plays no role in his account.

38. Benjamin (1983, 281–300). See also Asendorf (1993, 119–39).

39. E.g., Rabinbach (1992), Crary (1990), Chadarevian (1993), Lenoir
(1993), Brain and Wise (1994), Wise (1999), and Felsch (2007, 7–53).

40. See the scathing remarks of Ludwig (1865, 3) about the nostalgia for
vital forces and the necessity of introducing physiology to the "severe law" and
"implacable logic" of mechanisms. On the program of the graphical method, see
Norton Wise's masterful description: "Their program rested on the thesis that
all natural processes—whether physical, chemical, or physiological—involved
nothing other than conversions of physical 'force' from one form to another,
precisely like a steam engine converting steam to work. Helmholtz' conservation
paper generalized this principle from the analysis of steam engines by French
engineers Sadi Carnot and Emile Clapeyron, with the all-important change that

the work done by the engines derived not from a 'fall' of heat from high to low temperature but from the consumption of heat, which was itself nothing but the motion of atoms. With respect to physiology, muscles produced work and heat from 'force' released in chemical reactions. Helmholtz and Dubois-Reymond developed this perspective to great effect in their research on muscle action and nerve transmission in frogs" (Wise 1999, 134).

41. See Chadarevian (1993, 279–88) and Holmes and Olesko (1995). The large laboratory equipped with kymographs required a new organization akin to that of the factory floor; see Dierig (2001).

42. It can only be mentioned here—it deserves, of course, much deeper investigation—that Darwin's concept of evolution repeats the cylindrical inscription of life on the grandest possible scale: in conjoins the translational pull of biological time and extinction with the infinite variability of organisms adapting to their milieu.

43. See Millard (2005, 23–36) and Read and Welch (1976, 1–41). In the film version of *My Fair Lady*, Professor Higgins exclaims in exasperation: "I am not going to waste another cylinder on her!"

44. See Kittler (1999, 24).

45. On the intersection of intention, function, and aesthetics in the Forth Bridge, see Baxandall (1985, 15–36).

46. For a detailed description, see Genevro and Heineman (1991, 159–219) and Bradley (1972, 1–56). On the intricacies of screw cutting, see Rose (1877, 53–71).

47. Bredekamp (1995, 40); Reuleaux (1876, 493–97; Ger., 1875, 480–84) analyzed the lathe as a "form-changing" (as opposed to a "place-changing") machine.

48. On Watt's difficulties in obtaining true cylinders, see Ferguson (1962, 189–91) and B. Marsden (2002, 69–106).

49. On Maudslay's towering importance, see Roe (1916, 22–49), Nasmyth (1841), Rolt (1965, 83–121), and Paulinyi (1997, 328–52).

50. Buchanan (1841, 401); see also Babbage (1989b, 1–13).

51. See the crucial text by Schaffer (1994a) on the relation between intelligence (and intelligentsia), skill, and factory work in the first half of the nineteenth century.

52. Here is a description of this process through the eyes of Maudslay's apprentice Nasmyth (1883, 142–41): "It consisted in the employment of a knife-edged, hardened steel instrument, so arranged as to be set at any required angle, and its edge caused to penetrate the surface of a cylindrical bar of soft steel or brass. This bar being revolved under the incisive action of the angularly placed knife-edged instrument, it thus received a continuous spiral groove cut into its surface. . . . The production of perfect screws was one of Maudsley's highest ambitions and his principal technical achievement. . . . His screw-cutting lathe was moved by combination wheels, and by its means he could, by the one guide-screw, obtain screws of every pitch and diameter. As an illustration of its complete accuracy I may mention that by its means a screw of five feet in length and two inches in diameter was cut with fifty threads to the inch, the nut to fit on to it being twelve inches long and containing six hundred threads!"

53. Karl Marx shares this point of view—and the corresponding one that satisfying work is always unhurried work with the hand—not only with most nineteenth-century cultural critics (such as Carlyle and Ruskin) but also with more pessimistic twentieth-century thinkers like Spengler, and with that aspect of Heidegger's thought that casts machines out of the circle of authentic being. On Carlyle, Ruskin, and Morris, see the classic work by Leo Marx (2000, 145–226), and Knowles (2001); see also Spengler (1923, 1183–95). On the ambivalence in Heidegger's attitude toward technics, see (S. Weber 1989). For an excellent selection of writings on the nature of work in the nineteenth century, see Bradshaw and Ozment (2000).

54. This apparent breach of scientific objectivity is inherent in Marx's claim that the representation of laws of capitalist economy is coincidental with their critique: "It [Das Kapital] is at the same time representation [Darstellung] of the system and through the representation its critique." Karl Marx to Lassalle, quoted in Heinrich (2006, 31).

55. The key text of the mature Marx on the quantification of human work and its relation to mechanical work is chapter 15 of the first volume of Capital, "Machinery and Modern Industry" (K. Marx 1996, 374–508), chapter 13 in the German edition (1987, 330–457). The eulogy of work as "self-creation" of the individual as a species-being is in Marx (1975, 273–80); for an interpretation, see Elster (1985, 82–92). Like most interpreters, Rabinbach (1992, 72–81) recognizes a shift in Marx from an early, qualitative understanding of work to a later, quantitative and purely economic view and attributes it to a "marriage of Marx and Helmholtz" (72). But if such a marriage ever took place, it must have been exceedingly Victorian, for there are no traces—as Rabinbach admits—of Marx (in contrast to Engels) actually having read any of Helmholtz's (widely available) writings.

56. K. Marx (1996, 376; Ger., 1987, 332): "The tool or working machine is that part of the machinery with which the industrial revolution of the 18th century started. . . . On a closer examination of the working machine (Werkzeug-maschine) proper, we find in it, as a general rule, though often, no doubt, under very altered forms, the apparatus and tools used by the handicraftsman or manufacturing workman; with this difference, that instead of being human implements (Werkzeuge), they are the implements of a mechanism, or mechanical implements."

57. K. Marx (1996, 388; Ger., 1987, 343).

58. K. Marx (1996, 399, 450–62; Ger., 1987, 354, 403–15).

59. K. Marx (1996, 490–91; Ger., 1987, 442).

60. See Roe (1916, 22–32) and Johnson (1999, 576–80).

61. See Smiles (1861), for the eminent Scottish civil engineer Thomas Telford, and Johnson (1999, 541–76).

62. A classic modern case of the (mis-)understanding of mechanical work as manifest work can be found in Althusser and Balibar (1968, 2:131–34); for an anthropological view on the importance of rotational machines, see Leroi-Gourhan (1943, 98–114).

63. See also Babbage in 1832 (1989a, 48): "It would be possible for a very skillful workman, with files and polishing substances, to form a cylinder out of

a piece of steel; but the time which this would require would be so consider-able, and the number of failures would probably be so great, that for all prac-tical purposes such a mode of producing a steel cylinder might be said to be impossible. The same process by the aid of the lathe and the sliding-rest is the everyday employment of hundreds of workmen." The notion of replication as an alternative to creation has been advanced by Davis (1996a, 1–5).

64. Derrida (1994, 162); K. Marx (1996, 388–89; Ger., 1987, 343–44). In his description of machines as mythical monsters, Marx does not go so far as Samuel Butler (1998) in his wonderful chapter "On the Evolution of Machines and the Question Whether They Have a Reproductive System": "If this be taken to mean that they cannot marry, and that we are never likely to see a fertile union between two vapor-engines with the young ones playing about the door of the shed, however greatly we might desire to do so, I will readily grant it. But the objection is not a very profound one. No one expects that all the features of the now existing organizations will be absolutely repeated in an entirely new class of life" (249).

65. Kapp (1877, 204), in his enthusiastic appraisal of Reuleaux (1875, 165–208), manages to completely ignore Reuleaux's insistence on the kinematic and social novelty of machines; asking himself whether theoretical kinematics is in accordance with organ projection, he answers: "This question has to be affirmed as soon as one is convinced that machines are as much continuations of hand tools and of tools in general as these are continuations of the hand and of organs." (Die Frage ist bejahend zu beantworten, sobald man die Ansicht festhält, dass die Maschine ebenso die Fortsetzung des Handwerkzeugs und überhaupt des Werkzeugs ist, wie diese die Fortsetzung der Hand und der Organe.) Kapp (1877, 27) already reflects on the notion of "Zeug," which will become so important to Heidegger. Equally important for Heidegger is Fried-rich Georg Jünger's pamphlet Die Perfektion der Technik, which Heidegger read in manuscript during the war. It revolves around the rhetorical question: "Is technics anything else than the process of rationalization of manufactur-ing processes that in earlier times were performed by hands and hand tools?" (Ist die Technik etwas anderes als eine Rationalisierung von Arbeitsverfahren, zu denen früher Hände und Handwerkzeuge benötigt wurden?) (F. Jünger 1953, 21).

For a decisive criticism of Kapp's and others' theory of organ projection from a kinematic point of view, see Horwitz (1933–34). Mumford (1967, 140) adds another dimension to the critique of the projection hypothesis: "Many scholars who have no difficulty in recognizing that tools are mechanical counterfeits of the muscles and limbs of the male body—that the hammer is a fist, the spear a lengthened arm, the pincers the human fingers—seem prudishly inhibited against the notion that woman's body is also capable of extrapolation. They recoil from the notion that the womb is a protective container and the breast a pitcher of milk: for that reason they fail to give full significance to the appearance of a large variety of containers precisely at the moment when we know from other evidence that woman was beginning to play a more distinc-tive role as food provider and effective ruler than she had in the earlier foraging and hunting economies. The tools and the utensils, like the sexes themselves, perform complementary functions. One moves, manipulates, assaults; the other remains in place, to hold and protect and preserve."

66. It is the purpose of Stiegler (1998) to make this point from a vastly more comprehensive, philosophical point of view, tracing in Western metaphysics from Plato to Heidegger an exclusion of the technical conceived as prosthetic. In extensive critiques of Leroi-Gourhan, Simondon, Rousseau, Heidegger, and others, he wants to arrive at a point where the evolution of technical objects is no longer left to the blind progressivism of the markets. While acknowledging and benefiting from the power of Stiegler's project, the present work is much more closely focused on the kinematic properties of technical objects as a guiding thread to understand their history and cultural impact.

67. "Gespenstige Gegenständlichkeit" (K. Marx 1987, 72).

68. "Inhumanity" and "ghostliness" can be understood as variations on Derrida's concept of "spectrality" in his analysis of Marx's legacy as a (political) philosopher. In fact, the following argument about the presence of something that is neither human nor natural—the forced motions of cylindrical machines—and that introduces repetitive motions into the area of production is intended as a kinematically focused version of Derrida's argument that Marx's notion of use-value is equally haunted by an "originary iterability" (Derrida 1994, 162) that prevents its functioning as a point of unalienated origin.

69. The value-form analysis plays a crucial role in differentiating various schools of Marxist thought. One of the most penetrating analyses is Heinrich (2006).

70. The most extensive technical discussion of this law is in K. Marx (1998, 209–65); see also K. Marx (1953, 648–50).

71. K. Marx (1996, 407; Ger., 1987, 362).

72. See Elster (1985, 155–61) and Helberger (1974, 133–37).

73. The instances are too many to list; a particularly dense section is K. Marx (1996, 386–87; Ger., 1987, 342–43). The distinction, so pronounced in the German, is elided in the English translation as "radical change" *(Umwälzung)* and "revolution."

74. For the semantics of revolution in the eighteenth century, which still informs Marx's usage, see Cohen (1980, 39–51).

75. This essential fact can be derived from the mostly technical discussion of the composition of capital, the relation of surplus to profit, and the status of average profitability in Marxist economics. See Heinrich (1999, 329–37; 2006, 47–80).

6. KINEMATICS OF NARRATION I

1. See the opening chapter of Sternberger (1955) and K. Marx (1989, 375–76).

2. For the enormous popularity of carousels in the nineteenth century, see Braithwaite (1976); the symbolic power of steam hammers was such that Krupp not only named its largest steam hammer ("Hammer Fritz," of course) but also concealed its retirement when rolling replaced forging in steel manufacture; see Radkau (2008, 100).

3. In the opening scenes of Jean Renoir's film of Zola's *La bête humaine* (1938) the conjunction between the movement of the locomotive and that of the film camera is made explicit.

4. This is a technical and historical rewording of Ian Watt's (2001, 11) lapidary statement that "the novel's realism does not reside in the kind of life it presents, but in the way it presents it."

5. For the following summary observations on the kinematics of realism I have found considerable support in M. Brown (1981)—not only in the fearless way he synthesizes large swaths of nineteenth-century realism and its critical reception but also in the particular solution to the definition of realism he offers in his reconstruction of Hegel's logic of reality. Already the reading of Reuleaux's kinematics has shown that Hegel's dialectic of contingency, relative necessity, and absolute necessity can be read kinematically as the successive relation of translational, rotational, and helical motion. If the following pages attempt to describe this relation in the narrative elements of story, plot, and their intertwining, they do so on a "lower," more restricted level than Brown, but one that is fundamentally compatible with his paradigmatically wider and systematically more ambitious theory.

6. See Moseley (2005).

7. See for the following Couturier (1991, 145–92). Couturier interprets the rise of the novel in conjunction with the rise of printing techniques and copyright laws but ultimately dissolves these influences in an abstract notion of "bookhood."

8. See F. Schlegel (1968, 129 [Lyceums-Fragment # 89] and 140–41 [Athenaeums-Fragment # 116]), Bauer (2005, 41–43), and Lacoue-Labarthe and Nancy (1988, 90–99).

9. See Moretti (1987, 19): "The plot as 'ring,' or a 'network,' is the most significant of the many novelties introduced by Goethe in the second [and final] draft of Wilhelm Meister." For a genealogy of the *Bildungsroman* in which theme and form are intertwined, see Wellbery (2006, 70–117).

10. Significantly, Keller attempted to straighten out Heinrich's path in a revised ending written fifteen years later; rather than returning and dying, Heinrich now finds a way to integrate himself into the social and libidinal fabric of his hometown. On the importance of the cycloid, see Kassung (2007, 185–217), Berz (2001, 84–92), and the introduction to Reuleaux (1900).

11. See Genette (1982, 49–69) and his classic "Discours du récit" (1980, 65–273). More recently, see Abbott (2007), Herman (2007, s.v.), and Bauer (2005, 221–30 plus bibliography, 231–47).

12. Brooks (1992, 13). The entire discussion (3–36) is worth reading.

13. The most vociferous proponents of these inverse positions were, respectively, Lukacs (e.g., 1972, 1–19) and Roland Barthes (1989, 141–48).

14. For the following, see Butt (1971).

15. Dickens (2003, 43) (beginning of ch. 4).

16. For a description of this process—and discussion of its structuralist interpretation—see Miller (1991, 119–77).

17. Sterne (1986, 95) emphatically maintains: "Digressions, incontestably, are the sunshine;—they are the life, the soul of reading;—take them out of this

book, for instance,—you might as well take the book along with them;—one cold eternal winter would reign in every page of it; restore them to the writer;—he steps forth like a bridegroom,—bids All hail; brings in variety, and forbids the appetite to fail." Wellbery (2006, 7–41) shows how the practice of digression in Sterne is itself the enactment of a poetics of contingency that in turn is figured in the novel around the uncertainty in preformationist theories of generation and parentage. Realist narratives will actively transform each of these aspects: digression will be geared to the story, apparent contingency transformed into real continuity, and uncertain parentage into family coherence.

18. "Thus, the installment structure of *Romola* encouraged Victorian readers to expect that the author would narrate all significant actions within individual parts, skipping over less significant times, not between but within numbers" (Hughes and Lund 1991, 81).

19. For the relation of plot, shock, surprise, and suspense (and an acute critique of Benjamin's notion of shock as the fundamental experience of the nineteenth century), see Moretti (2005, 114–19). For an overview of research on narrative suspense, see Zillmann (1980).

20. See Ackroyd (1990, 174–200).

21. Dickens's memoranda for *Hard Times* give a vivid impression of his hesitations over introducing a character at the right moment; see Dickens (2001, 226–35).

22. See Turner (2005, 117). The precise description of London and its public houses had the same function; see Miller (1995, 105).

23. Hughes and Lund (1991, 4). Brooks (1992, 143–70) details the same condition, at the very same time (1836), for France; there the innovator is Eugène Sue: "Because publication of *Les Mystères de Paris* extended across some sixteen months—generally running four times weekly, but with some long interruption when Sue ran out of copy—and because Sue had no very precise outline for the yet unwritten pages, not only could readers express their responses to the novel, Sue could respond to their responses in future installments" (163). In his reflections on serialization in the *Passagen-Werk,* Benjamin (1983, 2:903–38) presents documents for the importance of serial publication in France of the 1830s and 1840s.

24. The similarities between nineteenth-century practices of shared interpretation of serial publications and current interpretation communities that form around television shows are obvious: viewers discuss the latest installments online and speculate about the development of a show's plot and characters. It is instructive to note that under these circumstances expressions or actions of a character can rarely be definitively understood (is Don Draper a homophobe because he said "you people" to Sal?), and that the tone of discussion—unlike that on political websites—is tempered precisely by this essential openness.

25. This is not to say that the *Poetics* does not recognize literature as written; it does (see *Poetics* 12.2), and it warns against histrionics (12.1).

26. For the relation of sensation fiction to the newly accelerated Victorian life, see Daly (2004, 34–55). For Collins's "plot of suspense" versus Dickens's "plot of surprise," see Brooks (1984, 168–70).

27. For the rootedness of secular hermeneutics in Christian exegesis, see Grondin (1994, 1–75). Early Romantic theory in Germany held that by articulating reflections contained within a work of art, art criticism *(Kunstkritik)* actually completes it. This theory, as well as the conviction that prose, not poetry, was the true language of art, appeared like visionary anticipations of the developments brought about by serialization, much as the panorama seems like an anticipation of cinema. For the notion of *Kunstkritik,* see Benjamin (1981a, 87–109).

28. In the afterword to *Our Mutual Friend*—which borrows its basic storyline from eighteenth-century comedies in which children rebel against the arrangement of their marriages, only to fall in love with the intended—Dickens acknowledges the difficulties of aligning the plot with the rhythm of serial publication: "To keep for a long time unsuspected, yet always working itself out, another purpose originating in th[e] leading incident, and turning it to a pleasant and useful account at last, was at once the most interesting and the most difficult part of my design. Its difficulty was much enhanced by the mode of publication; for it would be very unreasonable to expect that many readers, pursuing a story in portions from month to month through nineteen months, will, until they have it before them complete, perceive the relations of its finer threads to the whole pattern which is always before the eyes of the story-weaver at his loom" (1989, 821).

29. See, e.g., Bakhtin (1981, 259–300) and Wood (2008).

30. This is the stripped-down, "lower" version of an argument that in great philosophical and historiographical depth is being made by Rüdiger Campe (2009): that life and the novel stand in a much deeper relationship than the representation of man's "transcendental homelessness" diagnosed by Lukacs. Campe also goes back to Aristotle—not to book 8 of the *Physics* and its discussion of forms of motion, however, but to book 12 of the *Metaphysics* and its distinction between motion and life.

7. THE CYLINDER AS ENCLOSURE

1. The air pump is the subject of the legendary book by Shapin and Schaffer (1985, esp. 22–79).

2. See Dulken (2001, 146–47) for a full description of the "pneumatic railway" of 1867.

3. The difference between combustion and detonation is important for understanding the kinematics of nineteenth-century machines—there is no forced transmission of motion to be had from detonation. Unfortunately, the most imaginative contemporary account of the impact of machines on the life of nineteenth- and twentieth-century culture, Negt and Kluge's *Geschichte und Eigensinn* (1993; see in particular their description of bodily and mental discipline in large steel factories, 1:190–217) proceeds from this misunderstanding. The first volume, which is focused on the rise of industrial discipline and its impact both on social and on intimate interactions, sees (like Marx) machines exclusively as tools but claims that all of their actions are violent. The origin of this violence is in the motor (14): "The Otto-engine, for example, is based on

the principle of permanent explosions. Every single element of this invention is destructive." (Der Otto-Motor z.B. beruht auf dem Prinzip permanenten Explodierens. Alle Einzelkomponenten dieser Erfindung sind zerstörerisch.) Every car enthusiast knows that detonations ("knocking") in the cylinder are a sign of serious problems.

4. Mayer (1876); many of Kleist's novellas concern the disproportion between minute cause and huge effect. The first philosopher who was fully versed in these aspects of nineteenth-century physics was Friedrich Nietzsche (1988, 365), who had read Mayer carefully and proclaimed: "I am not a man, I am dynamite."

5. The history of modern firearms, their kinematics, and the complex interaction of research labs, machine shops, military commissions, and political actors leading to the machine guns of the First and Second World Wars are richly documented and brilliantly analyzed in Berz (2001).

6. See Rosen (1973, 625–67). Beyond the separation of sewage and water lay the idea—especially important in France—of collecting human manure and returning it to the soil as fertilizer. This idea—provoked in part by the "guano craze" in the 1840s and backed by recent discoveries in organic chemistry—sought to oppose the entropy envisioned by Malthus. Instead of more and more people competing for less food, the fertilized soil would yield an abundance of food, making man, by excreting rather than by working, the "reproducer of his own subsistence." See Simmons (2006).

7. On the notion of the "formless," see Bois and Krauss (1997).

8. On the emergence of the chemical industries and the enormous number of cylindrical contraptions upon which it was built, see Paulinyi (1997, 412–28), Singer et al. (1980, 235–83), and Routledge (1989, 618–63).

9. See Brimblecombe (1987, 1–89).

10. See Douet (1988, 12).

11. Images in Douet (1988). Benjamin Baker, the designer of the Forth Bridge, in an argument against William Morris and the aesthetics of arts and crafts, nicely summarized: "The marble columns of the Parthenon were beautiful where they stood, but if they took one and bored a hole through its axis and used it as a funnel of an Atlantic liner it would, to his [Morris's] mind, cease to be beautiful." Quoted in Baxandall (1985, 24). See also Baudelaire (1986, 379), who described smokestacks as "obélisques de l'industrie vomissant contre le firmament leurs coalitions de fumée." The most extensive meditation on the status of the column both as a measure of man and as the organizing principle of Western architecture is Rykwert (1996).

12. Benjamin (1999, 678) (Y4a, 3): " What makes the first photographs so incomparable is perhaps this: that they present the earliest image of the encounter of machine and man." For an overview of early cameras, see Nekes (2002). See also Plessen et al. (1993).

13. See Benjamin (1999, 530) (Q1a,8).

14. More precisely, the translational practice of Eadweard Muybridge, who captured the motion of galloping horses by setting up cameras parallel to their track resulting in a series of photographs, and the rotational setup of Marey, whose subjects ran in a circle and were photographed by a camera turning

around a central axis resulting in a single photograph, need to merge to produce cinematography.

Like the emergence of the kymograph, the rise of photographic and cinematographic techniques has been very well researched. The standard book on Marey's project is Braun (1992); her account of the relation between Marey and Muybridge and the emergence of commercial cinematography is on 229–63. Daston and Galison (2007, 115–90) have demonstrated the constitutive role of photographs in the emergence of "mechanical objectivity." See also Rabinbach (1992) and, concentrating on the impact of the transition from photography to film, Benjamin (2002, 101–33).

15. On the phenomenon of katoptic anamorphosis (where an upright cylindrical mirror de-skews a distorted drawing), see Baltrusaitis (1977, 131–58) and Füsslin and Hentze (1999, 46–117). On the *laterna magica,* see Nekes (2002, 134–57). For a topographic history of the panorama, see Comment (2000, 23–56). Goethe not only made the magic lantern a medium but also displayed it as a material object in his *Faust* (see Goethe 1999, 479–84); Marcel Proust's childhood reveries about the Guermantes were still induced by a "lanterne magique, dont, en attendant l'heure du dîner, on coiffait ma lampe" (2009, 136–42).

16. On the practices of drawing, projecting, and painting panoramas throughout the nineteenth century, see Oettermann (1997, 49–97). The whole process, in particular in the second half of the century, was organized like industrial fabrication, since the "work" could no longer be comprehended and executed by an individual painter. The continuity of the horizon was created by partitioning the canvas into segments that were conceived as tangent to the surface of the cylinder. The size of the segments depended on the radius of the panorama; see Plessen et al. (1993, 303).

17. For images of panorama constructions, see Comment (2000); see Oettermann (1997, 59–97), Stenger (1939), and Grau (2001, 66–137; 1983, 655–56), as well as the notorious "-rama" scene in Balzac (1994, 40–41). See also Benjamin's reminiscences of the "Kaiserpanorama" (2006a, 42–44); in this late variation, the spectators were placed on the outside of the cylinder looking in on stereoscopic photographs.

18. See Oettermann (1997, 32) ("democratization of perspective"), as well as Comment (2000, 119) (the panorama "became progressively more like . . . television, it became as much a tool of alienation as of emancipation"). The peculiar pathos of the panoramas is the subject of Walter Benjamin's reflections in Benjamin (1983, 2:657). Crary (1990, 67–96) has made the argument that the new "thermodynamic" physiology of Helmholtz and others (a physiology very much dependent on the use of kymographs) gradually did away with the Kantian idea of a transcendental ego processing all sensory input and that this accounts for the immersive abandonment to sensation in visual apparatuses of the nineteenth century.

19. See Comment (2000, 110–14) for the coincidence of distance and nearness. Horizontal infinity (which was often probed by telescopes provided by the panorama's operator) and vertical elation were equally visible in the way panoramas were painted: a host of assistant painters transferred the details onto the canvas (from a preparatory drawing or a photograph) while the chief painter directed them from a raised, moving platform in the center; see Oettermann (1997, 56).

20. See Kittler (1987, 203–12).

21. The wandering of attention, together with its opposite, the idée fixe, became of great interest to psychology; an important compendium was Ribot (1898) (French orig., 1888). See also the anthology edited by Haas, Nägele, and Rheinberger (1998). The psychology and topography of the ambulating flaneur is the subject of some of Walter Benjamin's most intense reflections; see, e.g., "Convolute M" (1:524–69) in *The Arcades Project* (Benjamin 1983).

22. See Bentham (1843, 96–170) and of course Foucault (1995, 195–228). On the literary use of these spaces, see the discussion of Balzac in chapter 8 below.

23. See Schormüller (1948) and Singer et al. (1980, 5:38–45) (on other forms of food preservation in the nineteenth century, see 26–38). The most productive reflections on the cultural ramifications of the shape of packaging can be found in Baxandall (1972, 86–94, 86): "It is an important fact of art history that commodities have come regularly in standard-sized containers only since the nineteenth century: previously a container—the barrel, sack or bale—was unique, and calculating its volume quickly and accurately was a condition of business."

24. See the somewhat disgruntled accounts in D'Eramo (2002, 41–51).

25. "Round silos . . . have greater relative capacity, and no form of silo can be built that to so great an extent facilitates the even settling of the silage" (Shaw 1913, 274).

26. See Singer et al. (1980, 5:137–40, 152–56).

27. For a description of the various types of gas holders, see Becher and Becher (1993, 7–9). There was widespread, and not entirely unfounded, fear in the early nineteenth century that these containers might explode; see Schivelbusch (1988, 33–37).

28. The Bechers also photographed spherical gasholders, used to store gas under high pressure. Two recent exhibitions at the Gasometer Oberhausen made artistic use of the cylinder's properties. In 1999, Christo and Jeanne Claude's *The Wall* cut the interior space in half by erecting a twenty-six-meter wall made out of cylindrical oil drums, thus relating the question of containment to that of the change in fuel from solid coal and gas to liquid oil; and in 2003 Bill Viola, in the installation *Five Angels for the Millennium,* projected videos onto the inside walls of the same gasholder, effectively turning the gasometer into a panorama.

29. See Evers (1939/1970, 96): "So setzen wir der nüchternen Theorie, die Säule sei eine Stütze, den Satz entgegen: Die Säule ist eine Hoheitsform, das größte Hoheitssymbol, welches die menschliche Baukunst kennt." Rykwert (1996) has written the history of the metaphysics of the column. On the significance of the Platonic polygons, see Pacioli (1980, 112), Kemp (1990, 53–64), and Vesely (2004, 156). On the sphere, see Kemp (1990, 295–303), Vidler (1990, 272–76, 315, 388), and Blumenberg (1998, 169).

30. Wiggin (2007, 49–50).

31. See Müller-Sievers (forthcoming).

32. See von Eelking (1962), who also reports that the first wearer of a top hat in London was arrested for causing public annoyance (36). See also Loschek (1994, 479–80).

33. Selenka (1900, 46). I am indebted to Spiros Papapetros for this reference.

34. Lotze (1887, 592–93). On Lotze's central place in nineteenth-century philosophy (including the claim that his philosophy influenced Du Bois and Martin Luther King), see Sullivan (2010).

35. On the geometry of linear perspective, see Kemp, (1990, 343); on its implications, see Panofsky (1994) (with the translator's preface), Damisch (1994), and Davis (1996c).

36. This is the implication of Mallarmé's analysis in "The Impressionists and Edouard Manet" (1876/1998). Of course, this ambulatory mode of viewing was a necessity in the salons, which were extremely crowded and displayed paintings often high up on the walls.

37. That Manet de-rhetoricizes painting and reduces its narrative structure to mere presentation is the main thrust in Bataille's reading of Manet's oeuvre; describing Manet's *Execution of Maximilian,* he says, "We get the impression of an all-engulfing numbness, as if a skillful practitioner had radically cured painting of a centuries-old ailment: chronic eloquence" (1983, 48). See also the famous quote reported by his friend (and model) Antonin Proust (1913, 30): "Il n'y a qu'une chose vraie. Faire du premier coup ce qu'on voit. Quand ça y est, ça y est. Quand ça n'y est pas, on recommence. Tout le reste est de la blague." The *Concert* can be studied in stunning detail on the website of the National Gallery in London: www .nationalgallery.org.uk/paintings/edouard-manet-music-in-the-tuileries-gardens.

38. Bataille (1983, 65).

39. For an interpretation of this painting in the context of Baudelaire's aesthetics, see Armstrong (2002, 121–33).

40. On the composition of the painting and its formal and social context, see Nochlin (1989, 75–94). In a remark to Antonin Proust after refinishing his portrait—dominated, as it is by the sitter wearing a top hat—Manet allegedly said, "Voici, ca y est, cette fois, et comme cela tourne dans le fond!" This is, as far as I know, Manet's only remark that could be read as a comment on the difficulties of painting a cylinder.

41. M. Fried (1996, 21) et al. Fried, concerned with the paintings of the 1860s, does not discuss the *Masked Ball.* With "strikingness" and other concepts, Fried seeks to bring nuance into the discussion of Manet's and modernism's chief feature, the acknowledgment of the essential flatness of the picture plane. Clement Greenberg had argued that around the middle of the nineteenth century, in order to resist absorption into mere decoration and entertainment, painting had begun to concentrate on its own medial presuppositions and hence to expose and integrate its two-dimensionality rather than to conceal it behind elaborate perspectival constructions. The relevant literature on this crucial debate is summarized in M. Fried (1996, 13–19).

42. Meier-Graefe (1912, 216).

43. Cézanne quoted in Doran (2001, 33); see also Boehme (1988, 153).

44. Quoted in Boehme (1988, 113).

8. KINEMATICS OF NARRATION II

1. On the relation between *mimesis* and *methexis* (partaking), see Gadamer (2007, 293–321).

2. Obviously, the tension between temporality and spatiality in narrative form, and with it the value of the distinction between story and plot (or discourse), is at the heart of most theoretical work on the novel. For a minimal account, see Friedman (2002). The present account seeks to add the kinematic perspective to this ongoing discussion.

3. Brooks (1992, 18) uses the word *overcoding* for these retardations. The two Hölderlin quotes are from his *Anmerkungen zum Oedipus* (1998, 2:310).

4. This is not to discount Ian Watt's analysis of *Tom Jones,* which concentrates on those elements that presage the fully integrated plots of realist novels; see especially Watt (2001, 260–89). On the equivalence of episodes as framed screens, see Koschorke (1990). On the function of the frames in relation to narrative tempo, see Stevenson (2008): "Digression and ekphrasis go naturally hand in hand. To break from the main action of a narrative . . . means immediately that a frame has been established, with the digression nested inside. Such strongly framed material, by the intricacy of design involved, should serve to focus attention on what is inside, which are miniature history paintings" (7). H. Brown (1979, 219) speaks of the "ever deflected lateral movement of the narration" engendered by the framed episodes.

5. This transcendental nostalgia informs Lukacs's early *Theory of the Novel,* as well his later essays on European realism, in which he reads realist novels as contributions to a master narrative of emancipation and return to communist ideals. In his view, the kinematic opposition between narration and description offers authors a choice to opt for the forces of progress or regress. Bersani (1970) works from the opposition of "centrifugal" and "centripetal" forces in French novels of the nineteenth century and beyond. Wellbery (2006, 70–117) analyzes this predicament as "the operation of ending."

6. On the relation between cylindricality and narration, see Seltzer (1984, 54).

7. See M. Butor's comments (1994, 296) on the relation between scalability and the recurrence of characters in Balzac: "The principle of recurring characters is thus first and foremost one of economy, but its consequences will fundamentally transform the very nature of novelistic work. Indeed, each individual novel will open onto others, the characters that appear in one novel will not be enclosed within it, they will refer to other novels in which we will discover additional information about them." See also the important essay by Warning (1980, 35, 37), who identifies in Balzac an "Achse der Vertikalität" that is complemented by a "horizonthafte Geschichte."

8. Blumenberg (2001c, 67): "Vom Wirklichkeitsproblem her ist ein entscheidender Unterschied zwischen der episch-linearen und der perspektivischen Wiederkehr von Personen; es entsteht ein ganz anderes Raumbewußtsein, eine subtilere Welthaftigkeit des Romans. Das perspektivische System des Balzacschen Romans erlaubt die Übersetzung der linearen Episodenfolge in die Gleichzeitigkeit. Es ist hier mehr gefordert als die bloße Widerspruchsfreiheit mit bereits aufgetretenen Prädikaten. . . . Das ist etwas grundsätzlich anderes als die längst bekannte gleichzeitig sich vollziehende Vorbereitung der einzelnen Romanpersonen auf ihr schließliches Zusammentreffen im Schnittpunkt der Handlung. Nicht mehr nur und nicht mehr vor allem die Personen des Romans bewegen sich durch die Ereignispunkte der Handlung, sondern der Leser

bewegt sich mit um das Massiv der imaginären Wirklichkeit und durchläuft die Möglichkeiten der Anblicke, die es zu bieten vermag." The contrast to the naturalism of Zola's *Les Rougon-Macquart* is instructive: although the individual works can also be read in random order, they are inscribed into a genealogy that flows only in one direction, and this degeneration is part of the wider argument Zola wants to make about his time.

9. On the "discovery of the horizon," its influence on the shape of narrative and poetic language, and its relation to the project of modernity, see the indispensible book by Koschorke (1990). As every reader of *Le Père Goriot* remembers, Balzac is not exactly subtle about his interest in the panorama (or any other –rama). See also Benjamin (1999, 535) (Q4,1).

10. See Barthes (1989, 56–64).

11. In accordance with his project to describe the "thought" of the novel, Pavel (2003, 282–87) sees in the disengagement of background and protagonists an anti-idealist attempt to reverse the *Bildungsroman* and instead portray the deformation of an individual.

12. Schivelbusch (1986, 52–68).

13. The richest "analysis" of this convergence of technical and narrative innovation in the practices of panoramic ordering can be found in Arno Schmidt's voluminous *Zettels Traum* (1963–69, 149–67), itself single-mindedly devoted to the destruction of panoramic totality.

14. The examples are from Balzac's *Les illusions perdues* and from Dickens's *Little Dorrit* respectively; surely one of the more intense descriptions of panoramic spaces (Balzac [1977, 823] calls it "pandémonium") comes toward the end of Balzac's *Splendeurs et misères des courtisanes*, when the narrator indulges in a long digression about the interior courtyard of the Conciergerie and the modes of communication it dictates.

15. For a traditional (and additional) interpretation of ambition, see Brooks (2005, 39): "By the nineteenth century, the picaro's scheming to stay alive has typically taken a more elaborate and socially defined form: it has become ambition. It may in fact be a defining characteristic of the modern novel (as of bourgeois society) that it takes aspiration, getting ahead, seriously, rather than simply as an object of satire (which was the case in much earlier, more aristocratically determined literature), and thus makes ambition the vehicle and emblem of Eros, that which totalizes the world as possession and progress." See also Moretti (2005, 111–29).

16. Benjamin (1983, 2:937) quotes Cassou: " Le développement du roman-feuilleton et la création des sciences sociales sont parallèles." A strong confirmation of the cylindricality of realist plots come from twentieth-century post mortems for literary realism. One is Joseph Frank's concept of "spatial form," through which he seeks to convey the tendency of modern and modernist fiction to achieve meaning by spatial juxtaposition rather than by temporal development. The market/seduction scene in *Madame Bovary* is one of his chief examples; it is the seed that will grow into fully spatialized forms such as Joyce's *Ulysses* (see Frank 1968 and Holtz 1977). The recurrence of characters in Balzac and the desire to provide a complete panorama are similar seeds of "spatial form."

9. GEARS AND SCREWS

1. Automata continue to accompany the rise of machines mostly as fantastical or polemical shadows; see Inglis (2008). It is misleading, however, to conflate the survival of these eighteenth-century figures with the emergence of the factory system, which is based on a different kinematic regime.

2. A separate species of mechanisms, hovering between automata and working machines, were the so-called philosophical machines of the eighteenth century. They were used to demonstrate and embody scientific arguments (about the vacuum, air pressure, electricity, the order of the solar system, etc.) when mathematical arguments didn't suffice. See the account in Schaffer (1994b).

3. See Rabinbach (1992, 239–70). The culmination of this effort to synchronize the movements of the worker and the motion of machines is Ernst Jünger's essay *Der Arbeiter* of 1932. His ideal is the "total mobilization" of the worker's "Gestalt" as the basis of a fully pair-closed body politic. See E. Jünger (1960).

4. See Norton (2004, 478).

5. On the nomenclature of gear design and the illustration of gear interaction, see Scott (1962, 4–48 [sec. 4.1]), and Beggs (1955, 64–118).

6. See Lewis (2009, 74–81).

7. On this important shift toward a new, conventional conception of precision, see Olesko (1995), Schaffer (1995), Porter (1995), and Wise (1995a, 1995b).

8. The number and analyses of primitive machines change over time and from author to author, but six seems the traditional number; see Siegert (1996, 300) and Nave (2010). Lawton in his monumental work admits further simple machines, such as cams and bearings, brakes and gears, but his definition is admirably precise: "A common feature of all machine elements, if friction losses are ignored, is that they change the magnitude of force and velocity without changing the power transmitted. They are devices for transmitting, rather than generating power, but prime movers could not be developed without them; and without prime movers slavery and human drudgery would continue still" (2004, 3–4). Leupold (1724), perhaps the first writer with a pronounced focus on kinematics, organized his treatise according to the primitive machines.

9. Or the most powerful, as Leupold (1724, 62) claims: "Ihren Effect und Vermögen nach übertrifft die Schraube alle andere Rüst-Zeuge oder Potentien . . . weil sie in einem so kleinen und kurtzen Begriff verfasset ist, und also durch eine Machine, die nur etliche Zoll im Umfang ist, mehr kann gethan werden, als durch andere . . . dannenhero ihr Nutzen und Gebrauch mit keiner Feder genugsam zu beschreiben, und also diese Erfindung vor eine der allernützlichsten in der Welt zu achten ist." (With regard to its effect and power, the screw exceeds all other machines or potentials . . . because it is contained in such a small and short concept and therefore by a machine of only a few inches in diameter more can be done than by any other . . . which is why no pen can sufficiently describe its convenience, and its invention must be regarded as the most useful in the world.)

10. Vitruvius (1999 [10.6]). On the screw in antiquity, see Deppert-Lippitz (1995).

11. For a general cultural history of the screw, see Kellermann und Treue (1962) and Rybczinski (2000, 55–72).

12. Kant (1968d, 381): "Ein Schraubengewinde, welches um seine Spille von der Linken gegen die Rechte geführt ist, wird in eine solche Mutter niemals passen, deren Gänge von der Rechten gegen die Linke laufen, obwohl die Dicke der Spindel und die Zahl der Schraubengänge in gleicher Höhe einstimmig wären."

13. The full ramifications of this argument, along with a selection of Kant's further writings on the problem, can be found in Van Cleve and Frederick (1991).

14. Kant (1968b, 403).

15. Burocker (1981). See also Müller-Sievers (2003, 21–49).

16. See Kant (1968e, 135) and Wedemeyer (1994).

17. See Alder (1995) and the extended analysis and case study in Alder (1997).

18. My translation. Leupold (1724, 64): "Alleine es findet sich mehrentheils, daß solche Leute zwar wissen, daß ein sehr groses damit [sc. mit der Schraube] kan praestiret werden, aber nicht wie und auf was Art es mit der Zeit verbunden, und daß unsägliche Zeit, und endlich eine solche Stärcke der Machinen, Räder und Wellen erfordert wird, die weder zu machen noch zu bekomen ist." On the tradition of the Theatres of Machines, to which Leupold is a late entrant, see Sawday (2007, 70–124), who, despite the title of his interesting chapter ("The Turn of the Screw"), does not reflect on the screw as such.

19. Leupold quoted in Kellermann and Treue (1962, 184–85): "Die Schraube ohne Ende ist eines der allerstärckesten und compendieusesten Hebezeuge, weil damit durch einen kleinen Apparat eine unsägliche Gewalt kan gethan werden. . . . Alleine in Ansehung der Zeit und Krafft ist nicht eines Haar breit vor allen andern damit zu erhalten."

20. Hegel (1986, 571–72).

21. Hölderlin (1998, 685–87); in a commentary to this notion, Heidegger (Heidegger and Fink 1996, 184–85), who has made ample use of the kinematic notion of *Gestell*, reflects on the very important distinction in German between *der Moment* (moment in time) and *das Moment* (potential force, later torque). *Das Moment* is a key notion in Hegel's logic.

22. "The straight and the crooked path of the fuller's comb is one and the same." Heraclitus, frag. 59, in Heraclitus (1912).

23. Goethe (1892, 37–68).

24. Goethe (1896, 74–124; quotes on 100–101).

25. Charles Darwin devoted considerable attention to what he called the "circumnutation of plants," claiming that "apparently every growing part of every plant is continually circumnutating" (1880, 3), but he did not draw any speculative consequences from this observation.

26. J. Phillips (2006, 2).

27. Ball (1900, 4). The year 1900 may seem fortuitous as the counterpoint to the year 1800, when Watt's patents expired and the epoch of cylindrical kinematics began; however, as Barus (1900, 1001) points out, Ball made ample use of Schell (1870, 7–100) and published on screw theory much earlier. Those for whom the following axioms and definitions at the beginning of Ball's treatise

are too dry may enjoy them sung here: http://helix.gatech.edu/ball2000/Song
OfTheScrew/screw128.mp3.

28. See, e.g., Poinsot (1834, 24–25).

29. Schell (1870, 13) calls the distinction between translation and rotation
"not at all necessary," since translation can be understood as rotation around an
infinite axis of rotation; a similar convergence operates in Paucellier's linkage,
which amplifies the rotation of the crank into the motion along a circle with
infinite circumference; see Kempe (1877, 12–17).

30. Ball (1900, 4–5).

31. Ball (1900, 7).

32. Ball (1900, 9).

33 . Ball (1900, 10).

34. There may be no better representation of this epochal difference in machine design than the difference between Wall-E and EVE in the eponymous
Pixar movie.

10. KINEMATICS OF NARRATION III

1. See Klein (2005).

2. For the English context, see Greiner and Kemmler (1997, esp. 52–116).
Anthony Trollope's autobiography is full of relentlessly technical advice, such
as his admonishment to writers to keep up the speed of their writing: "His
language must come from him like as music comes from the rapid touch of
the great performer's fingers; as words come from the mouth of the indignant
orator; as letters fly from the fingers of the trained compositors; as the syllables
tinkled out by little bells form themselves to the ear of the telegraphist" (Trollope 1999, 177).

3. The term mediating between the extremes of transcendence and contingency is *economy* in the sense of a conscious or unconscious justification of
events and decisions of equal probability. Joseph Vogl's path-breaking *Kalkül
und Leidenschaft* (2002) has shown how such an economy characterizes narratives of the eighteenth century until it gives way to a new vision of immeasurable productivity, credit, and debt.

4. This is Laurence Sterne (1986, 95) before screw theory: "The machinery
of my work is of a species by itself: two contrary motions are introduced into
it, and reconciled, which were thought to be at variance with each other. In a
word, my work is digressive, and it is progressive too,—and at the same time."
Here is Trollope (1999, 237) after it: "There should be no episodes in a novel.
Every sentence, every word, throughout all those pages, should tend to the telling of the story." On the motion of prose, see the wonderful essay by Ginsburg
and Nandrea (2006).

5. See Auerbach (1968, 468–82).

6. See Pascal (1977, 98–112), Price (1971), Finch (2004), and Moretti
(2006). Free indirect speech eliminates the power of symbols: by the time the
blind beggar—such a powerful Romantic symbol, for example, in Wordsworth's
Prelude—appears on the scene, he has become little more than an annoyance,
and as such a proximate cause rather than a harbinger of Emma's death.

7. One of the most insistently kinematic analyses of Flaubert's style remains Proust (1987), who is concerned with the rhythm and the interruptions of Flaubert's writing and famously compares it to the *trottoir roulant*, the moving walkway or conveyor belt of the 1900 World Fair.

8. See his (James 1984, 176) famous put-down of the *Education sentimentale*: "'Madame Bovary' was relatively spontaneous and sincere; but to read its successor is, to the finer sense, like masticating ashes and sawdust. 'L'Education Sentimentale' is elaborately and massively dreary. That a novel should have a charm seems to me the most rudimentary of principles, and there is no more charm in this laborious monument to a treacherous ideal than there is perfume in a gravel-heap." See also Hale (1998). See also James's criticism of Eliot's novels from 1873 (reprinted in G. Eliot 2000, 578–81, quotes on 578, 579): "*Romola* sins by excess of analysis; there is too much description and too little drama: too much reflection (all certainly of a highly imaginative sort) and too little creation. Movement lingers in the story, and with it attention stands still in the reader."

9. On the notion of anagnorisis in general and in Henry James in particular, see Cave (2002, 428–63). On Poe, see Baudelaire (1986, 594–639).

10. Poe (1906, 115). Poe was criticized even by his admirers for "slipshod writing, puerile thinking unsupported by wide reading or profound scholarship, haphazard experiments in various types of writing, chiefly under pressure of financial need, without perfection in any detail" (T. Eliot 1949, 327).

11. To James's consternation, his brother William was a prominent believer in psychic phenomena; see Tóibín (2004, 295–338). For the philosophical background of the reappearance of ghosts in the nineteenth century, see Andriopoulos (2006).

12. James (1999, 106).

13. A good cross section is available in the appendix to James (1999).

14. On the development of textual criticism and its relation to literary realism, see Müller-Sievers (2006). The "found manuscript" scenario is of course an old ploy, but one that gains entirely new importance with the rise of textual criticism of the Lachman school in the first half of the nineteenth century. It now suggests that if we can trace the provenance of a manuscript we also can trace the way certain events found their way into the text—whether from the writer's biography or from the surrounding historical context. A clamorous case in point is the editorial history of Georg Büchner's work. On the relation between psychoanalysis, philology, and archaeology, see the important pages in Downing (2006, 87–166).

15. James (1999, 118).

16. James (1999, 57, 68).

17. James (1999, 74).

18. See Kittler (1999). This disintegration was by no means experienced as the moment of trauma and loss that Kittler and, at times, Walter Benjamin describe. The most intimate account of the pleasures of narrative disintegration comes early in Proust's *Recherche*, when the narrator reflects on his youthful readings of the writer Bergotte—an account that performs what it praises by

interrupting the forward movement of the narration with extended metaphors, gnomic asides, and proleptic markers.

19. Beckett (1995, 202–23).

EPILOGUE

1. The most extensive reflection on the relation between historical and epochal distinctions can be found in Blumenberg (1983, 457–81) ("The Epochs of the Concept of an Epoch").

2. See S. Thompson (1898, 83–89).

3. Blühm and Lippincott (2000, 31).

4. Adams (1974, 353–55).

5. Warburg (1995, 54).

6. One of the great documents of kinematic motion at the time of its disappearance is the film *Berlin, Die Symphonie der Großstadt* (1927). The first act in particular shows an astonishing array of forced motions. The film can be downloaded (legally) at www.archive.org/details/BerlinSymphonyofaGreatCity.

7. Hansen (2000). The single greatest weakness of this attempt to furnish a "robust" account of technology is the lack of analysis of even a single machine.

8. Canguilhem (1975) and Simondon (1958) (for the first part of Simondon's pathbreaking book in translation, see Simondon 1980). On Simondon and Canguilhem, see Schmidgen (2001) and his afterword in Canguilhem (2006).

9. A notable exception is the work of Deleuze and Guattari (1998), but it is mostly concerned with late nineteenth- and twentieth-century literature.

10. For the German text and image, see Hölder (1803–4).

11. Schelling (1985, 536) and Hölderlin (1998, 309).

12. The idea of mechanically achieving balance in the rush of representations is more pronounced in the *Notes on Antigone* (Hölderlin 1998, 2:370; trans., 1988, 109): "For it is the end which has to be protected as it were against the beginning, and the equilibrium will consequently incline more toward the end (b) because the first half (c) extends further and the equilibrium occurs later. c_____/a____b."

13. Urs Strässle's excellent book *Heinrich von Kleist: Die keilförmige Vernunft* (Heinrich von Kleist: The Wedge-Shaped Reason [2002]) invokes the instances in which Kleist reflects on the shape of the wedge and the act of wedging apart, but it makes no mention of the "tragic wedge."

14. Hölderlin (1998, 310, 369–70). This is the holy grail of Hölderlin's poetics and has produced an infinite amount of interpretation. For a first orientation, see Fenves (2001, 3) and Nägele (2005, 135–48), who makes several important distinctions between the mechanical and the technical in Hölderlin's thinking. The appropriate illustration of Hölderlin's idea is the set of levers and weights in Leupold (1724, plate 6).

15. Schlaffer (2002) has remarked this fact, to great public consternation. It bears remembering that Gottfried Keller and Conrad Ferdinand Meyer were Swiss, that Adalbert Stifter was Austrian, and that all three were very much concerned with the role of narration and representation in their respective polities.

All three, together with the German writers Wilhelm Raabe and Theodor Storm, opted for the novella as their most convenient (though not exclusive) genre, which was designed to be read in a single sitting even when it was published in installments. These provisos serve to point out that the most insightful analysis of German realism, Downing (2000), not only deals with literature differently but also deals with different literature.

16. One of the best accounts of the importance of the tragic for German literature and criticism in the nineteenth century remains Szondi (1978, 151–260).

17. See Bakhtin (1981, 259–422).

18. Dickens famously rewrote the Fagan sections of *Oliver Twist* when it was pointed out him how offensive they were. That he did it is a question of character; that he could do it without bringing down the narrative machine is a fact of narrative kinematics.

19. Even the democrat and future Marx-collaborator Arnold Ruge felt in 1841 that Dickens's writing was so "chaotic" and "senseless" that it should be kept from pregnant women. Dickens lacked an "ideal element" and was, like his nation, incapable of writing the truth: "The reconciliation of life and the ideal is impossible for a nation . . . for which 'Philosophical Institute' is another name for gas factory." The quote is from Wolfgang Klein's entry "Realismus/realistisch," in the excellent encyclopedia *Ästhetische Grundbegriffe* (2005, 173).

20. Ferrari and Nancy (2003): "Da una pagina all' altra, il prosaico prosegue, è perennemente nell' atto di passare, mentre il poetico si interrompe. Il romanzo è esattamente questa impossibilità di arrestarsi, di chiudere nella pagine l'infinito. Non la ricerca sfinente di un cattivo infinito, cioè la ricerca infinita di un senso in sé completo e ab-soluto, ma l'esperienza stessa, a fior di pagina, dell' esperienza della finitezza del senso. Nel corpus del romanzo, sulla pelle delle sue pagine, è in gioco il senso finito e fragile dell' esistenza quotidiana, il quotidiano passare tra altri corpi, a loro volta finiti e in sé perfetti. Non c'è inizio né fine alla scrittura finita del romanzo, perché non c'è un senso assoluto della storia al di fuori di essa e perché ogni corpo espone sulla sua pelle, ai confini della sua esistenza, tutto il senso che c'è."

21. Beckett (1995, 216).

Works Cited

Abbott, H. Porter. 2007. "Story, Plot, and Narration." In *The Cambridge Companion to Narrative,* edited by David Herman, 39–51. Cambridge: Cambridge University Press.

Ackroyd, Peter. 1990. *Dickens.* New York: HarperCollins.

Adams, Henry. 1974. *The Education of Henry Adams.* Boston: Houghton Mifflin.

Adelung, Johann Christoph. 1811. *Grammatisch-kritisches Wörterbuch der hochdeutschen Mundart.* Vienna: Bauer.

Alberti, Leon Battista. 1988. *On the Art of Building in Ten Books.* Translated by Joseph Rykwert, Neil Leach, and Robert Tavenor. Cambridge, MA: MIT Press.

Alder, Ken. 1995. "A Revolution to Measure: The Political Economy of the Metric System in France." In *The Values of Precision,* edited by M. Norton Wise, 39–71. Princeton: Princeton University Press.

———. 1997. *Engineering the Revolution: Arms and Enlightenment in France, 1763–1815.* Princeton: Princeton University Press.

Althusser, Louis, and Etienne Balibar. 1968. *Lire le Capital.* 2 vols. Paris: Maspero.

Ampère, André-Marie. 1834/1856. *Essai sur la philosophie des sciences ou Éxposition analytique d' une classification naturelle de toutes les connaissances humaines.* Paris: Mallet-Bachelier.

Andriopoulos, Stefan 2006. "Die Laterna magica der Philosophie: Gespenster bei Kant, Hegel und Schopenhauer." *Deutsche Vierteljahresschrift für Literaturwissenschaft und Geistesgeschichte* 80 (2): 173–211.

Aquinas, Thomas. 1934. *Summa contra Gentiles.* London: Burns, Oates, and Washbourne.

Aristotle. 1984. *The Complete Works of Aristotle*. Edited by Jonathan Barnes. 2 vols. Vol. 2. Princeton: Princeton University Press.

Armstrong, Carol. 2002. *Manet Manette*. New Haven: Yale University Press.

Asendorf, Christoph. 1993. *Batteries of Life: On the History of Things and Their Perception in Modernity*. Berkeley: University of California Press.

Auerbach, Erich. 1968. *Mimesis*. Princeton: Princeton University Press.

Babbage, Charles. 1989a. *On the Economy of Machinery and Manufactures*. Edited by Martin Campbell-Kelly. Vol. 8 of *The Works of Charles Babbage*. London: Pickering.

——. 1989b. *Scientific and Miscellaneous Papers*. Edited by Martin Campbell-Kelly. Vol. 5 of *The Works of Charles Babbage*. London: Pickering.

Bachelard, Gaston. 1994. *The Poetics of Space: The Classic Look at How We Experience Intimate Spaces*. Boston: Beacon Press.

Baines, Edward. 1835. *History of the Cotton Manufacture in Great Britain*. London: Fisher.

Bakhtin, Michail. 1981. *The Dialogic Imagination*. Austin: University of Texas Press.

Ball, Robert Stawell. 1900. *A Treatise on the Theory of Screws*. Cambridge: Cambridge University Press.

Baltrusaitis, Jurgis. 1977. *Anamorphic Art*. Cambridge: Chadwyck-Healey.

Balzac, Honoré de. 1977. *La comédie humaine*. Vol. 6. Paris: Gallimard.

——. 1994. *Père Goriot*. Edited by Peter Brooks. Translated by Burton Raffel. Norton Critical Edition. New York: Norton.

——. 2001. *Lost Illusions*. New York: Modern Library.

Barnert, Arno. 1997. "Polizei—Theater—Zensur: Quellen zu Heinrich von Kleists 'Berliner Abendblättern.'" *Brandenburger Kleist-Blätter* 11:29–367.

Barnikel, Helfried. 1965. *Friedrich Koenig, ein früher Industriepionier in Bayern*. Munich: Dissertations-Druckerei Charlotte Schön.

Barsanti, Giulio. 1992. *La scala, la mappa, L'albero: Immagini e classificazioni della natura fra Sei e Ottocento*. Florence: Sansoni.

Barthes, Roland. 1989. *The Rustle of Language*. Berkeley: University of California Press.

Bartsch, Shadi. 2006. *The Mirror of the Self: Sexuality, Self-Knowledge, and the Gaze in the Early Roman Empire*. Chicago: University of Chicago Press.

Barus, Carl. 1900. Review of *A Treatise on the Theory of Screws*, by Robert Stawell Ball. *Science* 12 (313): 1001–3.

Bashforth, Reginald. 1957. *Iron Production*. Vol. 1 of *The Manufacture of Iron and Steel*. London: Chapman and Hall.

——. 1959. *Steel Production*. Vol. 2 of *The Manufacture of Iron and Steel*. London: Chapman and Hall.

——. 1962. *The Mechanical Treatment of Steel*. Vol. 4 of *The Manufacture of Iron and Steel*. London: Chapman and Hall.

Bataille, Georges. 1983. *Manet*. London: Macmillan.

Baudelaire, Charles. 1986. *Curiosités esthetiques: L'art romantique*. Classiques Garnier. Paris: Garnier.

——. 1995. *The Painter of Modern Life*. London: Phaidon.

Bauer, Matthias. 2005. *Romantheorie und Erzählforschung*. Stuttgart: Metzler.

Baxandall, Michael. 1972. *Painting and Experience in Fifteenth-Century Italy*. Oxford: Clarendon Press.

———. 1985. *Patterns of Intention: On the Historical Explanation of Pictures*. New Haven: Yale University Press.

Becher, Bernd, and Hilla Becher. 1993. *Gas Tanks*. Cambridge, MA: MIT Press; Munich: Schirmer/Mosel.

Becker, Bernhard. 1875. *Scientific London*. New York: Appleton.

Beckett, Samuel. 1974. "Dante . . . Bruno. Vico . . . Joyce." In *An Exagmination of James Joyce: Analysis of the Work in Progress (Finnegan's Wake)*. New York: Haskell House.

———. 1995. *The Complete Short Prose*. New York: Grove Press.

Beggs, Joseph. 1955. *Mechanism*. New York: McGraw-Hill.

Behler, Constantin. 1995. *Nostalgic Teleology: Friedrich Schiller and the Schemata of Aesthetic Humanism*. Stanford German Studies 26. Frankfurt: Peter Lang.

Beiser, Frederick. 2005. *Schiller as Philosopher: A Re-Examination*. Oxford: Oxford University Press.

Benjamin, Walter. 1981a. *Gesammelte Schriften*. Vol. 1, pt. 1. *Abhandlungen*. Frankfurt: Suhrkamp.

———. 1981b. *Gesammelte Schriften*. Vol. 4, pt. 1. *Kleine Prosa*. Frankfurt: Suhrkamp.

———. 1983. *Das Passagen-Werk*. 2 vols. Frankfurt: Suhrkamp.

———. 1999. *The Arcades Project*. Cambridge, MA: Belknap Press.

———. 2002. "The Work of Art in the Age of Its Technological Reproducibility." In *Selected Writings*. Vol. 4. *1935–1938*, edited by Michael William Jennings, 101–33. Cambridge, MA: Harvard University Press.

———. 2006a. *Berlin Childhood around 1900*. Cambridge, MA: Belknap Press.

———. 2006b. *The Writer of Modern Life: Essays on Charles Baudelaire*. Edited by Michael William Jennings. Cambridge, MA: Harvard University Press.

Bentham, Jeremy. 1843. *Works*. Edinburgh: Tait.

Berger, Christian. 2000. *Bewegungsbilder: Kleists Marionettentheater zwischen Poesie und Physik*. Paderborn: Schoeningh.

Berghahn, Klaus L. 2004. "An Aesthetic Revolution." In *A New History of German Literature*, edited by David E. Wellbery and Judith Ryan, 455–59. Cambridge, MA: Harvard University Press.

Bersani, Leo. 1970. *Balzac to Beckett: Center and Circumference in French Fiction*. New York: Oxford University Press.

Berti, Enrico. 1985. "La suprématie du mouvement locale selon Aristote: Ses conséquences et ses apories." In *Aristotles: Werk und Wirkung*, vol. 1, *Aristoteles und seine Schule*, edited by Jurgen Wiesner, 123–50. Berlin: Walter de Gruyter.

Berz, Peter. 2001. *08/15: Ein Standard des 20. Jahrhunderts*. Munich: Fink.

Bevilacqua, Fabio. 1993. "Helmholtz's *Ueber die Erhaltung der Kraft:* The Emergence of a Theoretical Physicist." In *Hermann von Helmholtz and the Foundations of Nineteenth-Century Science,* edited by David Cahan, 291–333. Berkeley: University of California Press.

Biagioli, Mario. 2003. "Stress in the Book of Nature: The Supplemental Logic of Galileo's Realism." *Modern Language Notes* 118:557–85.

Blühm, Andreas, and Louise Lippincott, eds. 2000. *Light! The Industrial Age, 1750–1900.* London: Thames and Hudson.

Blumenberg, Hans. 1983. *The Legitimacy of the Modern Age.* Cambridge, MA: MIT Press.

———. 1987. *The Genesis of the Copernican World.* Cambridge, MA: MIT Press.

———. 1998. *Paradigmen zu einer Metaphorologie.* Frankfurt: Suhrkamp.

———. 2001a. "Nachahmung der Natur: Zur Vorgeschichte des schöpferischen Menschen." In *Ästhetische und metaphorologische Schriften,* edited by Anselm Haverkamp, 9–46. Frankfurt: Suhrkamp.

———. 2001b. "Neoplatonismen und Pseudoplatonismen in der Kosmologie und Mechanik der frühen Neuzeit." In *Ästhetische und metaphorologische Schriften,* edited by Anselm Haverkamp, 291–326. Frankfurt: Suhrkamp.

———. 2001c. "Wirklichkeitsbegriff und Möglichkeit des Romans." In *Ästhetische und metaphorologische Schriften,* edited by Anselm Haverkamp, 47–73. Frankfurt: Suhrkamp.

———. 2009. *Geistesgeschichte der Technik.* Frankfurt: Suhrkamp.

———. 2010. *Paradigms for a Metaphorology.* Ithaca: Cornell University Press.

Boehm, Gernot. 1988. *Paul Cézanne: Montagne Saint-Victoire.* Frankfurt: Insel.

Bois, Yve-Alain, and Rosalind Krauss. 1997. *Formless: A User's Guide.* New York: Zone Books.

Bradley, Ian. 1972. *A History of Machine Tools.* Norwich: Model and Allied.

Bradshaw, David, and Suzanne Ozment, eds. 2000. *The Voice of Toil: Nineteenth-Century British Writings about Work.* Athens: Ohio University Press.

Brain, Robert, and M. Norton Wise. 1994. "Muscles and Engines: Indicator Diagrams and Helmholtz's Graphical Method." In *Universalgenie Helmholtz,* edited by Lorenz Krüger, 124–45. Berlin: Akademie Verlag.

Braithwaite, David. 1976. *Fairground Architecture: The World of Amusement Parks, Carnivals, and Fairs.* London: Evelyn.

Brantly, John. 1971. *History of Oil Well Drilling.* Houston, TX: Gulf Publications.

Braun, Marta. 1992. *Picturing Time: The Work of Etienne-Jules Marey (1830–1904).* Chicago: University of Chicago Press.

Bredekamp, Horst. 1993. *Antikensehnsucht und Maschinenglauben: Die Geschichte der Kunstkammer und die Zukunft der Kunstgeschichte.* Berlin: Wagenbach.

———. 1995. *The Lure of Antiquity and the Cult of the Machine: The Kunstkammer and the Evolution of Nature, Art, and Technology.* Princeton, NJ: Marcus Wiener.

Brimblecombe, Peter. 1987. *The Big Smoke: A History of Air Pollution in London since Medieval Times*. London: Methuen.

Bröcker, Walter. 1964. *Aristoteles*. Frankfurt: Klostermann.

Brooks, Peter. 1992. *Reading for the Plot: Design and Intention in Narrative*. Cambridge, MA: Harvard University Press.

———. 2005. *Realist Vision*. New Haven: Yale University Press.

Brown, Homer Obed. 1979. "Tom Jones: The 'Bastard' of History." *boundary 2* (7): 201–34.

Brown, Lloyd. 1998. "John Harrison's 'Ticking Box.'" In *The Art and Science of Analog Circuit Design*, edited by Jim Williams, 233–50. Woburn: Newnes.

Brown, Marshall. 1981. "The Logic of Realism: A Hegelian Approach." *PMLA* 96 (2): 224–41.

Brush, Stephen G. 1978. *The Temperature of History: Phases of Science and Culture in the Nineteenth Century*. New York: Franklin.

Buchanan, Robertson. 1841. *Practical Essays on Mill Work and Other Machinery*. 3rd ed. London: John Weale.

Buckley, Donald H. 1985. "Tribology." In *Tribology: The Story of Lubrication and Wear*, edited by Donald H. Buckley et al., 3–20. NASA Technical Memorandum 101430. http://gltrs.grc.nasa.gov/reports/1985/TM-101430.pdf.

Burocker, Jill. 1981. *Space and Incongruence: The Origins of Kant's Idealism*. Dordrecht: Kluwer.

Butler, Samuel. 1998. *Erewhon*. Amherst, NY: Prometheus Books.

Butor, Michel. 1994. "Balzac and Reality." In *Père Goriot,* edited by Peter Brooks, translated by Burton Raffel, 294–300. Norton Critical Edition. New York: Norton.

Butt, John. 1971. "The Serial Publication of Dicken's Novels: *Martin Chuzzlewit* and *Little Dorrit*." In *The Victorian Novel: Modern Essays in Criticism,* edited by Ian Watt, 70–82. London: Oxford University Press.

Camp, J.M., and C.B. Francis. 1951. *The Making, Shaping and Treating of Steel*. Pittsburgh, PA: United Steel Company.

Campe, Ruediger. 2009. "Von der Theorie der Technik zur Technik der Metapher. Blumenbergs systematische Eröffnung." In *Metaphorologie: Zur Praxis von Theorie,* edited by Anselm Haverkamp and Dirk Mende. Frankfurt: Suhrkamp.

Canguilhem, Georges. 1975. "Machine et organisme." In *La connaissance de la vie*. Paris: Vrin.

———. 2006. *Wissenschaft, Technik, Leben*. Berlin: Merve.

Cardwell, D.S.L. 1971. *From Watt to Clausius: The Rise of Thermodynamics in the Early Industrial Age*. Ithaca: Cornell University Press.

———. 1972. *Turning Points in Western Technology: A Study of Technology, Science, and History*. New York: Science History Publications.

Carnegie, Andrew. 1905. *James Watt*. Garden City: Doubleday.

Cave, Terence. 2002. *Recognitions: A Study in Poetics*. Oxford: Clarendon Press.

Celaya, Juan de. 1525. *Expositio magistri Joannis de Celaya, Valentini, in primum tractatum Summularum magistri Petri Hispani nuperrime impressa, et quam diligentissime ab eodem sua integritati restituta.* http://gallica.bnf .fr/ark:/12148/bpt6k109374h.

Chadarevian, Soraya de. 1993. "Graphical Method and Discipline." *Studies in the History and Philosophy of Science* 24 (2): 267–91.

Chastel, André. 1991. "The Artist." In *Renaissance Characters*, edited by Eugenio Garin, 180–206. Chicago: University of Chicago Press.

Clagett, Marshall. 1959. *The Science of Mechanics in the Middle Ages.* Publications in Medieval Science. Madison: University of Wisconsin Press.

Cohen, I. Bernhard. 1980. *The Newtonian Revolution.* Cambridge: Cambridge University Press.

Comment, Bernard. 2000. *The Painted Panorama.* Rev. and expanded ed. New York: Abrams.

Copernicus, Nicolaus. 1995. *On the Revolutions of the Heavenly Spheres.* New York: Prometheus.

Couturier, Maurice. 1991. *Textual Communication: A Print-Based Theory of the Novel.* London: Routledge.

Crary, Jonathan. 1990. *Techniques of the Observer.* New York: Zone Books.

Crone, Robert. 1999. *A History of Color: The Evolution of Theories of Light and Color.* Documenta Ophtalmologica. Dordrecht: Kluwer.

Crump, Thomas. 2007. *A Brief History of the Age of Steam.* London: Carroll and Graf.

Daly, Nicholas. 2004. *Literature, Technology, and Modernity, 1860–2000.* Cambridge: Cambridge University Press.

Damisch, Hubert. 1994. *The Origin of Perspective.* Cambridge, MA: MIT Press.

Darwin, Charles. 1880. *The Power of Movement in Plants.* London: John Murray.

Daston, Lorraine, and Peter Galison. 2007. *Objectivity.* New York: Zone Books.

Davis, Whitney. 1996a. *Pacing the World: Construction in the Sculpture of David Rabinowitch.* Cambridge, MA: Harvard University Press.

———. 1996b. *Replications: Archaeology, Art History, Psychoanalysis.* University Park: Pennsylvania State University Press.

———. 1996c. "Virtually Straight." *Art History* 19 (3): 434–44.

de Lubac, Henri. 1998. *Medieval Exegesis.* 2 vols. Grand Rapids, MI: Eerdmans.

Deleuze, Gilles, and Félix Guattari. 1998. *Anti-Oedipus: Capitalism and Schizophrenia.* Minneapolis: University of Minnesota Press.

de Man, Paul. 1984. *The Rhetoric of Romanticism.* New York: Columbia University Press.

Deppert-Lippitz, Barbara, ed. 1995. *Die Schraube zwischen Macht und Pracht: Das Gewinde in der Antike.* Sigmarinen: Jan Thorbecke.

d'Eramo, Marco. 2002. *The Pig and the Skyscraper: Chicago, a History of Our Future.* London: Verso.

Derrida, Jacques. 1994. *Specters of Marx: The State of the Debt, the Work of Mourning, and the New International.* New York: Routledge.

Descartes, René. 1991. *Principles of Philosophy.* Dordrecht: Kluwer.

Dickens, Charles. 1989. *Our Mutual Friend*. Oxford: Oxford University Press.

———. 2003. *The Posthumous Papers of the Pickwick Club*. New York: Modern Library.

———. 2001. *Hard Times*. New York: Norton.

Dickinson, H. W. 1958. "The Steam Engine to 1830." In *A History of Technology*, edited by Charles H. Singer, E. J. Holmyard; A. R. Hall, and Trevor I. Williams, 4:173–87. New York: Oxford University Press.

———. 1963. *A Short History of the Steam Engine*. London: Cass.

Dickinson, H. W., and Rhys Jenkins. 1919/1989. *James Watt and the Steam Engine*. London: Encore Editions.

Dierig, Sven. 2001. "Nach Art einer Fabrik: Der 'eiserne Arbeiter' und die Mechanisierung des Labors." *Technikgeschichte* 68 (1): 1–20.

Doran, Michael, ed. 2001. *Conversations with Cézanne*. Berkeley: University of California Press.

Douet, James. 1988. *Going Up in Smoke: The History of the Industrial Chimney*. London: Victorian Society.

Downing, Eric. 2000. *Double Exposures: Repetition and Realism in Nineteenth-Century German Fiction*. Stanford: Stanford University Press.

———. 2006. *After Images: Photography, Archaeology, and Psychoanalysis and the Tradition of Bildung*. Detroit: Wayne State University Press.

Drinker, Henry. 1878. *Tunneling, Explosive Compounds, and Rock Drills*. New York: Wiley.

Dulken, Stephen van. 2001. *Inventing the 19th Century: 100 Inventions That Shaped the Victorian Age, from Aspirin to the Zeppelin*. New York: New York University Press.

Dyck, Joachim. 1977. *Athen und Jerusalem: Die Tradition der argumentativen Verknüpfung von Bibel und Poesie im 17. und 18 Jahrhundert*. Munich: Beck.

Edgerton, Samuel Y. 1987. "'How Shall This Be?' Reflections on Filippo Lippi's Annunciation in London, Part II." *Artibus et Historiae* 8 (16): 45–53.

Eichberg, Henning. 1980. "Die Rationalität der Technik ist veränderlich. Festungsbau im Barock." In *Technik-Geschichte: Historische Beitrage und neuere Ansätze*, edited by Ulrich Troitzsch and Gabriele Wohlauf, 212–40. Frankfurt: Suhrkamp.

Eliot, George. 2000. *Middlemarch*. New York: Norton.

Eliot, T. S. 1949. "From Poe to Valéry." *Hudson Review* 2 (3): 327–42.

Elster, Jon. 1985. *Making Sense of Marx*. Cambridge: Cambridge University Press.

Evers, Hans Gerhard. 1939/1970. *Tod, Macht und Raum als Bereiche der Architektur*. Munich: Fink.

Felsch, Philipp. 2007. *Laborlandschaften: Physiologische Alpenreisen im 19. Jahrhundert*. Göttingen: Wallstein.

Fenves, Peter. 2001. *Arresting Language: From Leibniz to Benjamin*. Stanford: Stanford University Press.

Ferguson, Eugene. 1962. "Kinematics of Mechanisms from the Time of Watt." *United States National Museum Bulletin* 228:185–230.

Ferrari, Federico, and Jean-Luc Nancy. 2003. "Il ritratto del romanziere." In *Il romanzo*, edited by Franco Moretti. Milan: Einaudi.

Ficino, Marsilio. 1576/1959. *In Timaeum commentaria, Opera omnia*. Turin: Bottega d'Erasmo.

Field, J.V. 1997. *The Invention of Infinity: Mathematics and the Art of the Renaissance*. Oxford: Oxford University Press.

Finch, Alison. 2004. "The Stylistic Achievements of Flaubert's Fiction." In *The Cambridge Companion to Flaubert*, edited by Timothy Unwin, 145–64. Cambridge: Cambridge University Press.

Forbes, R.J. 1958. "Power to 1850." In *A History of Technology*, edited by Charles H. Singer, E.J. Holmyard, A.R. Hall, and Trevor I. Williams, 4: 230–57. New York: Oxford University Press.

Foucault, Michel. 1995. *Discipline and Punish*. New York: Vintage.

———. 2002. *The Order of Things*. London: Routledge.

Fox, Robert. 1990. "Laplacian Physics." In *Companion to the History of Modern Science*, edited by R.C. Olby, G.N. Cantor, J.R.R. Christie, and M.J.S. Hodge, 278–94. London: Routledge.

Frank, Joseph. 1968. *The Widening Gyre: Crisis and Mastery in Modern Literature*. Bloomington: Indiana University Press.

Frautschi, Steven, Richard Olenick, Tom Apostol, and David Goodstein. 2008. *The Mechanical Universe: Mechanics and Heat*. Cambridge: Cambridge University Press.

Fried, Frederick. 1964. *A Pictorial History of the Carousel*. New York: Barnes.

Fried, Michael. 1996. *Manet's Modernism, or, The Face of Painting in the 1860s*. Chicago: University of Chicago Press.

———. 2002. *Menzel's Realism: Art and Embodiment in Nineteenth-Century Berlin*. New Haven: Yale University Press.

Friedman, Susan Stanford. 2002. "Spatialization: A Strategy for Reading Narrative." In *Narrative Dynamics: Essays on Time, Plot, Closure, and Frames*, edited by Brian Richardson, 217–28. Columbus: Ohio State University Press.

Frost, Harwood. 1910. *The Art of Roadmaking*. New York: Engineering News Publishing.

Füsslin, Georg, and Ewald Hentze. 1999. *Anamorphosen: Geheime Bilderwelten*. Stuttgart: Füsslin.

Gadamer, Hans-Georg. 2007. *The Gadamer Reader*. Evanston: Northwestern University Press.

Gauss, Herrmann. 1961. *Philosophischer Handkommentar zu den Dialogen Platos*. Bern: Lang.

Genette, Gérard. 1980. *Narrative Discourse*. Ithaca: Cornell University Press.

———. 1982. "Frontiers of Narrative." In *Figures of Literary Discourse*, 127–44. New York: Columbia University Press.

Genevro, George, and Stephen Heineman. 1991. *Machine Tools: Processes and Applications*. New York: Prentice Hall.

Gerhardt, Claus. 1975. *Der Buchdruck*. 4 vols. Vol. 2. *Geschichte der Druckverfahren*. Stuttgart: Hiersemann.

Ghins, Michel. 1990. *L'inertie et l'espace-temps absolu de Newton à Einstein: Une analyse philosophique*. Brussels: Académie Royale de Belgique.

Giedion, Siegfried. 1948. *Mechanization Takes Command: A Contribution to Anonymous History*. New York: Oxford University Press.

Gillispie, Charles Coulston. 1990. *The Edge of Objectivity: An Essay in the History of Scientific Ideas*. Princeton: Princeton University Press.

Ginsburg, Michal, and Lorri Nandrea. 2006. "The Prose of the World." In *The Novel*, edited by Franco Moretti. Princeton: Princeton University Press.

Goethe, Johann Wolfgang von. 1892. *Goethes Werke*. Weimar: Böhlau.

———. 1999. *Maxims and Reflections*. London: Penguin.

Grafton, Anthony. 2000. *Leon Battista Alberti: Master Builder of the Renaissance*. New York: Hillary and Wang.

Grau, Oliver. 2001. *Virtuelle Kunst in Geschichte und Gegenwart*. Berlin: Reimer.

Greiner, Walter, and Fritz Kemmler, eds. 1997. *Realismustheorien in England, 1692–1919*. Tübingen: Gunter Narr.

Grondin, Jean. 1994. *Introduction to Philosophical Hermeneutics*. New Haven: Yale University Press.

Gutsche, Fritz. 1937. "Die Entwicklung der Schiffschraube." *Technikgeschichte* 26:37–50.

Haas, Norbert, Rainer Nägele, and Hans-Jörg Rheinberger, eds. 1998. *Aufmerksamkeit*. Liechtensteiner Exkurse. Lichtenstein: Isele.

Hale, Dorothy. 1998. "Henry James and the Invention of Novel Theory." In *The Cambridge Companion to Henry James*, edited by Jonathan Friedman, 79–101. Cambridge: Cambridge University Press.

Hankins, James. 2005. "Plato's Psychogony in the Later Renaissance." In *Platons Timaios als Grundtext der Kosmologie in Spätantike, Mittelalter und Renaissance*, edited by Thomas Leinkauf, 387–406. Leuven: Leuven University Press.

Hansen, Mark. 2000. *Embodying Technesis: Technology beyond Writing*. Ann Arbor: University of Michigan Press.

Harrisberger, Lee. 1961. *Mechanization of Motion: Kinematics, Synthesis, Analysis*. New York: Wiley and Sons.

Hartenberg, Richard, and Jacques Denavit. 1964. *Kinematic Synthesis of Linkages*. New York: McGraw-Hill.

Haverkamp, Anselm, and Dirk Mende, eds. 2009. *Metaphorologie: Zur Praxis von Theorie*. Frankfurt: Suhrkamp.

Hawkins, Nehemiah. 1904. *New Catechism of the Steam Engine*. New York: Audel.

Hegel, Georg Wilhelm Friedrich. 1986. *Wissenschaft der Logik II*. Frankfurt: Suhrkamp.

Heidegger, Martin. 2004. *Vorträge und Aufsätze*. Stuttgart: Klett-Cotta.

———. 2009. *Leitgedanken zur Entstehung der Metaphysik, der neuzeitlichen Wissenschaft und der modernen Technik*. Frankfurt: Klostermann.

Heidegger, Martin, and Eugen Fink. 1996. *Heraklit: Seminar Wintersemester 1966/1967*. Frankfurt: Klostermann.

Heimann, P.M. 1974. "Conversion of Forces and Conservation of Energy." *Centaurus* 18 (2): 147–61.

Heinrich, Michael. 1999. *Kritik der politischen Ökonomie: Eine Einführung.* Stuttgart: Schmetterling.

———. 2006. *Die Wissenschaft vom Wert.* Münster: Westfälsiches Dampfboot.

Helberger, Christof. 1974. *Marxismus als Methode.* Frankfurt: Athenäum.

Helmholtz, Herrmann von. 1847. *Ueber die Erhaltung der Kraft: Eine physikalische Abhandlung.* Berlin: G. Reimer.

———. 1995. "On the Conservation of Force." In *Science and Culture: Popular and Philosophical Essays,* edited by David Cahan, 96–126. Chicago: University of Chicago Press.

Henderson, William. 1941. *Modern Paper-Making.* Oxford: Blackwell.

Heraclitus. 1912. "The Fragments." Translated by John Burnet. In *Early Greek Philosophy,* edited by John Burnet. Philoctetes (English, French, and Greek versions), http://philoctetes.free.fr/heraclite.pdf.

Herman, David, ed. 2007. *The Routledge Encyclopedia of Narrative Theory.* London: Routledge.

Herzog, Reinhart, and Reinhart Koselleck, eds. 1987. *Epochenschwelle und Epochenbewusstsein.* Munich: Fink.

Hogarth, William. 1997. *The Analysis of Beauty.* Edited by Ronald Paulson. New Haven: Yale University Press.

Hölder, Christian Gottlieb. 1803–4. "Kleists (?) Dramentheorie." In *Meine Reise über den Gotthard nach den Borromäischen Inseln und Mailand; und von da zurück über das Val Formozza, die Grimsel und das Oberland im Sommer 1801,* 2:173–78. Stuttgart: Steinkopf. www.textkritik.de/bka/dokumente/dok_h/hoelder.htm.

Hölderlin, Friedrich. 1988. *Essays and Letters on Theory.* Edited and translated by Thomas Pfau. Albany: SUNY Press.

———. 1998. *Sämtliche Werke und Briefe.* 3 vols. Edited by M. Knaupp. Vol. 2. Darmstadt: Wissenschaftliche Buchgesellschaft.

Holmes, Frederic L., and Kathryn M. Olesko. 1995. "The Images of Precision: Helmholtz and the Graphical Method in Physiology." In *The Values of Precision,* edited by M. Norton Wise, 198–221. Princeton: Princeton University Press.

Holtz, William. 1977. "Spatial Form in Modern Literature." *Critical Inquiry* 4 (2): 271–283.

Horstmann, Rolf-Peter. 1990. *Wahrheit aus dem Begriff.* Frankfurt: Anton Hain.

Horwitz, Hugo. 1933–34. "Die Drehbewegung und ihre Bedeutung für die Entwicklung der materiellen Kultur." *Anthropos* 28:721–57 and 29:99–125.

Hrones, John, and George L. Nelson. 1951. *Analysis of the Four-Bar Linkage: Its Application to the Synthesis of Mechanisms.* Cambridge, MA: MIT Press.

Hughes, Linda, and Michael Lund. 1991. *The Victorian Serial.* Charlottesville: University Press of Virginia.

Hunt, K.H. 1978. *Kinematic Geometry of Mechanisms.* Oxford: Clarendon Press.

Hunter, Dard. 1978. *Papermaking: The History and Technique of an Ancient Craft*. New York: Dover.

Inglis, Katherine. 2008. "Becoming Autonomous: Automata in *The Old Curiosity Shop* and *Our Mutual Friend*." *Interdisciplinary Studies in the Long Nineteenth Century* 6.

James, Henry. 1984. *Literary Criticism*. New York: Library of America.

———. 1999. *The Turn of the Screw*. Norton Critical Edition. New York: Norton.

Jammer, Max. 1997. *Concepts of Mass in Classical and Modern Physics*. Mineola: Dover.

Johnson, Paul. 1999. *The Birth of the Modern: World Society, 1815–1830*. New York: HarperCollins.

Jünger, Ernst. 1932/1960. *Der Arbeiter*. Stuttgart: Klett.

Jünger, Friedrich Georg. 1953. *Die Perfektion der Technik*. Frankfurt: Klostermann.

Kahn, David. 1967. *The Codebreakers: The Story of Secret Writing*. New York: Macmillan.

Kanitschneider, Bernulf. 1984. *Kosmologie: Geschichte und Systematik in philosophischer Perspektive*. Stuttgart: Reclam.

Kant, Immanuel. 1968a. "Allgemeine Naturgeschichte und Theorie des Himmels." In *Kants Werke*, edited by Königlich Preussische Akademie der Wissenschaften, 1:215–368. Berlin: Walter de Gruyter.

———. 1968b. "De mundi sensibilis atque intelligibilis forma et principiis." In *Kants Werke*, edited by Königlich Preussische Akademie der Wissenschaften, 1:385–419. Berlin: Walter de Gruyter.

———. 1968c. "Untersuchung der Frage, ob die Erde in ihrer Umdrehung um die Achse, woďurch sie die Abwechslung des Tages und der Nacht hervorbringt, einige Veränderung seit den ersten Jahren ihres Ursprungs erlitten habe." In *Kants Werke*, edited by Königlich Preussische Akademie der Wissenschaften, 1:183–92. Berlin: Walter de Gruyter.

———. 1968d. "Von dem ersten Grunde des Unterschieds der Gegenden im Raume." In *Kants Werke*, edited by Königlich Preussische Akademie der Wissenschaften, 2:375–84. Berlin: Walter de Gruyter.

———. 1968e. "Was heisst: Sich im Denken orientiren?" In *Kants Werke*, edited by Königlich Preussische Akademie der Wissenschaften, 8:131–48. Berlin: Walter de Gruyter.

———. 2005. *Allgemeine Naturgeschichte und Theorie des Himmels*. Edited by Harri Deutsch. Ostwalds Klassiker der Exakten Naturwissenschafte. Frankfurt: Ostwald.

———. 2008. *Universal Natural History and Theory of the Heavens*. Translated by Ian Johnston. http://records.viu.ca/~johnstoi/kant/kant2e.htm.

Kapp, Ernst. 1877. *Grundlinien einer Philosophie der Technik*. Braunschweig: Westermann.

Kassung, Christian. 2001. *EntropieGeschichten: Robert Musils "Der Mann ohne Eigenschaften" im Diskurs der modernen Physik*. Munich: Fink.

———. 2007. *Das Pendel: Eine Wissensgeschichte*. Munich: Fink.

Kellermann, Rudolf, and Wilhelm Treue. 1962. *Die Kulturgeschichte der Schraube*. Munich: Bruckmann.

Kemp, Martin. 1990. *The Science of Art: Optical Themes in Western Art from Brunelleschi to Seurat*. New Haven: Yale University Press.

Kempe, Alfred. 1877. *How to Draw a Straight Line: A Lecture on Linkages*. London: Macmillan.

Kent, Dale. 2002. "Michele del Giogante's House of Memory." In *Society and Individual in Renaissance Florence*, edited by William J. Connell, 110–36. Berkeley: University of California Press.

Kepler, Johannes. 1938. *Mysterium cosmographicum*. Edited by Max Caspar. Vol. 1 of *Gesammelte Werke*. Munich: Beck.

———. 1981. *The Secret of the Universe*. Norwalk, CT: Abaris.

Kittler, Friedrich A. 1987. "Weltatem: On Wagner's Media Technology." In *Wagner in Retrospect: A Centennial Reappraisal*, edited by Leroy Robert Shaw, Nancy R. Cirillo, and Marion S. Miller, 203–12. Amsterdam: Rodopi.

———. 1999. *Gramophone, Film, Typewriter*. Stanford: Stanford University Press.

Klein, Wolfgang. 2005. "Realismus/realistisch." In *Ästhetische Grundbegriffe*, edited by Karlheinz Barck et al., vol. 5. Stuttgart: Metzler.

Kleist, Heinrich von. 1990. *Erzählungen, Anekdoten, Gedichte, Schriften*. Edited by K. Müller-Salget. Frankfurt: Deutscher Klassiker Verlag.

———. 1997a. *Brandenburger Ausgabe*. Vol. 2, pt. 7. Frankfurt: Stroemfeld; Marburg: Roter Stern.

———. 1997b. "On the Marionette Theater." Translated by Carol Jacobs. *Connecticut Review* 19 (1): 49–55.

———. 1997c. *Selected Writings*. Edited by David Constantine. London: Dent.

Knowles, Rob. 2001. "Carlyle, Ruskin, and Morris: Work across the 'River of Fire'." *History of Economics Review* 34:127–45.

König, Wolfgang. 1999. *Künstler und Strichezieher: Konstruktions- und Technikkulturen im deutschen, britischen, amerikanischen und französischen Maschinenbau zwischen 1850 und 1930*. Frankfurt: Suhrkamp.

Koschorke, Albrecht. 1990. *Die Geschichte des Horizonts*. Frankfurt: Suhrkamp.

———. 2000. "Selbststeuerung: David Hartleys Assoziationstheorie, Adam Smiths Sympathielehre und die Dampfmaschine von James Watt." In *Das Laokoon-Paradigma: Zeichenregime im 18. Jahrhundert*, edited by Inge Baxmann, Michael Franz, and Wolfgang Schäffner. Berlin: Akademie Verlag.

Koyré, Alexandre. 1957. *From the Closed World to the Infinite Universe*. Baltimore: Johns Hopkins University Press.

———. 1965. *Newtonian Studies*. London: Chapman and Hall.

Kuhn, Thomas. 1959. "Energy Conservation as an Example of Simultaneous Discovery." In *Critical Problems in the History of Science: Proceedings of the Institute for the History of Science, 1957*, edited by Marshall Clagett, 321–56. Madison: University of Wisconsin Press.

Lacoue-Labarthe, P., and J.-L. Nancy. 1988. *The Literary Absolute: The Theory of Literature in German Romanticism*. Albany: State University of New York Press.

Lalla, Sebastian. 2003. "Kants allgemeine Naturgeschichte und Theorie des Himmels (1755)." *Kant Studien* 94 (4): 426–53.

Landes, David. 2003. *The Unbound Prometheus: Technological Change and Industrial Development in Western Europe from 1750 to the Present.* 2nd ed. Cambridge: Cambridge University Press.

Langendorff, Oskar. 1891. *Physiologische Graphik: Ein Leitfaden der in der Physiologie gebräuchlichen Registrirmethoden.* Leipzig: Deuticke.

Lawton, Bryan. 2004. *The Early History of Mechanical Engineering.* Leiden: Brill.

Leinkauf, Thomas. 2005. "Aspekte und Perspektiven: Die Rezeption des Timaios in Renaissance und Früher Neuzeit." In *Platons Timaios als Grundtext der Kosmologie in Spätantike, Mittelalter und Renaissance,* edited by Thomas Leinkauf, 363–86. Leuven: Leuven University Press.

Lenoir, Timothy. 1992. *Politik im Tempel der Wissenschaft.* Frankfurt: Campus.

———. 1993. "Helmholtz and the Materialities of Communication." *Osiris* 9:183–207.

Leroi-Gourhan, André. 1943. *Évolution et techniques: L'homme et la matière.* Paris: Albin Michel.

Leupold, Jacob. 1724. *Theatrum Machinarum Generale: Schau-Platz des Grundes mechanischer Wissenschaften.* 3 vols. Leipzig: Gleditsch.

Lewis, Elmer. 2009. *Masterworks of Technology.* Amherst, MA: Prometheus Books.

Loschek, Ingrid. 1994. *Reclams Mode- und Kostümlexikon.* Stuttgart: Reclam.

Lotze, Rudolph Hermann. 1887. *Microcosmus: An Essay concerning Man and His Relation to the World.* Vol. 1. Edinburgh: T and T Clark.

Lowell, Donald. 1971. *From Watt to Clausius: The Rise of Thermodynamics in the Early Industrial Age.* Ithaca: Cornell University Press.

Ludwig, Carl. 1865. *Die physiologischen Leistungen des Blutdrucks.* Leipzig: Hirzel.

Lukacs, Georgy. 1972. *Studies in European Realism.* London: Merlin Press.

Magdanz, Teresa. 2006. "The Waltz: Technology's Muse." *Journal of Popular Music Studies* 18 (3): 251–81.

Mallarmé, Stephane. 1876/1998. "The Impressionists and Édouard Manet." Reprinted in *Mallarmé via Manet (De "The Impressionists and Edouard Manet" a "Crise de Vers"),* 19–91, by Pascal Durand. Leuven: Peeters.

Mannoni, Laurent. 2002. "Geburt und Kommerzialisierung der Chrono-photographie." In *Ich sehe was, was du nicht siehst: Sehmaschinen und Bilderwelten. Die Sammlung Werner Nekes,* edited by Bodo von Dewitz, 362–78. Göttingen: Steidl.

Marsden, Ben. 2002. *Watt's Perfect Engine.* New York: Columbia University Press.

Marsden, Richard. 1888. *Cotton Spinning: Its Development, Principles, and Practice.* London: Bell.

Martin, Alexis. 1855. "Physiologie de l'asphalte." *Le Bohème* 1 (3).

Martínez, Alberto. 2009. *Kinematics: The Lost Origins of Einstein's Relativity.* Baltimore: John Hopkins University Press.

Marx, Karl. 1953. *Grundrisse der Kritik der politischen Ökonomie.* Frankfurt: Europäische Verlagsanstalt.

———. 1975. *Economic and Philosophic Manuscripts of 1844.* Vol. 3 of Karl Marx and Frederick Engels, *Collected Works.* New York: International Publishers.

———. 1987. *Das Kapital. Kritik der Politischen Ökonomie. Erster Band, Hamburg 1972.* Sec. II, vol. 6, of *Marx-Engels Gesamtausgabe,* edited by the International Marx Engels Foundation. Berlin: Dietz.

———. 1989. *Das Kapital: Kritik der politischen Ökonomie. Erster Band, Hamburg 1883.* Sec. II, vol. 8, of *Marx-Engels Gesamtausgabe,* edited by the International Marx Engels Foundation. Berlin: Dietz.

———. 1996. *Capital I.* Vol. 35 of Karl Marx and Frederick Engels, *Collected Works.* New York: International Publishers.

———. 1998. *Capital III.* Vol. 37 of Karl Marx and Frederick Engels, *Collected Works.* New York: International Publishers.

Marx, Leo. 2000. *The Machine in the Garden: Technology and the Pastoral Ideal in America.* Oxford: Oxford University Press.

Maxwell, J. Clerk. 1876. *Matter and Motion.* New York: Van Nostrand.

Mayer, Julius Robert. 1876. "Ueber Auslösung." *Staatsanzeiger für Württemberg,* March 22, 1876, special supplement, 104–7.

McKitterick, David. 2003. *Print, Manuscript and the Search for Order, 1450–1830.* Cambridge: Cambridge University Press.

Meier-Graefe, Julius. 1912. *Édouard Manet.* Munich: Piper.

Millard, A. J. 2005. *America on Record: A History of Recorded Sound.* Cambridge: Cambridge University Press.

Miller, J. Hillis. 1991. *Victorian Subjects.* Durham: Duke University Press.

———. 1995. *Topographies.* Stanford: Stanford University Press.

Moon, Francis. 2003. "Franz Reuleaux: Contributions to 19th Century Kinematics and Theory of Machines." *Applied Mechanics Reviews* 56 (2): 261–85.

———. 2007. *The Machines of Leonardo da Vinci and Franz Reuleaux.* Vol. 2. *History in Mechanism and Machine Science.* Dordrecht: Springer.

Moretti, Franco. 1987. *The Way of the World: The Bildungsroman in European Culture.* London: Verso.

———. 2005. *Signs Taken for Wonders: On the Sociology of Literary Forms.* London: Verso.

———, ed. 2006. *The Novel.* Princeton: Princeton University Press.

Moseley, C. W. R. D. 2005. "Waiting for the Death of Little Nell: Gas, Flong, and the Nineteenth Century Novel." *TRANS: Internet-Zeitschrift für Kulturwissenschaften,* no. 16. www.inst.at/trans/16Nr/09_6/moseley16.htm.

Muirhead, James. 1859. *The Life of James Watt with Selections from His Correspondence.* London: Murray.

Müller-Sievers, Helmut. 1997. *Self-Generation: Biology, Philosophy, and Literature around 1800.* Stanford: Stanford University Press.

———. 2003. *Desorientierung: Anatomie und Dichtung bei Georg Büchner.* Göttingen: Wallstein.

———. 2006. "Reading without Interpreting: German Textual Criticism and the Case of Georg Büchner." *Modern Philology* 103 (4): 498–518.

———. 2009. "Drehmoment: Lebendigkeit und Bewegung im 19. Jahrhundert." In *Vita aesthetica: Szenarien ästhetischer Lebendigkeit*, edited by Armen Avanessian, Winfried Menninghaus, and Jan Völker, 227–36. Zurich: Diaphanes.

———. Forthcoming. "Die Roman-Maschine: Narration im 19. Jahrhundert." *Compar(a)ison*.

Müller-Wille, Staffan. 1999. *Botanik und weltweiter Handel*. Edited by O. B. M. Weingarten. Vol. 3. *Studien zur Theorie der Biologie*. Berlin: Verlag für Wissenschaft und Bildung.

Mumford, Lewis. 1967. *The Myth of the Machine*. New York: Harcourt Brace.

Nägele, Reiner. 2005. *Hölderlins Kritik der poetischen Vernunft*. Basel: Engeler.

Nasmyth, James. 1841. "Remarks on the Introduction of the Slide Principle." In *Practical Essays on Mill Work and Other Machinery*, edited by Robertson Buchanan, 393 (Essay VIII, Appendix B). London: John Weale.

———. 1883. *John Nasmyth Engineer: An Autobiography*. New York: Harper and Brothers.

Nave, Rod. 2010. "Simple Machines." In *Hyperphysics*. http://hyperphysics .phy-astr.gsu.edu/hbase/mechanics/simmac.html.

Negt, Oskar, and Alexander Kluge. 1993. *Geschichte und Eigensinn*. 3 vols. Frankfurt: Suhrkamp.

Nekes, Werner. 2002. *Ich sehe was, was du nicht siehst: Sehmaschinen und Bilderwelten. Die Sammlung Werner Nekes*. Edited by Bodo von Dewitz. Göttingen: Steidl.

Neubauer, John. 1982. "The Freedom of the Machine: On Mechanism, Materialism, and the Young Schiller." *Eighteenth Century Studies* 15 (3): 275–90.

Newton, Isaac. 1995. *Texts, Backgrounds, Commentaries*. Edited by I. Bernard Cohen and Richard S. Westfall. Norton Critical Edition. New York: Norton.

Nicholas of Cusa. 2001. *Complete Philosophical and Theological Treatises of Nicholas of Cusa*. Minneapolis: Arthur Banning Press.

Nietzsche, Friedrich. 1988. *Ecce Homo*. Munich: dtv.

Nochlin, Linda. 1989. *The Politics of Vision: Essays on Nineteenth-Century Art and Society*. Boulder, CO: Westview Press.

Norton, Robert. 2004. *Design of Machinery: An Introduction*. Boston: McGraw Hill.

Oettermann, Stephan. 1997. *The Panorama: History of a Mass Medium*. New York: Zone Books.

Oken, Lorenz. 1847. *Elements of Physiophilosophy*. London: Ray Society.

Olesko, Kathryn M. 1995. "The Meaning of Precision: The Exact Sensibility in Early Nineteenth-Century Germany." In *The Values of Precision*, edited by M. Norton Wise, 103–34. Princeton: Princeton University Press.

Oliver, Simon. 2005a. *Philosophy, God, and Motion*. Radical Orthodoxy. New York: Routledge.

———. 2005b. "The Sweet Delight of Virtue and Grace in Aquinas' Ethics." *International Journal of Systematic Theology* 7 (1): 52–71.

Ong, Walter. 1958. *Ramus, Method, and the Decay of Dialogue.* Cambridge, MA: Harvard University Press.

Oschmann, Dirk. 2007. *Bewegliche Dichtung: Sprachtheorie und Poetik bei Lessing, Schiller und Kleist.* Munich: Fink.

Osten, Manfred. 2002. "'Alles Veloziferisch': Goethes Ottilie und die beschleunigte Zeit." In *Goethe und das Zeitalter der Romantik,* edited by Walter Hinderer, 213–30. Würzburg: Königshausen und Neumann.

Otis, Laura, ed. 2002. *Literature and Science in the Nineteenth Century: An Anthology.* Oxford: Oxford University Press.

Pacioli, Luca. 1980. *Divine Proportion: Oeuvre nécessaire à tous les esprits perspicaces et curieux, où chacun de ceux qui aiment à etudier la philosophie, la perspective, la peinture, la sculpture, l'architecture, la musique et les autres disciplines mathématiques, trouvera une très délicate, subtile et admirable doctrine et se délectera de diverses questions touchant une très secrète science.* Paris: Librairie du Compagnonnage.

Panofsky, Erwin. 1994. *Perspective as Symbolic Form.* New York: Zone Books.

Parker, Patricia. 1990. "Metaphor and Catachresis." In *The Ends of Rhetoric: History, Theory, Practice,* edited by John Bender and David E. Wellbery, 60–76. Stanford: Stanford University Press.

Pascal, Roy. 1977. *The Dual Voice.* Manchester: Manchester University Press.

Paulinyi, Akos. 1997. "Die Umwälzung der Technik in der industriellen Revolution zwischen 1750 und 1840." In *Propyläen Technikgeschichte,* edited by Wolfgang König, 3:271–513. Berlin: Propyläen.

Pavel, Thomas. 2003. *La pensée du roman.* Paris: Gallimard.

Phillips, Bill. 2005. *The Complete Book of Locks and Locksmithing.* New York: McGraw-Hill.

Phillips, Jack. 2006. *Freedom in Machinery.* Cambridge: Cambridge University Press.

Plato. 2003. *Timaeus.* Translated by B. Jowett. http://www.ellopos.net/elpenor/physis/plato-timaeus/default.asp.

Plessen, Marie-Louise, Ulrich Giersch, and Kunst- und Ausstellungshalle der Bundesrepublik Deutschland. 1993. *Sehsucht: Das Panorama als Massenunterhaltung des 19. Jahrhunderts.* Basel: Stroemfeld; Frankfurt: Roter Stern.

Poe, Edgar Allan. 1906. *The Poetical Works of Edgar Allan Poe.* Boston: Educational Publishing.

Poinsot, Louis. 1834. *Outline of a New Theory of Rotary Motion.* Cambridge: Newby.

———. 1837/1877. *Éléments de statique.* 2nd ed. Paris: Gauthier-Villars.

Porter, Theodore M. 1995. "Precision and Trust: Early Victorian Insurance and the Politics of Calculation." In *The Values of Precision,* edited by M. Norton Wise, 173–97. Princeton: Princeton University Press.

Price, Martin. 1971. "The Irrelevant Detail and the Emergence of Form." In *Aspects of Narrative: Selected Papers from the English Institute,* edited by J. Hillis Miller, 69–91. New York: Columbia University Press.

Proust, Antonin. 1913. *Éduard Manet: Souvenirs.* Paris: Renouard.

Proust, Marcel. 1987. *Sur Baudelaire, Flaubert et Morand.* Brussels: Éditions Complexe.

———. 2009. *A la recherche du temps perdu.* Kindle ed. West Roxbury, MA: B&R Samizdat Express.

Pynchon, Thomas. 1997. *Mason & Dixon.* New York: Holt.

Rabinbach, Anson. 1992. *The Human Motor: Energy, Fatigue, and the Origins of Modernity.* Basic Books.

Radkau, Joachim. 2008. *Technik in Deutschland.* Frankfurt: Campus.

Ray, John. 1682. *Methodus plantarum nova.* London: Faitborne and Kersey.

Read, Oliver, and Walter Welch. 1976. *From Tinfoil to Stereo: Evolution of the Phonograph.* Indianapolis: Sama.

Reid, Henry. 1877. *The Science and Art of the Manufacture of Portland Cement.* London: Spon.

Reuleaux, Franz. 1875. *Theoretische Kinematik: Grundzüge einer Theorie des Maschinenwesens.* Braunschweig: Vieweg.

———. 1876. *The Kinematics of Machinery.* Translated by A. Kennedy. London: Macmillan.

———. 1900. *Lehrbuch der Kinematik.* Vol. 2. *Die praktischen Beziehungen der Kinematik zu Geometrie und Mechanik.* Braunschweig: Vieweg.

Rheinberger, Hans-Joerg. 1997. *Towards a History of Epistemic Things.* Stanford: Stanford University Press.

———. 2005. "A Reply to David Bloor: 'Toward a Sociology of Epistemic Things.'" *Perspectives on Science* 13 (3): 406–10.

Ribot, Théodule-Armand. 1898. *The Psychology of Attention.* Chicago: Open Court.

Riedel, Wolfgang. 1985. *Die Anthropologie des jungen Schiller: Zur Ideengeschichte der medizinischen Schriften und der "Philosophischen Briefe."* Epistemata. Würzburg: Königshausen und Neumann.

Ringwalt, Luther. 1981. *American Encyclopedia of Printing.* New York: Garland.

Robinson, Eric. 1972. "James Watt and the Law of Patents." *Technology and Culture* 13 (2): 115–39.

Roe, Joseph Wickham. 1916. *English and American Tool Builders.* New Haven: Yale University Press.

Rolt, L.T.C. 1959. *Isambart Kingdom Brunel: A Biography.* New York: St. Martin's Press.

———. 1965. *A Short History of Machine Tools.* Cambridge, MA: MIT Press.

———. 1970. *Victorian Engineering.* London: Penguin.

Rose, Joshua. 1877. *The Complete Practical Machinist.* Philadelphia: Baird.

Rosen, George. 1973. "Disease, Debility, and Death." In *The Victorian City,* edited by Jim Dyos and Michael Wolff, 625–67. London: Routledge.

Routledge, Robert. 1989. *Discoveries and Inventions of the Nineteenth Century.* New York: Crescent Books.

Rühlmann, Moritz. 1875. *Allgemeine Maschinenlehre.* Vol. 1. Leipzig: Baumgärtners.

Ruprecht, Lucia. 2006. *Dances of the Self in Heinrich von Kleist, E. T. A. Hoffmann and Heinrich Heine.* Aldershot: Ashgate.

Rybczynski, Witold. 2000. *One Good Turn: A Natural History of the Screwdriver and the Screw.* New York: Scribner.

Rykwert, Joseph. 1996. *The Dancing Column: On Order in Architecture.* Cambridge, MA: MIT Press.

Sabin, Louis Carlton. 1904. *Cement and Concrete.* Boston: Stanhope.

Sachs, Joe. 1995. *Aristotle's Physics: A Guided Study.* New Brunswick: Rutgers University Press.

Sawday, Jonathan. 2007. *Engines of the Imagination.* London: Routledge.

Schaffer, Simon. 1986. "Scientific Discoveries and the End of Natural Philosophy." *Social Studies of Science* 16 (3): 387–420.

———. 1994a. "Babbage's Intelligence: Calculating Engines and the Factory System." *Critical Inquiry* 21 (1): 203–27.

———. 1994b. "Machine Philosophy: Demonstration Devices in Georgian Mechanics." *Osiris* 9:157–82.

———. 1995. "Accurate Measurement Is an English Science." In *The Values of Precision,* edited by M. Norton Wise, 135–72. Princeton: Princeton University Press.

Schell, Wilhelm. 1870. *Theorie der Bewegung und der Kräfte.* Leipzig: Teubner.

Schelling, Friedrich Wilhelm Joseph. 1985. "Philosophie der Kunst." In *Ausgewählte Schriften,* edited by Manfred Frank. Frankfurt: Suhrkamp.

———. 2000. *Von der Weltseele.* Edited by Jörg Jantzen. Vol. 6. *Werke: Historisch-Kritische Ausgabe.* Stuttgart: Frommann-Holzboog.

———. 2001. *Erster Entwurf eines Systems der Naturphilosophie.* Edited by Wilhelm G. Jacobs and Paul Ziche. Vol. 7. *Werke: Historisch-Kritische Ausgabe.* Stuttgart: Frommann-Holzboog.

Schild, Erich. 1967. *Zwischen Glaspalast und Palais des Illusions.* Berlin: Ullstein.

Schiller, Friedrich. 1962. "Ueber Anmuth und Wuerde." In *Werke (Nationalausgabe),* edited by Benno von Wiese. Weimar: Böhlau.

———. 1967. *On the Aesthetic Education of Man.* Oxford: Clarendon Press.

———. 2005. *Schiller's "On Grace and Dignity" in Its Cultural Context: Essays and a New Translation.* Edited by Jane V. Curran and Christophe Fricker. Rochester: Camden House.

Schivelbusch, Wolfgang. 1986. *The Railway Journey: Trains and Travel in the 19th Century.* Berkeley: University of California Press.

———. 1988. *Disenchanted Night: The Industrialization of Light in the Nineteenth Century.* Berkeley: University of California Press.

Schlaffer, Heinz. 2002. *Die kurze Geschichte der deutschen Literatur.* Munich: Hanser.

Schlegel, Friedrich. 1968. *Dialogue on Poetry and Literary Aphorisms.* University Park: Pennsylvania State University Press.

Schmidgen, Henning. 2001. "Der Psychologe der Maschinen: Über Gilbert Simondon und zwei Theorien technischer Objekte." In *Grenzgängerin—Bridges between Discourses: Festschrift für Irmingard Staeuble,* edited by C. Kraft Alsop, 265–87. Heidelberg: Asanger.

Schmidt, Arno. 1963–69. *Zettels Traum*. Frankfurt: Fischer.

Schneider, Helmut. 2000. "Standing and Falling in Heinrich von Kleist." *Modern Language Notes* 115 (3): 502–18.

Schoenflies, Arthur Moritz. 1901–8. "Kinematik." In *Encyclopädie der mathematischen Wissenschaften mit Einschluss ihrer Anwendungen,* edited by C. M. Felix Klein. Leipzig: Teubner.

Schormüller, J. 1948. "Die Konservendose, ihre Entwicklung und ihre Bedeutung für die Lebensmittelerhaltung." *Zeitschrift für Lebensmittel-Untersuchung und -Forschung* 88 (2): 154–74.

Scott, Gerald. 1962. "Elements of Gears and Basic Formulas." In *Gear Handbook,* edited by Darle W. Dudley. New York: McGraw-Hill.

Selenka, Emil. 1900. *Der Schmuck des Menschen*. Berlin: Vita.

Seltzer, Mark. 1984. *Henry James and the Art of Power*. Ithaca: Cornell University Press.

Serres, Michel. 1974. *Hermes III: La traduction*. Paris: Minuit.

———. 1975. Introduction to *Cours de philosophie positive,* by Auguste Comte. Edited by Michel Serres. 2 vols. Paris: Herrmann.

———. 1992. *Hermes III: Übersetzung*. Berlin: Merve.

Shapin, Steven, and Simon Schaffer. 1985. *Leviathan and the Air-Pump: Hobbes, Boyle, and the Experimental Life*. Princeton: Princeton University Press.

Shaw, Thomas. 1913. *Soiling Crops and the Silo*. New York: Orange Judd.

Siegert, Bernhard. 1996. "Carnotmaschinen: Zur Genese von Umkehrbarkeit und Wiederholung als Maschinenschreibweise." In *Wunschmaschine Welterfindung: Eine Geschichte der Technikvisionen seit dem 18. Jahrhundert,* edited by Brigitte Felderer, 296–313. New York: Springer.

———. 1998. "Switchboards and Sex: The Nut(t) Case." In *Inscribing Science: Scientific Texts and the Materiality of Communication,* edited by Timothy Lenoir, 78–90. Stanford: Stanford University Press.

———. 1999. *Relays: Literature as an Epoch of the Postal System*. Stanford: Stanford University Press.

———. 2003. *Passagen des Digitalen*. Berlin: Brinkmann und Bose.

Simmons, Dana. 2006. "Waste Not, Want Not: Excremental Economy in Nineteenth Century France." *Representations* 96 (1): 73–98.

Simondon, Gilbert. 1958. *Du mode d'existence des objets techniques*. Paris: Aubier.

———. 1980. "On the Mode of Existence of Technical Objects." Translated by Ninian Mellamphy. University of Western Ontario. www.scribd.com/doc/23928820/Gilbert-Simondon-On-The-Mode-Of-Existence.

Sindall, R. W. 1920. *Paper Technology*. London: Griffin.

Singer, Charles H., E. J. Holmyard, A. R. Hall, and Trevor I. Williams, eds. 1980. *A History of Technology*. Vol. 5. Oxford: Oxford University Press.

Slaughter, Mary M. 1982. *Universal Languages and Scientific Taxonomy in the Seventeenth Century*. Cambridge: Cambridge University Press.

Smiles, Samuel. 1861. *Lives of the Engineers*. Vol. 2. London: Murray.

Smith, Crosbie. 1998. *The Science of Energy: A Cultural History of Energy Physics in Victorian Britain*. London: Athlone Press.

Smith, Crosbie, and Norton Wise. 1989. *Energy and Empire: A Biographical Study of Lord Kelvin*. Cambridge: Cambridge University Press.

Spengler, Oswald. 1923. *Der Untergang des Abendlandes: Umrisse einer Morphologie der Weltgeschichte*. Munich: Beck.

Staengle, Peter. 1997. "'Berliner Abendblätter': Chronik." *Brandenburger Kleist-Blätter* 11:369–411.

Steinberg, Leo. 1987. "'How Shall This Be?' Reflections on Filippo Lippi's 'Annunciation' in London, Part I." *Artibus et Historiae* 8 (16): 25–44.

Steinberg, S.H. 1996. *Five Hundred Years of Printing*. Edited and revised by John Trevitt. London: British Library.

Stenger, Erich. 1939. "Das Pleorama." *Technikgeschichte* 28:127–32.

Sternberger, Dolf. 1955. *Panorama oder Ansichten vom 19. Jahrhundert*. Hamburg: Claassen.

Sterne, Laurence. 1986. *The Life and Opinions of Tristram Shandy, Gentleman*. Harmondsworth: Penguin.

Stevenson, John. 2008. *The Real History of Tom Jones*. New York: Palgrave.

Stiegler, Bernard. 1998. *Technics and Time 1: The Fault of Epimetheus*. Stanford: Stanford University Press.

Strässle, Urs. 2002. *Heinrich von Kleist: Die keilförmige Vernunft*. Würzburg: Königshausen und Neumann.

Sullivan, David. 2010. "Hermann Lotze." In *The Stanford Encyclopedia of Philosophy*, Fall 2010 ed. Ed. Edward N. Zalta. http://plato.stanford.edu/entries/hermann-lotze/.

Summers, David. 2007. *Vision, Reflection, and Desire in Western Painting*. Chapel Hill: University of Carolina Press.

Sylvester, James. 1875. "On Recent Discoveries in Mechanical Conversion of Motion." *Notices of the Proceedings at the Meetings of the Members of the Royal Institiution of Great Britain* 7:179–98.

Szondi, Peter. 1978. *Schriften 1*. Frankfurt: Suhrkamp.

Tartaret, Pierre. 1493. *Expositio magistri Petri Tatereti suoper textu Logices Aristotelis*. http://gallica.bnf.fr/ark:/12148/bpt6k52888x.

Theissen, Gerd. 2007. "Protestantische Exegese: Plädoyer für einen neuen vierfachen Schriftsinn." *Sacra Scripta: Journal of the Center for Biblical Studies, Babes-Bolyai University* 5:164–91.

Thompson, John. 1904. *History of Composing Machines*. Chicago: Inland.

Thompson, Silvanus. 1898. *Michael Faraday*. London: Cassell.

Thurston, Robert. 1884. "Theory of the Sliding Friction of Rotation." *Van Nostrand's Engineering Magazine*, December, 441–47.

———. 1902. *A History of the Growth of the Steam Engine*. New York: Appleton.

Toíbín, Colm. 2004. *The Master*. Toronto: McClelland and Stewart.

Trollope, Anthony. 1999. *An Autobiography*. Oxford: Oxford University Press.

Turner, Mark. 2005. "'Telling of My Weekly Doings': The Material Culture of the Victorian Novel." In *A Concise Companion to the Victorian Novel*, edited by Francis O'Gorman, 113–33. Oxford: Balckwell.

Van Cleve, James, and Robert Frederick, eds. 1991. *The Philosophy of Left and Right: Incongruent Counterparts and the Nature of Space*. Dordrecht: Kluwer.

Vesely, Dalibor. 2004. *Architecture in the Age of Divided Representation*. Cambridge, MA: MIT Press.

Vidler, Anthony. 1990. *Claude-Nicholas Ledoux*. Cambridge, MA: MIT Press.

Vitruvius. 1999. *Ten Books on Architecture*. Translated by I.D. Rowland. Cambridge: Cambridge University Press.

Vogl, Joseph. 2002. *Kalkül und Leidenschaft: Poetik des ökonomischen Menschen*. Munich: Sequenzia.

von Eelking, Baron. 1962. *Das Bildnis des eleganten Mannes: Ein Zylinderbreview von Werther bis Kennedy*. Berlin: Herbig.

von Matt, Peter. 1971. *Die Augen der Automaten: E.T.A. Hoffmanns Imaginationslehre als Prinzip seiner Erzählkunst*. Tübingen: Niemeyer.

von Wiese, Benno. 1967. "Das verlorene und wieder zu findende Paradies: Eine Studie über den Begriff der Anmut bei Goethe, Kleist und Schiller." In *Kleists Aufsatz über das Marionettentheater: Studien und Interpretationen*, edited by Helmut Sembdner, 196–220. Berlin: Erich Schmidt.

Warburg, Aby. 1995. *Images from the Region of the Pueblo Indians of North America*. Ithaca: Cornell University Press.

Warning, Rainer. 1980. "Chaos und Kosmos. Kontingenzbewältigung in der Comedie Humaine." In *Honoré de Balzac*, edited by Hans Ulrich Gumbrecht, Karlheinz Stierle, and Rainer Warning, 9–15. Munich: Fink.

Watt, Ian. 2001. *The Rise of the Novel*. Berkeley: University of California Press.

Weber, Samuel. 1989. "Upsetting the Set Up: Remarks on Heidegger's Questing after Technics." *Modern Language Notes* 104 (5): 977–92.

———. 2008. *Benjamin's Abilities*. Cambridge, MA: Harvard University Press.

Weber, Wolfhard. 1997. "Verkürzung von Zeit und Raum." In *Propyläen Technikgeschichte*, edited by Wolfgang König, 4:11–261. Berlin: Propyläen.

Wedemeyer, Arndt. 1994. "Kant: Spacing Out." *Modern Language Notes* 109:372–98.

Weigel, Sigrid. 1997. *Enstellte Ähnlichkeit: Walter Benjamins theoretische Schreibweise*. Frankfurt: Fischer.

Weihe, Carl. 1925. *Franz Reuleaux und seine Kinematik*. Berlin: Springer.

Wellbery, David. 2006. *Seiltänzer des Paradoxalen: Aufsätze zur ästhetischen Wissenschaft*. Munich: Hanser.

White, Lynn. 1966. *Medieval Technology and Social Change*. New York: Oxford University Press.

Wiggin, Kate. 2007. *Froebel's Gifts*. New York: Cook Press.

Wild, Christopher. 2002. "Wider die Marionettenfeindlichkeit." In *Kleist-Jahrbuch 2002*, edited by Günter Blamberger, 109–41. Stuttgart: Metzler.

———. 2003. *Theater der Keuschheit—Keuschheit des Theaters*. Freiburg: Rombach.

Willis, Robert. 1870. *Principles of Mechanism*. London: Longmans.

Wise, M. Norton. 1995a. "Precision: Agent of Unity and Product of Agreement. Part I—Traveling." In *The Values of Precision*, edited by M. Norton Wise, 92–102. Princeton: Princeton University Press.

———. 1995b. "Precision: Agent of Unity and Product of Agreement. Part II—The Age of Steam and Telegraphy." In *The Values of Precision*, edited by M. Norton Wise, 222–38. Princeton: Princeton University Press.

———. 1999. "Architecture for Steam." In *The Architecture of Science*, edited by Peter Galison, 107–40. Cambridge, MA: MIT Press.

Wittkower, Rudolf. 1953. "Brunelleschi and 'Proportion in Perspective.'" *Journal of the Warbourg and Courtauld Institutes* 16 (3/4): 275–91.

Wood, James. 2008. *How Fiction Works*. New York: Farrar, Straus and Giroux.

Yates, Frances A. 1966. *The Art of Memory*. Chicago: University of Chicago Press.

Zillmann, Dolf. 1980. "The Anatomy of Suspense." In *The Entertainment Functions of Television*, edited by Percy Tannenbaum. Hillsdale, NJ: Erlbaum Associates.

Zimmerman, John. 1962. *Elementary Kinematics of Mechanisms*. New York: Wiley and Sons.

Zola, Émile. 1966. *La bête humaine. Les Rougon-Macquart. Histoire naturelle et sociale d'une famille sous le seconde Empire*. Bibliothèque de la Pléiade. Paris: Gallimard.

Zumbusch, Cornelia. 2004. *Wissenschaft in Bildern*. Berlin: Akademie Verlag.

Index

readers, and serialization, 110–11, 112, 197n23, 197nn23–24. *See also* audiences' sensations

realist novel: overview and description of, 104, 196n4; biographical writing and, 106–7, 208n14; catharsis and, 111; central perspective and, 155; cycloids and narrative discussion and, 104, 106; digressions in, 109, 133, 152–53, 196n17, 203n4; discovered manuscript device and, 107–10, 134, 156, 208n14; epistolary novel and, 107–8; fantastic stories and, 109, 132, 153; Germany and, 5, 162–67, 172n4; *Gestell* as external to narration and, 156; ghostly presence and, 154–55, 156–57, 208n11; helix of screw thread and, 150, 152–53, 155–57, 162, 207n6, 208n7; journalism versus, 108, 132, 190n20; kinematics dimension and, 12, 39, 83, 105, 196n5; narration devices and, 105–9, 112; panopticons and, 130, 137, 138, 204n14; panoramic narratives and, 134–36, 138, 204n9; plot and story relation and, 83, 108, 112, 153–57, 166, 208n8, 208n10; printing press and narratives relation and, 75; prose/poetry relation and, 12–13, 162, 198n27; representational complexities and paradoxes of, 152, 207nn2–4; as semitechnical object, 166–67; senses of motion and, 104–5; story and, 107–10, 112; temporality and spatiality in narrative discussion and, 132–33, 134–38, 136, 138, 203nn2–4, 204n9, 204n16; tragedy incorporation and, 165–67. *See also* romantic novel; serialization

reason cult, 5–6, 172n6

reciprocating motion, 3, 27, 34, 173n22, 179n22

rectilinear motion, 45, 48, 53. *See also* translational motion

reeling motion, 77–78

Renger-Patzsch, Albert, 19, 68, 69, 72, 73, 90, 116

representing attribute, 124–30, 129, 201n32, 202nn36–37, 202nn40–41

repulsive force, 50–51, 186n34

restoration of grace, 4–5, 6–14, 17–18, 182n10, 182nn12–13, 183n14

Reuleaux, Franz, and topics discussed: automobiles and, 64; centrodes and, 31–32, 33, 149–50, 180n31, 181n32; cosmos and machines, 34, 38; cylinder

chains and, 22–23; cylindrical shape and, 39; desmodromic valve design and, 36, 181n43; devaluation of human work and kinematically efficient machines, 38–39; exclusion/inclusion of cosmic forces in kinematics dimension and, 23–24, 35–37, 181n43; freedom and, 149–50; friction and, 22; *Gestell* and, 16, 27, 29, 78–79, 174n32; historic context of kinematics dimension and, 30–33, 36–37, 39, 180n28; kinematics dimension and, 22, 23–24, 39, 177n14; linkage, 29; logic for generality of kinematics dimension and, 35, 181n42; pair-closed chain and, 34–36, 35; pedagogy in German and, 30–31; rails as part of steam locomotives motion and, 62; reciprocity of rolling motion and, 34; rolling motion and, 31–34, 67, 180n29, 180n31, 181n33; screw-nut pair and, 142; screw theory effects and, 149–50; synthesis of machine design and kinematics, 30, 35, 40; terminology for kinematics dimension and, 35–36, 181n42; Watt's steam engine and kinematics dimension, 177nn16

revolution: overview and use of term, 68, 101; political change due to machine-based capitalist production and, 68, 93–94, 98–100, 101, 180n29, 193n54, 195n75; transmission of motion and, 15–16. *See also* political dimension

rhythm of narrated time and serial publications, 105, 109, 110, 197n18, 197n23. *See also* time

rivets, 89–90, 90

roads and automobiles relation, 37–38, 72, 161

robots, 140, 150, 207n34. *See also* automata

rolling mills, 67–70, 69, 188nn4–6, 189n8

rolling motion: overview and definition of, 3–4, 23, 66–67, 176n12, 177n13; axial rotation and, 34; centrodes and, 31–32, 33, 149–50, 180n31, 181n32; crank-driven mechanisms and, 173nn21–22; cycloids and, 33; epochs and, 67, 69, 189n4; flying machine invention and, 171n1; *Gestell* and, 31; historic context and, 31–34, 39, 180n31, 181n33; kinematics dimension and, 31–34, 67–68, 132, 180n31, 181n33; oppositions concept and, 4; plot and story relation and, 132; reciprocity of, 34; screws and,

COVER DESIGN
Claudia Smelser

TEXT
10/13 Sabon

COMPOSITOR
BookComp

INDEXER
Naomi Linzer

PRINTER & BINDER
IBT Global

S